The Book of Yōkai

The Book of Yōkai

MYSTERIOUS CREATURES OF
JAPANESE FOLKLORE

Michael Dylan Foster

With Original Illustrations by Shinonome Kijin

UNIVERSITY OF CALIFORNIA PRESS

University of California Press, one of the most distinguished university presses in the United States, enriches lives around the world by advancing scholarship in the humanities, social sciences, and natural sciences. Its activities are supported by the UC Press Foundation and by philanthropic contributions from individuals and institutions. For more information, visit www.ucpress.edu.

University of California Press
Oakland, California

Library of Congress Cataloging-in-Publication Data

Foster, Michael Dylan, 1965– author.
  The book of yokai : mysterious creatures of Japanese folklore / Michael Dylan Foster ; with original illustrations by Shinonome Kijin.
    pages   cm
  Includes bibliographical references and index.
  ISBN 978-0-520-27101-2 (cloth : alk. paper)
  ISBN 978-0-520-27102-9 (pbk. : alk. paper)
  ISBN 978-0-520-95912-5 (ebook)
  1. Yokai (Japanese folklore).   I. Shinonome, Kijin, illustrator.
II. Title.
  GR340.F66   2015
  398.20952—dc23
                                        2014025479

Manufactured in the United States of America

23 22 21
10 9

In keeping with a commitment to support environmentally responsible and sustainable printing practices, UC Press has printed this book on Natures Natural, a fiber that contains 30% post-consumer waste and meets the minimum requirements of ANSI/NISO Z39.48-1992 (R 1997) (*Permanence of Paper*).

In memory of three masterful, monsterful, inspirational teachers:

Geraldine Murphy (1920–1990)
Alan Dundes (1934–2005)
Miyata Noboru (1936–2000)

Contents

Illustrations

Water Goblin Tales

PREFACE AND ACKNOWLEDGMENTS

Long ago, there was a *kappa*. A water goblin. It was about two inches tall, green, made of some sort of durable ceramic material, and it sat atop the small refrigerator in my studio apartment in California. It was just an inexpensive charm from a shrine that somebody must have given to me when I lived in Japan for the first time. Or perhaps I bought it myself. Either way, I had never actually given it much thought. But then one day, I was opening the refrigerator to get a beer and, for some reason, the kappa caught my attention. I began to inspect it carefully, turning it over in my hands. What was a kappa anyway? I knew that it was a little monster from Japanese folklore, a nasty, threatening creature that pulled people and animals into the water. But that didn't really explain anything. The little goblin was inviting me on a quest to explore an otherworld of fantastic beings and to try to understand how this otherworld might also be part of our own world.

I was in graduate school at the time, in Asian studies, and I ended up writing my master's thesis about kappa. I wasn't able to answer all the questions the creature raised, but I did learn that in Japan such water creatures fit into a larger category called *yōkai,* and the world of yōkai offers insight into the world of humans. Yōkai are an age-old part of belief and, simultaneously, at the cutting edge of knowledge and contemporary expression. In 1929, the physicist and writer Terada Torahiko (1878–1935) explained that the desire to understand yōkai is at the core of innovation because it inspires investigation within all sorts of fields. And this investigation never ends: the moment a mystery is solved, yōkai assume different shapes, evolving right alongside humans and inspiring us to keep asking questions.[1]

The creature on my refrigerator guided me into the otherworld of yōkai, and I have been exploring it ever since. I went on to write a doctoral dissertation on yōkai, and in 2009 I published a book called *Pandemonium and Parade: Japanese Monsters and the Culture of Yōkai,* which is a cultural history of discourses of the weird and mysterious over the last four hundred years.

The Book of Yōkai is a very different endeavor. Although it builds on what I learned while working on *Pandemonium and Parade* and in the years since its publication, the present book focuses more explicitly on yōkai as forms of folkloric expression and communication that are simultaneously part of long-standing historical traditions and also very much alive and changing today. It also travels further back, into the earliest known texts in Japanese history, exploring a range of ideas and discussing some key individuals, from Abe no Seimei to Lafcadio Hearn, who contributed in different ways to shaping understandings of the supernatural world. *The Book of Yōkai* also introduces many of the yōkai themselves— some already famous beyond Japanese shores, and others almost unknown outside the small villages in which their legends developed.

Yōkai are part of folklore and popular culture in Japan, of course, but in recent years they have also started to garner attention elsewhere, including North America and Europe. In large part because of manga, anime, gaming, and the global influence of Japan's "soft power," more and more people have heard of yōkai and are interested in their folkloric roots. Although *The Book of Yōkai* does not focus explicitly on contemporary popular culture and media, I hope it will be useful to people engaged in these dimensions, as well as to anybody interested more generally in questions of belief, the monstrous, and the uncanny.

I wrote *The Book of Yōkai* while living in two very different locations in Japan: the city of Kyoto and the island of Shimo-Koshikijima in Kagoshima Prefecture. Kyoto, of course, is a historic capital and was a center of elite power and cultural production for much of Japanese history. In contrast, the island of Shimo-Koshikijima, with fewer than three thousand people, is far removed from the historical seats of power and, for that matter, from many of the amenities of urban life today. Yet both these places are entirely fitting locations to contemplate yōkai, because yōkai are equally at home in the metropolitan centers of the nation and in its rural peripheries. And in both places, my thinking about this project benefited immensely from conversations with friends and colleagues and teachers—though, of course, responsibility for any mistakes is entirely my own.

Kyoto is the home of the International Research Center for Japanese Studies (Nichibunken), a research facility that houses one of the largest collections of material on yōkai in the world; the current director, Komatsu Kazuhiko, has been the leading academic researcher on yōkai for the last several decades. I finished drafting this book while in residence there in 2013 and was fortunate to have access to all these resources, as well as to the wisdom of Komatsu-sensei and the members of his various *kenkyū-kai* (research workshops). My profound gratitude goes to Komatsu-sensei and to Professor Yamada Shōji, who sponsored me while I was there as a visiting research scholar. I am also indebted to Nakano Yōhei, Tokunaga Seiko, and the other denizens of the "yōkai project room," to Egami Toshinori and the Nichibunken library staff, and to Hayashi Hiroko, Nishiyama Akemi, No Sung-hwan, Ted Mack, and Kasumi Yamashita for many hours of excellent company and conversation.

For the first half of 2012, I lived on Shimo-Koshikijima, in the village of Teuchi, in order to research a ritual that I have written about elsewhere. But while on the island, I also began writing this book. A few of the local yōkai made it into the pages that follow; but more important, the experience of living in a small rural community gave me a deeper understanding of the kind of village lifestyle that was, and still is, characteristic of many parts of Japan. My friends on the island, many of whom I have known for over a decade, helped me understand viscerally the intimate connection of people with place, and the living relationship between history and the present. I am indebted to too many people to name them individually, but

I am especially grateful to Hironiwa Yoshitatsu and Hironiwa Yasuko for many hours of insightful conversation and exquisite food (and *imo-jōchū*). My deep appreciation also goes to my good friend Ozaki Takakazu and his family; to Shirasaki Hiroki, Shirasaki Sugako, Kawabata Tsuyoshi, Kawabata Yoriko, Hironiwa Hirokazu, Hironiwa Masako, Megurida Toshifumi, Megurida Chiriko, Hashiguchi Yoshitami, Hashiguchi Kyoko, Hironiwa Mamoru, Hironiwa Eiko, and their families; and to the fishermen of Aose.

Reed Malcolm, editor at the University of California Press, originally suggested this book—I am grateful to him and Stacy Eisenstark for their support throughout the project. My great thanks also goes to Chalon Emmons for her clear editorial guidance and to Bonita Hurd for her impeccable and perceptive copyediting. I also thank Makiura Yoshitaka for patiently assisting me with relevant aspects of copyright. Jon Kay and Hannah Davis of Traditional Arts Indiana graciously worked with me on last-minute technical issues as I prepared images, and Suzy Cincone provided careful (and bilingual) proofreading. Throughout this project it has been an honor to work with Shinonome Kijin, the illustrator who drew the original images in this book; he is not only a brilliant artist but also a true scholar of yōkai.

I am indebted to the Fulbright Foundation, which generously funded me in 2012 as the writing began to take shape; I particularly thank Jinko Brinkman and the other members of the JUSEC staff for their constant, good-natured support. I am profoundly grateful to my colleagues in the Department of Folklore and Ethnomusicology and the Department of East Asian Languages and Cultures at Indiana University, as well as to my graduate students there, for allowing me to escape campus duties for long enough to do a little yōkai hunting. In the United States and Japan, many people have supported my work, both intellectually and through pleasant distractions. There is no space to thank them all by name, but I would like to mention Ariga Takashi, Christopher Bolton, Dylar Kumax, Paul Manning, Steve Stuempfle, Denise Stuempfle, Suga Yutaka, Tsukahara Shinji, and the members of the Shingetsukai Research Society.

My deep gratitude also goes to my family. Adam Foster, Ann Ayton, Suzuki Tatsuo, Suzuki Yumi, and Suzuki Ken'ichirō were all remarkably patient and supportive throughout the research and writing process. My father, Jerry Foster, passed away in July 2014, while I was doing the final editing of the manuscript. Although he did not live to hold the finished book in his hands, for me every page is infused with his memory. His intellectual curiosity, encyclopedic knowledge, and extraordinary capacity to appreciate facts and ideas will always inspire me.

Finally, I am infinitely grateful to Michiko Suzuki, who has kept my work, and my life, centered. She has read all my drafts with crystalline perception and constantly challenged me to write more clearly and think more deeply. Without her, nothing would make sense.

Names, Dates, Places

A NOTE ON JAPANESE NAMES AND TERMS

Throughout this book, Japanese proper names are noted in Japanese order, with family name first. Where appropriate, I follow the Japanese convention of referring to certain writers, scholars, and artists by their pseudonyms or given names. For example, Toriyama Sekien is called Sekien rather than Toriyama. Japanese words and place-names that appear in standard English-language dictionaries are written in Roman script with no macrons (e.g., Tokyo, Shinto); other Japanese words are written with macrons to indicate long vowels. Japanese words used frequently throughout the text are italicized only in their first appearance.

DATES AND TIME PERIODS

Although I use Western-style dates, I also refer to several of the major Japanese time periods and eras.

Classical

Nara	710–794
Heian	c. 794–1185

Medieval

Kamakura	1185–1333
Muromachi	1392–1573

Early Modern

Edo (or Tokugawa)	c. 1600–1868

Modern

Meiji	1868–1912
Taishō	1912–1926
Shōwa	1926–1989
Heisei	1989–

PLACES

Throughout the book, I mention a variety of places by name. Below are some of the most common ones. (Please note, I omit the macrons for these particular place-names.)

Edo	The old name for Tokyo (before 1868)
Hokkaido	The second-largest and northernmost major island of Japan
Honshu	The largest of the four main islands of Japan, and the location of the cities Tokyo, Osaka, and Kyoto and the majority of the prefectures

Kansai	The region of western Japan, including Kyoto, Osaka, Nara, Kobe, and neighboring areas
Kanto	The region of eastern Japan, including Tokyo and nearby prefectures and cities
Kyushu	The third-largest island of Japan, located in the south-west
Okinawa	The southernmost prefecture in Japan, located south of Kyushu and encompassing the main island of Okinawa as well as many of the smaller islands in the Ryukyu Island group
Shikoku	The smallest of the four major islands of Japan, containing four prefectures
Tohoku	The northeast of Japan, including Akita, Aomori, Fukushima, Iwate, Miyagi, and Yamagata Prefectures

PART I Yōkai Culture

1 Introducing Yōkai

About fifteen years ago, I lived for a time in a small coastal village in rural Japan, where I was researching a local festival. I rented a rickety old wooden house literally a stone's throw from the ocean. Until a few months earlier, a family had lived there, and a lot of their belongings were still in the house: old furniture, pots and pans, kitchen utensils, drawers overflowing with clothes. A single Japanese-style room with worn tatami flooring served as my living room and became my bedroom when I unfolded my futon at night. There was a television in one corner and a Buddhist altar in another, and high on the wall was a row of framed black-and-white portraits of men and women looking down at me with severe expressions. These were the ancestors of the family who owned the house.

I'm not sure why the family had left. I rented the house from a distant relative of the owners, a kind old woman who lived nearby and saw that I was comfortable during my stay. And for the most part I was. I would fall asleep to the endless singsong of the waves. A few times, in the middle of the night, I awoke to rustling sounds in my tiny kitchen: a stray cat had snuck in through a hole in the floor and was rummaging around for scraps of food. And once or twice, when a storm blew in from the ocean, I could hear waves crashing on the beach with an eerie and purposeful violence.

The wind would shriek through the outer walls of the house and rattle the flimsy shoji doors inside.

But once, something really strange happened. I had been out late, drinking with friends and discussing the festival. When I got home around midnight, I diligently wrote up the day's events in my field notes and then laid out my futon. I promptly fell into a deep sleep.

When I opened my eyes, the room was glowing faintly. The framed photos of the ancestors glinted. It was dawn, that deep, quiet time of transition from darkness to light, from night to day. I wondered why I had woken up so suddenly and so early. Perhaps the cat had snuck into my kitchen again.

But then I heard voices—a woman, speaking quietly but with authority, and a man responding. I sat up wide awake now and looked around.

The voices were coming from the television. I watched the end of a weather report and the beginning of the morning news. There was nothing particularly scary about this until I started to wonder why the television was on in the first place. The remote control was on a table, a few feet from my futon, so it is unlikely I had turned it on accidentally while sleeping. Had I left it on the previous night? Perhaps I had been drunker than I thought, but I had no recollection of watching TV. Could there have been a weird electrical surge? Was something like that possible? Or perhaps it was a sign, some kind of message. Maybe somebody was trying to tell me something. I watched the news carefully, but could not figure out what message was being conveyed to me, other than the fact that the world was in its usual turmoil.

Eventually, I turned the television off and went back to sleep for another hour or two. Later that day, I mentioned the experience to several of my friends in the village. They had no explanation.

YŌKAI, FOLKLORE, AND THIS BOOK

I begin with this inconclusive story, a mundane modern mystery, because it raises the simple question of how we interpret our world. In particular, how do we explain occurrences that don't easily fit our everyday understandings of the way things work? When we ask who or what turned on the television, we are intimating that there is a living being or animated force interacting with us even though we cannot see it. We may visualize this force as a monster or a spirit or a ghost or a shape-shifting animal. In Japan such a force, and the form it takes, is often called a *yōkai*.

And yōkai, notoriously, take many different forms. They are commonly associated with folklore, and with small villages or old cities or deserted mountain passes, but they have also long populated literature and visual imagery. Today they are found throughout Japanese anime, manga, video games, movies, and role-playing games. Particularly in these latter formats, they have crossed oceans and continents to become part of popular culture in countries far from Japan. So what is a yōkai? For now, let us just say that a yōkai is a weird or mysterious creature, a monster or fantastic being, a spirit or a sprite. As this book will show, however, yōkai are ultimately more complicated and more interesting than these simple characterizations suggest. Yōkai may emerge from questions such as who turned on the television when nobody was around, but from there they take us on a kaleidoscopic journey through history and culture.

About This Book

One common characteristic of yōkai is their liminality, or "in-betweenness." They are creatures of the borderlands, living on the edge of town, or in the mountains between villages, or in the eddies of a river running between two rice fields. They often appear at twilight, that gray time when the familiar seems strange and faces become indistinguishable. They haunt bridges and tunnels, entranceways and thresholds. They lurk at crossroads.

It is appropriate that this book about yōkai also fits somewhere *in between*. While it is based on years of academic research and fieldwork, it is not intended only for scholars of Japan or experts on supernatural folklore. I hope it will contribute to their discussions, of course; but more important, I hope anybody with even a passing curiosity about these subjects will find it of interest. I have tried to present my ideas as clearly as possible, with little technical language; at the same time, I have strived to do justice to the depth and complexity of the topic.

The book, then, occupies a space between the academic and the popular, a position, in fact, similar to that of many books written about yōkai, and other subjects, in Japan. While Japan has a long tradition of publishing highly academic monographs with small print runs, many scholarly books—particularly about popular subjects such as yōkai—are also published by commercial presses and available at bookstores throughout the country. A diverse, well-educated public regularly consumes serious works on history, archaeology, folklore, media, literature, religion, and even philosophy.

This book is also situated at a crossroads between cultures. One objective is to introduce Japanese yōkai and Japanese scholarship on the subject to an English-language readership. In the West over the last several decades, the monstrous has increasingly become a subject of scholarly and popular fascination.[1] While much of the writing on these topics is insightful, rarely is there any mention of Japanese monsters. But as will become apparent in the pages that follow, in Japan the study of the monstrous—of yōkai—has long been a vibrant field. Like much other work within the humanities, yōkai research in Japanese simply has not been translated into English. This book is by no means a translation, but it is informed by rich Japanese research on the topic, which I hope to make accessible to people studying the monsters of other cultures. At the same time, I give all this my own particular interpretation and analysis, adding my voice to the conversation on these subjects.

Serious research on yōkai in English and other languages may be limited, but yōkai themselves are becoming more and more familiar to people in countries outside of Japan. Part and parcel of Japan's so-called soft power, these strange creatures have started to invade the rest of the world. For many of my students in the United States, for example, the terms *yōkai* and *Japanese folklore* are practically synonymous; they have encountered *kappa* or *kitsune* or *tengu* in manga and anime, films and video games, usually in English translation. This exposure inspires them to delve further into folklore, to find the "origins" of the yōkai of popular culture that they have come to love. And that is another purpose of this book, to provide some folkloric grounding for yōkai they might encounter. Although it is often impossible to trace the roots of particular creatures, I can offer a sense of the diverse influences and complex cultural histories that breathe life into them.

It will become clear, I think, that there has always been a great deal of interaction between yōkai in folklore, literature, art, manga, and so on, and it is meaningless to draw sharp distinctions between these forms of communication. But for the most part, I leave analysis of the most contemporary popular-culture appearances of yōkai to readers—who are probably more familiar with these versions than I am. I also do not explicitly treat Western-born manifestations of yōkai, such as English-language manga and fan fiction. My own research has focused on yōkai as they are expressed *in* Japan; I hope those with interests located elsewhere will build on what I present here or use it for comparative purposes.

With all this in mind, I have divided the text into two parts. Part 1, "Yōkai Culture," provides a cultural history of yōkai folklore and yōkai studies and explores some of the concepts that inform how yōkai and humans interact. Part 2, "Yōkai Codex," is a bestiary, a compendium of various yōkai, that helps illustrate many of the concepts discussed in part 1. These two parts are really interdependent—yōkai discussed in part 2 appear in part 1, and texts mentioned in part 1 show up in part 2. Getting the full picture may require flipping back and forth.

"Yōkai Culture" is divided into three chapters, each with several sections. Because there is a lot of information in each of these chapters, the sections are short and each one includes a number of subheadings. The current chapter presents key concepts related to yōkai and their study. I explain a little about folklore in general and then trace the words that historically have been used for yōkai. Finally, I explore some of the ways we can define yōkai and think about how they come into existence.

Chapter 2, "Shape-Shifting History," introduces the big names—both people and texts—through which we know about yōkai today. The simple premise of this chapter is that yōkai would not exist without the human beings who told of them, studied them, wrote about them, and in some cases tried to subdue them. Yōkai have played an important role, often in the shadows, as Japan developed from one period to the next. This chapter is divided into four sections, each dealing with a particular historical era.

Chapter 3, "Yōkai Practice/Yōkai Theory," has two sections. The first provides a brief journey through what I call the "yōkai culture network"—a web of people who are closely involved with the production of yōkai knowledge today. And the final section suggests further approaches to understanding yōkai in the abstract and to exploring their meanings within a larger global context.

Part 2, "Yōkai Codex," is designed like a small encyclopedia. One way people have commonly dealt with yōkai is by labeling, organizing, and classifying them. Perhaps this is because yōkai are so varied and plentiful: maybe the only way to really define them is by listing examples. So this part is a bestiary with information about selected yōkai: the list is long but really only scratches the surface, because, as I argue throughout the book, yōkai are diverse and abundant and always changing or being reborn. In the codex, I have tried to include all the best-known creatures, as well as a smattering of more obscure ones, but inevitably many have been left out. This bestiary is designed for easy sampling and for easily looking up particular yōkai, but it can also be read straight through, which may reveal surprising connections between different creatures.

Researching Yōkai

Yōkai dwell in the contact zone between fact and fiction, between belief and doubt. They inhabit a realm of narrative in which laws of nature are challenged. And yōkai themselves are always changing, from place to place and generation to generation. Because of this mutability, broad generalizations or simplistic statements about them are tempting. With something so elusive and shape-shifting, how can anybody say you are wrong? How do we prove anything about these creatures?

Indeed, one is faced with a problem when writing about yōkai: unlike historical figures, political events, or economic changes, yōkai rarely make it into the authoritative public record. They slip through the cracks of official history. They don't belong to anybody. Rather, they are a kind of communal intellectual property: anybody can play with them, change them, believe in them, and make new versions of them to be sent out into the world. Of course, these are all reasons why yōkai are deeply revealing. They are a part of culture that tends to be dismissed as "just folklore." So how do you study something that emerges anonymously, exists in multiple versions, and circulates widely over time and space? What do you do when there is no *original*? How do you research yōkai?

A young woman would walk up to people on the street. She was attractive, but she wore a large white surgical mask over her mouth. She would tap a stranger on the shoulder and ask, "Am I pretty?" Then she would remove the mask. Her mouth was slit at the corners all the way up to her ears. "Even like this?"

This is a legend I heard one day from a Japanese friend. She had heard it as a child and recalled being afraid to walk home from school alone. This frightening female yōkai came to be known as the *kuchi-sake-onna,* or the "slit-mouthed woman," and for a few months back in 1979 the very thought of her terrified children throughout much of Japan. In the codex, I have a longer entry on the kuchi-sake-onna, but I mention her now because, as a modern urban yōkai, she serves as a good example of how one goes about researching yōkai in general.

In my experience there are three general approaches, each one informing the others. First there is ethnography: talking with people, asking them about yōkai they grew up with or encountered in their communities, their hometowns, their apartment buildings, or even in manga and anime. That is how I first learned of the kuchi-sake-onna—and then I followed up by asking almost everybody I met for their versions of the legend and memories of what it had meant to them. Sometimes this sort of research can be easy: you just hang out in a bar and chat with customers. But it can also require contacting a village historian, formally interviewing a publisher or novelist, or making an appointment at a shrine to talk with the priest. It can entail participating in a public festival or getting permission to attend a ritual or private ceremony. In some cases, this kind of research requires living in a community for a long time and gradually learning about people's everyday lives.

A complementary form of research is archival—digging through primary sources. This might mean reading old texts written in Sino-Japanese *kanbun* or examining Edo-period images or illustrated books. It can also entail reading popular magazines or analyzing novels or contemporary manga and anime. These materials can be found in research libraries or museums, and sometimes in local communities or private households. The kuchi-sake-onna, for example, did not appear in any of the official historical documents I looked at, but I found dozens of references to her when I combed through popular magazines and tabloids from 1979 and the early 1980s; I also came upon all sorts of other data that helped me understand what she might have meant to people at that time. I found most of these sources in archives in Tokyo, but I also got some firsthand information from a record producer whose company had once recorded a song about the kuchi-sake-onna.

And finally, in Japan there has already been a great deal of research on yōkai. Fortunately, highly trained scholars have sorted through difficult old texts, sometimes translating them into modern Japanese. They have looked through images, and woodblock prints, and community records and tracked down the yōkai lurking there. Japanese scholarship on monsterdom is perhaps the most active in the world. This means there are a great many secondary sources—dictionaries, anthologies, collected art, and documents, as well as insightful analyses. University professors in Japan, in fact, have written numerous works on yōkai, and today several freelance writers make a living by writing and lecturing about yōkai. The legend of the kuchi-sake-onna is recounted in a number of contemporary legend collections; there is at least one doctoral dissertation discussing her; and several scholars have written about how she links to different female yōkai from earlier periods or reflects sociocultural concerns. I did not always agree with the analyses I read, of course, but they helped me think more deeply and develop my own interpretations.

As the kuchi-sake-onna example demonstrates, investigating yōkai entails a mix of all three of these approaches—ethnographic, archival, and secondary research. For the majority of yōkai in this book, I relied in part on archival materials and a great deal on the wealth of secondary scholarship available in Japan. I have also benefited immensely from getting to know some of the researchers personally; they have made suggestions, introduced me to primary materials, and engaged thoughtfully with my ideas and interpretations.

Throughout this book, I try to be as accurate as possible in my reporting and analysis. *Accuracy* may seem a strange word to use when talking about yōkai, but it is precisely because of their elusiveness that it is all the more important to note where the data and ideas come from. That is why I provide so many references and footnotes. Most sources, inevitably, are in Japanese, but whenever possible I also cite material in English, either translations or original research, so that English-language readers can know where to find more information. Unless otherwise indicated, all translations from Japanese-language sources are my own.

About Folklore

The word *folklore* in English is bandied about relatively freely. It is a concept people tend to feel they understand—until they try to explain it. Folklore has actually always been difficult to define and indeed has changed a great deal since 1846, when the neologism *Folk-Lore* was introduced by William J. Thoms to describe "the manners, customs, observances, superstitions, ballads, proverbs, &c., of the olden time."[2] All these things are still considered folklore, but the "&c." (etc.), of course, is all but endless. It includes verbal folklore, everything from myth, legends, and folktales to jokes, anecdotes, memorates, and even slang. And material folklore—the making of things—can encompass the throwing of a ceramic pot to folding origami to baking a cake or carving a pumpkin. Another broad genre is customary folklore: rituals, festivals, and beliefs that are themselves often made up of, or expressed through, a combination of verbal and material culture. Think of a wedding, for instance, with its symbolic exchange of rings or other objects, formulaic utterance of vows, and eating of special foods.

One aspect of folklore that is often emphasized is *traditionality*—the idea that something has added value because of its association with the past ("the olden time," as Thoms would say). But tradition, too, is tricky to define; I characterize it as referring to behaviors and beliefs that are infused with special meaning or value in the *present* because of a sense of continuity with the *past* and also with the *future*. Traditions are constantly changing, even though they retain (or seem to retain) some connection with the way they were performed in past years or by previous generations. And they are practiced in the present only because they have (or seem to have) some bearing on the future. Traditions, we might say, are creative continuity.

The process by which folklore operates is a kind of tug-of-war between two forces—the conservative pull of the past versus the immediate pull of present (and future) needs. Within this process there is also a contrast between the communal voice that has developed over the years and the innovative personal voice of the individual performer or participant. It is out of this tension between conservatism and dynamism that the folklore of the present is shaped and experienced.[3]

This pull between past and present is one of the forces in the creation and re-creation of yōkai through time. To a certain extent, this tug-of-war applies more or less to any process of creation—nothing is ever wholly new, and nothing is ever exactly the same as what came before. But one reason folklore is distinct from, say, fine art or a best-selling novel is that it tends to be unofficial and noninstitutional: folklore is not controlled by formal authorities, such as governments, schools, or established religious institutions. This is not to say that there is no overlap between folklore and these more official forms of organization, but the things we call folklore usually fly under the radar of these formal establishments. This is one reason folklore is able to change so easily—because nobody controls it.

Similarly, in principle, folklore is noncommercial. No author or designer or professional artist dictates what is correct or incorrect. Folklore does not *belong* to an individual creator or a single group—it belongs to all the people who engage with it.[4] Of course, none of this is cut-and-dried: these are not definitions as much as they are tendencies or orientations. In reality, as yōkai demonstrate, there has always been a dynamic and symbiotic relationship between folklore and commercial and popular culture. But in general, folklore is free to travel and reproduce—or rather, people can freely reproduce and reinvent folklore, transmitting it from person to person across time and space. And this is why any "single" item of folklore tends to have multiple versions and variants. As we will see, almost every type of yōkai exists in more than one place at a given time (and more than one time in a given place). Yōkai are characterized by these local and historical versions: they are the same but different wherever and whenever you find them.

And where do we find the yōkai of folklore? Often they reside within some kind of story—usually a legend or a folktale. While these two forms of narrative are related and often overlap, folklorists generally make a simple distinction. Legends tend to be thought of as true, or possibly true, by the teller or listener or both. At the very least, there is a question of truth or believability at their core. They often include specific details of time and place, as well as the names of characters (sometimes historical people). Sometimes they are recounted as hearsay, something about a "friend of a friend" (an FOAF, in folklorist parlance). On the other hand, folktales are related as fictional stories for purposes of entertainment;

they take place "once upon a time" or "deep in the woods," and the characters are often "an old man and an old woman" rather than specific people. Yōkai are found in both these kinds of stories, and they are also found in shorter anecdotes and beliefs shared by people in a particular community.

We should also remember that not all folklore is transmitted by word of mouth; today we accept that folklore has always also been passed along through writing, drawing, and the making of objects. Yōkai in particular seem to inhabit visual media, such as picture scrolls and woodblock prints, and also work their way into books of all sorts. In contemporary culture, social networking, texting, and other digital means of transmission increase the creative ways in which beliefs, narratives, rumors, memorates, ideas, fears, jokes, and so on are communicated from person to person.

Finally, the notion of "folk" has also changed radically since the early days of folklore studies. The folk are no longer considered—as they once were—uneducated, rural people. They are, to quote American folklorist Alan Dundes, "any group of people whatsoever who share at least one common factor. It does not matter what the linking factor is—it could be a common occupation, language or religion—but what is important is that a group formed for whatever reason will have some traditions which it calls its own."[5]

Which brings us back to yōkai. While many of the yōkai in this book have been around for a long time, this does not mean they are only a thing of the past. Of course, the *folk* for whom yōkai are relevant are long-ago warriors from the Heian (794–1185) or Kamakura period (1185–1333), or urban merchants from the Edo period (c. 1600–1868), or perhaps even contemporary farmers working in small rural villages. But the folk are also sleekly dressed commuters in Japan's thriving postmodern metropolises, and people like you and me who share a common interest in these mysterious, ever-changing phenomena. While some yōkai may already be gone and faded from memory, new yōkai and new versions of old yōkai are always being born, or reborn, and infused with fresh energy. Recall the kuchi-sake-onna story: a modern legend, in an urban setting, told by everyday people, and written about in popular magazines. All this is to say that as long as human culture persists, so too, in one form or another, yōkai will flourish. If we are a folk group linked by an interest in yōkai, then we are connected with people in other places whom we have never met, and we are also connected with people who are long dead, and people who have not yet been born.

THE LANGUAGE OF YŌKAI

Yōkai begin where language ends.

Mysterious sounds. Lights flitting through the graveyard. A flood that destroys one village and leaves another unscathed. A feeling that something is watching you in the darkness. How do we speak of things that are ungraspable, anomalous? What words can we use to signify things that evade established categories and seemingly refuse to conform to the laws of nature?

In Japan, as elsewhere, inexplicable occurrences and supernatural creatures have been part of the cultural imagination for as long as history has been recorded. Broadly speaking, these diverse mysterious phenomena and weird "things" have come to be called yōkai. In a sense, *yōkai* is nothing more than a convenient label to indicate a whole range of otherwise ineffable experiences that might, in English, be translated with the words *spirits, goblins, phantoms, specters, sprites, shape-shifters, demons, fantastic beings, numinous occurrences, the supernatural,* and perhaps most commonly today, *monsters.* This wide variety of possible translations speaks to the open-endedness of the word and hints at the many different ideas and nuances associated with it. Because of the danger of narrowing the definition too much, in this book I generally avoid translations and just use the word itself—and maybe, like *sushi* or *tofu,* it will take root in other languages as well.

Mysterious Words
MONO-NO-KE 物の怪

In popular culture and scholarly literature in Japan today, *yōkai* has become the umbrella term for an entire panoply of mysterious phenomena and weird creatures. But the common use of the word actually began relatively recently; during different historical periods other terms have been used. In the Heian period, for example, spooky and unexplainable "things" were often called *mono-no-ke*. We find *mono-no-ke*, for instance, in Murasaki Shikibu's *Genji monogatari* (*The Tale of Genji*, early eleventh century), the most famous literary text of the Heian period, where they tend to "take an invisible form imagined to signify human spirits."[6] A direct translation of *mono-no-ke* is difficult, but *mono* usually refers to "thing" or "matter" and *ke* to something mysterious, suspicious, or troubling. Some scholars suggest that in early texts *mono* did not refer to concrete things as it does in modern Japanese but to amorphous or ghostly things such as souls or spirits.[7] Although this interpretation is disputed, we can compromise by thinking of *mono* as the essence of something and, therefore, characterize *mono-no-ke* as a sense of spookiness and mystery. However we translate it, though, *mono-no-ke* during the Heian period indicated danger, uncertainty, and terror—something lurking out there, just beyond reach, intending to do you harm.

ONI 鬼 AND HYAKKIYAGYŌ 百鬼夜行

Another term used to signify danger and fear was *oni*, generally translated today as "demon" or "ogre." During the Heian period, *oni* was a default label for any sort of nasty and threatening creature, usually but not always humanlike in shape. For example, oni (in this case pronounced *ki*) is embedded in the word, *hyakkiyagyō* (alternatively pronounced *hyakkiyakō*), which can be translated as "night procession of one hundred oni." In Heian-period texts, *hyakkiyagyō* usually refers to a procession of dangerous beings passing through the Heian capital (present-day Kyoto). Warnings that the hyakkiyagyō would be out on a given evening were provided by the Onmyōryō, the Bureau of Divination, staffed by practitioners of Onmyōdō, a complex system of divination and geomancy based on principles of yin and yang. When the hyakkiyagyō was on the move, it was to be avoided: suddenly the familiar space of the city was possessed by wild, unpredictable, dangerous demons. For a short time, *this* world and the *other* world would intersect and the usual rules of human culture were invalid.

It was also possible for people traveling outside the city to inadvertently stumble into alien territory possessed by demons. One tale from *Uji shūi monogatari* (*A Collection of Tales from Uji,* c. 1220?; hereafter *Tales from Uji*) tells of a monk traveling alone through the province of Settsu (near the present-day city of Osaka). Coming upon a deserted temple, he decides to settle in for the night and begins chanting an incantation to the guardian deity Fudō. But suddenly, "a crowd some hundred strong came surging into the temple, every one of them with a torch in his hand. When they got close, he saw that they were fantastically weird creatures, not men at all; there were all sorts of them, some with only one eye, some with horns, while their heads were more terrible than words can describe." The monk spends a terrifying night, surviving only because Fudō protects him. After the gang of oni finally leaves and the sun rises, the monk is shocked to discover that there is actually no temple at all and he cannot even find the path that brought him there. Eventually, he meets some travelers who inform him that he is in the province of Hizen—hundreds of miles from Settsu![8]

In some cases even just looking at hyakkiyagyō could be fatal. *Ōkagami* (*The Great Mirror,* c. 1100), for example, recounts an episode in which a nobleman named Morosuke encounters hyakkiyagyō while traveling through the capital. After commanding his entourage to set down his carriage, he lowers the blinds and recites a protective incantation. After the danger finally passes, he raises the blinds and continues his journey. (Interestingly, the passage suggests that only Morosuke, as a member of the nobility, is endangered by looking at the procession of demons; apparently his servants cannot even see them.)[9]

Given the danger and fear associated with looking upon this night procession, it is ironic that in succeeding generations hyakkiyagyō would become the subject of numerous illustrations, many of them lighthearted and not in the least frightening. Perhaps the most famous are a number of picture scrolls, many of which are simply called *Hyakkiyagyō emaki.* Because the images in these picture scrolls often allude to earlier versions (and the artists were clearly aware of each other's work), collectively they can be thought of as a kind of series, with the *Hyakkiyagyō emaki* label broadly applying to the genre itself. The oldest (known) of these scrolls, believed to be by Tosa Mitsunobu (1434?–1525?), dates from the Muromachi period. It features a chaotic panoply of weird creatures and, although the narrative is not entirely clear, concludes with the appearance of a gigantic red fireball (probably the sun), which causes the yōkai to scatter.[10]

TSUKUMOGAMI 付喪神

Notably, many of the weird creatures parading through Tosa's scroll are household items and other everyday objects animated with legs, arms, eyes, and occasionally a tail. There are, for example, a number of musical instruments, such as a red-limbed creature with a *biwa* (Japanese-style lute) for a head, dragging what looks like a *koto* with legs and a reptilian tail.[11] Such yōkai-ified everyday objects are called *tsukumogami*. The morphing of normal utensils (*kibutsu*) into yōkai seems to have been the fate of objects that had survived a hundred years. Later on, I discuss this further, but I'll mention here that these images transform the riot of oni and other frightening creatures from the earlier Heian period into a playful parade of household objects, including musical instruments, rice containers, and tools for cooking. On one hand, this trivializes the whole idea of the hyakkiyagyō as a terrifying otherworldly threat that must not be looked at; at the same time, it also brings the threat right into the home, with the implication that even common household goods possess the potential to become animated monsters.

The expression *hyakkiyagyō*, therefore, took on new meanings over time, eventually becoming a catchall for all sorts of fantastic creatures, from truly terrifying oni to comical musical instruments and everything in between. It was a word associated with danger but also, simultaneously, with a carnivalesque topsy-turvy parade in which all manner of creatures and objects danced riotously, musically, through the streets. These picture scrolls not only demonstrate great playfulness but also show a huge assortment of yōkai of all different shapes and sizes. All these elements—the tension between the fearful and comic, the repulsive and appealing, as well as the emphasis on playfulness, variety, and abundance—remain influential in the yōkai world to this day. What is missing from the images are humans: for a short time at least, the streets belonged to these wild, lawless creatures.

BAKEMONO 化物 AND OBAKE お化け

During the Edo period, another word, *bakemono*, began appearing in all sorts of contexts, from illustrated books to Kabuki plays to *misemono*

Figure 1. Hyakkiyagyō (tsukumogami). Original illustration by Shinonome Kijin.

spectacle shows. Meaning literally "changing thing" or "thing that changes," *bakemono* emphasizes transformation, a characteristic common to many yōkai. But its usage was not limited only to shape-shifting things: *bakemono* also applied to all sorts of strangely formed, frightening, or anomalous creatures. Even today, *bakemono* is commonly used in casual conversation and sometimes in academic and literary discussions. A related word, *obake*, is still popular as well, particularly among children.[12] Both *bakemono* and *obake* are also similar to the English word *monster* and can refer to an evil person or to somebody or something extremely large, as in "look at that monster pumpkin!"

YŌKAI 妖怪

In recent years, however, *yōkai* has become the word of choice. The term itself is made up of two Chinese characters (kanji) both of which denote strangeness, mystery, or suspicion. The word has roots in China but appears in Japan as early as the eighth-century mythohistorical text *Shoku Nihongi*, where it is stated that because of a "yōkai"—inferably a strange or unfortunate occurrence of some sort—a purification ceremony was held at the Imperial Court.[13] The word is rare during the classical and medieval periods but starts to appear with increasing frequency during the mid-Edo period, when it was sometimes glossed with the pronunciation "bakemono."

However, it was not until the Meiji period (1868–1912), most prominently in the work of Inoue Enryō, that *yōkai* gradually became a technical term for all things beyond the realm of explanation. In the first part of the twentieth century, folklorist Yanagita Kunio used *yōkai* as a kind of catchall word in his academic writing, and in the late twentieth century it became the word of choice for the popular manga artist Mizuki Shigeru. Today *yōkai* appears frequently in both academic and popular writing, where, as noted earlier, it is an umbrella signifier for things we generally translate with terms such as *monster, spirit, goblin, demon, phantom, specter, fantastic being, lower-order deity,* or *unexplainable occurrence.*[14]

Gods, Monsters, Strange Beasts, Ghosts
YŌKAI AND KAMI 神

A key concept associated with yōkai is *kami* (often used with an honorific suffix: *kami-sama*), meaning "god" or "deity." Translations like this, however, can be misleading: kami in Japan may be worshipped and prayed to, but they do not have the all-powerful status attributed to gods in monotheistic religions. Rather, there are multitudes of kami inhabiting all sorts of things in the natural world. A large or striking feature of the landscape, like a mountain or a waterfall or an ancient tree, may contain (or actually be) a kami; in other cases, kami may lodge in something small and local, like a boulder, or a stone, or a trickling creek. Kami are abundant and varied and all around: almost anything, potentially, can possess a spirit.

I should note here that religion in Japan is notoriously complex; the very idea of "religion" as such is really a modern "invention."[15] Generally speaking, the two dominant strains of thought are Buddhism and Shintoism; but historically, and even now, these are intertwined with each other. The kami worship described earlier is often characterized as part of the "Shinto religion," but in practice Shinto is anything but an integrated and institutionalized system. Rather, it may be thought of "as a series of attempts at imposing a unifying framework upon disparate kami cults, or at creating a distinct religious tradition by transforming local kami cults into something bigger."[16] Whether we call them kami cults or folk religious practices or localized belief traditions, worship of kami at natural sites and in small communities continues to be part of everyday life in many parts of Japan. It is always important to remember the plurality and disparity of these traditions; the meaning of a kami in one time and place is not (necessarily) the same as in the next. As scholars of Shinto history put it, "The paths of the kami through Japanese history have been manifold."[17]

It is also important to remember that individual kami may be powerful, but they are not necessarily *good* in the moral sense. In fact, some kami are known for a short temper and violence; the line between deity and demon is rarely distinct and often depends on the perspective of the humans affected. Similarly, Buddhism has numerous figures of monstrous proportions who are both frightening and benevolent. Broadly speaking, in the early historical period in Japan the spirit of something could assume either of two distinct attitudes: it could be angry and rough, and would be known as an *aratama,* or gentle and beneficial, known as a *nigitama.* Rough spirits were sometimes labeled *oni,* and as we have already seen, oni are clearly related to yōkai.[18]

In short, although it is tempting to think in terms of a simple opposition—kami good and yōkai bad—the line between the two is blurry. Yanagita Kunio, the father of folkloristics in Japan, suggested that yōkai are kami that have "degraded" over time, an idea that suggests an intimate relationship between the two. Moreover, although yōkai are often considered mischievous and even murderous, they are not necessarily defined by bad behavior. An individual kami/yōkai can be evaluated positively or negatively depending on one's perspective: a water spirit, for example, may be worshipped as a kami by families for whom the river provides irrigation, and despised as a yōkai by families who suffer drought. An act that benefits one person may hurt another. Folklorist-anthropologist Komatsu Kazuhiko has suggested that yōkai are "unworshipped" kami and kami are "worshipped" yōkai.[19]

Both kami and yōkai reflect a way of thinking often called animistic, meaning that the things in the world around us—rocks, rivers, even musical instruments—can possess animating forces or spirits. In Japan, this way of thinking has been important historically and may, as Komatsu suggests, still be part of the consciousness of many people today.[20] Within such an animistic world, we can imagine a continuum. On one end, where yōkai cluster, we have everything that seems troublesome, undesirable, unworshipped. The other end contains helpful, desirable, and worshipped things—generally called kami. But these are extremes, and any individual entity can move along this continuum. If a "bad" yōkai does something "good," we might consider it a kami, and vice versa.

In other words, these identities are not set in stone; they are contingent on the perspectives of the humans interacting with them. Through appropriate human action, such as rituals of pacification, a rough spirit might be transformed into a gentle spirit. The very thing that threatens human enterprises and society (aratama, yōkai) can be changed into a beneficial and cooperating power (nigitama, kami) in these same enterprises. One famous example of transformation is Sugawara no Michizane (845–903), a Heian-period scholar and poet who was banished for political reasons to an undesirable post in Kyushu. After his death, it is said, he became a vengeful spirit (onryō) and proceeded to cause a series of terrible misfortunes, including untimely deaths, floods, and lightning storms. Eventually, through government proclamations and pacification ceremonies, he was deified, transformed into the kami called Tenjin-sama. The calamities ceased.[21] To this day, there are shrines throughout Japan dedicated to Tenjin-sama, considered the kami of learning because of

Michizane's status in life as a great scholar. Every year thousands of students flock to these shrines to pray for success on their school entrance exams.

In the case of Michizane, then, human agency transformed a murderous spirit into a beneficial kami who, among other things, helps students. And this is an important point, because ultimately judgments of good/bad, troublesome/helpful, desirable/undesirable, and worshipped/unworshipped are based on human interpretation. Komatsu suggests, for example, that we can imagine a scenario in which a bright object appears in the sky and seems to fall somewhere. Everybody would agree that this is a mysterious occurrence, but whether it is read as a good omen or as a portent of ill fortune is up to the observers. If it is taken as a bad sign, then we might classify it as a kind of yōkai.[22] Ultimately then, yōkai provide insight into the way humans, at different historical moments and in different circumstances, choose to interpret the world around them.

MONSTERS AND KAIJŪ 怪獣

The idea that a yōkai might be read as an omen aligns well with the English word *monster*, deriving as it does from the Latin *monstrum*, a term that "to the Romans signified generally a supernatural event thought to be a portent from the gods, a warning of some sort."[23] In this sense, "monster" is certainly a convenient translation for *yōkai*, but at the same time the characteristics of yōkai can also be quite different from those commonly associated with monstrousness in the West today. In contemporary culture, monsters are often portrayed as physically intimidating or frighteningly grotesque; some yōkai are similar, but many others express themselves through more spiritual, haunting forms of mischief. In fact, those things that fit under the rubric of *yōkai* run the gamut from tangible creatures to intangible phenomena, from the solid and embodied to the spiritual and ephemeral and everything in between. In general, then, yōkai is a more inclusive and amorphous concept than monster. Throughout this book, I mostly use *yōkai* to refer to the things I am discussing and leave it to the reader to determine how (or if) they differ from monsters and similar things in other languages and cultures.

We should, however, recognize another common Japanese term often translated as "monster": *kaijū. Kaijū* shares a kanji (*kai*) with yōkai and might be translated as "strange beast." The difference between kaijū and yōkai is murky, but kaijū usually encompass gigantic creatures such as Godzilla, Mothra, and Gamera that appear in *kaijū eiga*, or "monster movies." Kaijū do not often, if ever, appear in local folktales and legends. Generally speaking, then, kaijū are physically giant creatures whose origins are traceable not to folk roots but to commercial sources—usually a movie. So even though Godzilla (or Gojira as it is known in Japan) is one of Japan's most globally infamous monsters, in Japan Godzilla is not a yōkai.[24]

YŪREI 幽霊

Finally, one more relevant word is *yūrei*, generally translated as "ghost." A question that frequently comes up when discussing yōkai is how they are distinct from yūrei—that is, how do yōkai and ghosts differ? As with all questions relating to concepts as elusive as these, the answer depends on factors such as the historical period under discussion.

Writing in 1936, Yanagita Kunio argued that in the past people were clear about the difference between ghosts (yūrei) and obake/bakemono (by which we can assume he means yōkai). He points out distinctions with regard to place, victim, and time. Yōkai, he explains, "generally appeared in set locations. If you avoided these particular places you could live your entire life without ever running into one." On the other hand, yūrei were not associated with particular locations but would chase after you wherever you happened to be. Connected to this is the fact that yōkai were not particular about *who* they tormented: "They did not choose their victims; rather, they targeted the ordinary masses." In contrast, a yūrei "only targeted the person it was concerned with." Finally, yōkai could appear any time of day or night but preferred the "dim light" of twilight or dawn. Yūrei only came out during the time of *ushimitsu*, the third quarter of the hour of the ox, about 2:00–2:30 A.M., when night was at its darkest.[25]

Subsequent scholars have challenged Yanagita's distinctions, finding exceptions and pointing out that more often than not a yūrei is associated with a human being who has died. Given the broad definition of yōkai, then, the best solution perhaps is to consider ghosts a subset of the larger category of yōkai. This is what Komatsu Kazuhiko suggests, explaining that ghosts can be thought of as a special subcategory of yōkai just as we think of human beings as a special subcategory of animals. Because humans are animals who possess a particular kind of culture, they tend to receive special attention within the wider study of living things. So too ghosts, as yōkai with a particular relationship to humans, have received special attention within the wider study of yōkai.

Komatsu further points out that ghosts in Japanese history and culture can be roughly divided into two related "types." The first is what we might call folkloric ghosts: people who have died harboring a lingering attachment or with unfinished business of some sort. They wander about in the present world appearing much as they did when they were alive. If you did not know they were dead, you might not notice anything odd about them. Such ghosts often harbor a deep resentment toward a particular individual, or perhaps unquenchable feelings of love or friendship. In some cases, a person becomes a ghost because he or she has died suddenly with no opportunity to make peace with the world. This type of ghost is common in legends and personal-experience narratives, in which the plot revolves around the sudden, shocking realization that a person who seems very much alive is actually dead.

The second type of ghost, which overlaps with the first, is common in drama and art. Its distinguishing feature is that it clearly appears as somebody who has already passed to the other side; he or she might be dressed in a funeral shroud or have no feet—a particularly common trope for Japanese ghosts. When you see one of these ghosts, you know right away that you are dealing with a dead person. This type of ghost makes for good theater and artwork but rarely appears in folk narratives or local legends. A significant aspect of both these types of ghosts is that they are not just some vague scary presence, but rather they are associated, often by name, with a specific person who once was living.[26]

EVENT BECOMES OBJECT

By exploring various words relevant to yōkai, we get a sense of both the history and the parameters of the concept and the way it fits into particular cultural contexts. But words get us only so far. So now I would like to take one step back and think a little about the basic cognitive processes that, in theory at least, give birth to yōkai. These processes, of course, are not specific to Japan. Whether they call them monsters or spirits or demons or whatever, it is likely that all cultures have traditions involving something that fits what we are calling yōkai. Thinking about the genesis of yōkai, then, is really a philosophical problem; it helps us explore how human beings struggle to grasp, interpret, and control the world around them.

Imagine you are alone at night in an old house in the countryside. You are lying in bed trying to fall asleep. All of a sudden, you hear rattling sounds coming from the windows and something scratching against the walls. Perhaps it is only the wind, you think, and you get up and walk to the window to listen more carefully. The sounds stop. You open the window and peer out into the darkness, but there is nothing, not even a breeze.

You go back to bed. The sounds begin again. Could it be an animal? Maybe there is a squirrel or possum in the attic, or something outside scratching against the side of the house. But again, the instant you get up to check, the sounds stop.

What if this went on night after night? During the day, you inspect the house thoroughly, hoping for clear evidence of an animal or maybe a tree brushing against the eaves. But you find nothing at all. What now? You are confronted with something that makes no sense, a phenomenon that does not follow the rules of nature and the laws of science as you have come to know them. But there *must* be an explanation. Perhaps some human is causing this. Are there mischievous kids in the neighborhood? Is somebody trying to torment you? As far as you know, you have done nothing to anger anybody.

At this point, when all possibilities in the *known* world are exhausted, you might venture into the *unknown*. Maybe something is trying to contact you. Are these mysterious noises some sort of a sign? A warning to leave the house? Or maybe they are a message of comfort, a signal that you are protected and not alone? Is it possible that something happened in this house long ago—somebody died, perhaps—and the memory of that time is somehow expressed by these strange sounds? The possibilities are endless, and disconcerting, and along with the sounds themselves they keep you awake at night.

Then late one evening when you finally fall asleep, utterly exhausted, you dream of little demonlike figures, each one with a hammer in its hand, banging away at the foundations of your house, climbing the walls, scratching with clawlike hands, rattling the windows. When you awaken, you know that this is the cause of the noise—these little creatures—and you call them *yanari*, meaning "house sounders." You have not necessarily solved the noise problem, but now you have a name to associate with it, and an image of the creatures causing it. It is no longer just some vague mystery but an identifiable mystery. You are being kept awake at night by yanari. And now you can start thinking of how to make them go away.

Of course, the narrative here is imaginary—although there *is* a yōkai called yanari that causes strange noises in the house. But the point is that we can imagine a simple process of reasoning through which an odd experience—mysterious noises at night—is gradually transformed into an identifiable thing with a body and a name. Moreover, perhaps this identifiable thing with a body and a name is already part of common sense; when you tell a friend about the strange sounds, she immediately identifies the culprit as yanari and then describes them as little demonlike figures with hammers. Your own imagination is informed by this knowledge, and when you hear these sounds again, all you see in your mind's eye are yanari. In a sense, this is folklore at work: commonly shared knowledge (lore) passed from person to person helps us make sense of new and unfamiliar experiences. It also can provide a solution: since you now know the cause of the problem, you may be able to find a special charm or incantation to rid you of these mischievous demons.

Take another example. You have spent all day cutting wood in the forest. It is dark now. You are hungry and exhausted and you have a long way to travel. So you hoist your pack onto your shoulders and set off through the mountains. You walk and walk, and then suddenly, at a certain point, you just cannot take another step forward. It feels like something is blocking you, as if you have walked into a solid but invisible wall. And in fact there is a yōkai, called a *nurikabe* (plaster wall), described in just this way: an invisible wall that prevents you from moving forward. In the second half of the twentieth century, manga artist Mizuki Shigeru illustrated this nurikabe—giving it legs and arms and two little eyes. It would soon become a standard character in his manga and anime, known to children and adults throughout Japan. So we can see here the process by which a strange *phenomenon* (not being able to move forward anymore) becomes a *yōkai* (the nurikabe) and eventually even becomes a famous *character.*

In an interesting parallel, marathon runners are often said to "hit a wall" around the twentieth mile of their race. Certainly *hitting a wall* is a powerful image for the sudden fatigue that overtakes a runner who no longer has energy to continue. Literally speaking, of course, there is no wall. But that is just the point—we do not always speak *literally*. Rather, we often speak *figuratively*, drawing on metaphor and other figures of speech to accurately and gracefully express our ideas or feelings. Here the runner projects an internal experience (from inside the body) onto the external world. The violent image of hitting the wall is a vivid, memorable, and effective way to articulate a sense of helplessness.

The runner's experience dovetails neatly with the idea of bumping into a nurikabe. If *hitting the wall* itself is a metaphorical expression, then *nurikabe* is a slightly more concrete (no pun intended) metaphor, in which the phenomenon is not just described by alluding to the feeling of hitting a wall but is given its own special name and personality. (By calling a yōkai a metaphor, I am by no means saying it is not real—it is as real as any other "thing" for which we have a word or figure of speech.)

But of course, scientists would not explain sudden energy loss as "nurikabe." Rather, they might say that the experience of "hitting the wall" occurs when the body's "glycogen supplies have been exhausted and energy has to be converted from fat."[27] Does this mean that the nurikabe is just an explanation for people who know nothing about biology or medicine? Of course, how you explain something depends on your background and culture—your education, interests, values, beliefs. We could just as easily say that "glycogen depletion" is how people who know nothing about yōkai explain the experience of meeting a nurikabe! In some ways, in fact, this might be the most persuasive explanation—after all, I can draw a picture of a nurikabe, but I have no idea where to begin with glycogen.

All this is to say that by exploring yōkai we challenge ourselves to ponder issues of belief, both personal and cultural, as well as metaphysical and phenomenological questions about the ways we experience and perceive our lives. Although belief in the supernatural is often debunked as irrational or unscientific, for example, we can actually consider the processes through which yōkai are created to be, in a sense, rational. The unknown, the feared, those things that overwhelm us with anxiety, are carefully identified, given form, and labeled. Only then can we grapple with them. Whether we label something with the name of a yōkai or a disease, whether we call it nurikabe or glycogen depletion, identifying it helps us work out an appropriate response—which of course is a pretty rational way to deal with a problem.

The creation of yōkai is a process through which fear, mystery, the unknown, is transformed into something concrete. The hyakkiyagyō discussed earlier, for example, started out as a terrifying and amorphous experience but was shaped over time into something that could be illustrated and eventually even laughed at. We can think of this process as a gradual movement from pandemonium to parade, from chaotic fear of the intangible unknown to an orderly and lighthearted display of identifiable creatures.

Event, Presence, Object

With all the foregoing in mind, I will briefly introduce the way Komatsu Kazuhiko, probably the leading academic authority on the supernatural in Japan, analyzes the development of yōkai within Japanese history. In part, I review Komatsu's ideas here because they have influenced my own thinking about the subject, but more importantly because they reflect and have influenced the ideas of a great many scholars currently working in Japan. Komatsu's books are often read by the general public as well, so they also have an effect on popular notions of yōkai throughout the country. Komatsu presents a kind of structural analysis, dividing yōkai into three "realms" or "domains": yōkai as event, as presence, and as object.

YŌKAI AS EVENT

This domain of yōkai is entered when you experience something strange, mysterious, or weird through one (or more) of your five senses. When you feel that this phenomenon (genshō) or event (dekigoto) is caused by an "undesirable supernatural thing" (nozomashikunai chōshizenteki na mono), you are positing the intervention of a "yōkai." In theory, any of the five senses—sight, hearing, smell, touch, or taste—can play a role in the experience, but the majority are perceived through the eyes and ears.

Komatsu tells of somebody spending the night in a hut in the countryside. Late at night he hears a tree being chopped down in the distance, but when he investigates he finds no evidence of a felled tree. It turns out that there has long been folklore about this sort of phenomenon; it is known as *furusoma*. So with this knowledge, an odd event takes on the name of a yōkai called furusoma, about which there are already legends and beliefs. Through narrative and exchange, shared knowledge about this yōkai develops and gradually becomes part of a communal yōkai culture.

YŌKAI AS PRESENCE

The second domain is presence (*sonzai*). All around us are "things," such as animals and other presences, some of which we interpret as "supernatural." Within the generally animistic worldview that has long been part of the Japanese cultural imagination, not only do all things possess souls or spirits (*rei* or *tama*), but also we personify these spirits, attributing to them the kind of emotions we know from ourselves and other humans. They can be angry or sad, grateful or happy, and these emotions directly affect the human world: anger can be expressed in stormy weather or disease, and happiness expressed by a good catch or bountiful harvest. Komatsu stresses that during the ancient period (*kodai*) most natural phenomena were attributed to the machinations of a limited number of yōkai, such as oni, tengu, kitsune, and *tanuki*.

YŌKAI AS OBJECT

For the third realm, Komatsu uses the word *zōkei*, which I render as "object," but which could also be translated as "figure," "image," or "sculpted item"—that is, it refers to a created physical thing of some sort. With the introduction of Buddhism to Japan (in the sixth century) people created figures of deities and other spirits. During the Heian period, picture scrolls became a popular form of artistic-literary expression among the courtier classes, and certain yōkai-like creatures were illustrated for the first time. During the Muromachi period, a variety of illustrated texts became popular with merchant and working classes as well, and folk narratives featuring yōkai proliferated within these visual formats.

This creation of images was profoundly important for the cultural history of yōkai. As image-making continued through the years, many of the yōkai pictured did not come from local beliefs; rather, they were invented for purposes of recreation, pleasure, and amusement. This process of illustrating yōkai had two critical effects. First, certain yōkai became fixed with regard to how they were depicted—oni, for example, were illustrated with horns and a tiger-skin loincloth—and these images became the accepted, shared understanding of the yōkai in question. At the same time, however, the creativity involved in image-making also led to a major increase in the number and kinds of yōkai.[28]

Questioning Yōkai

Komatsu's brief summary here neatly prefigures the historical discussion in the next part of this book. It also encapsulates the processes through which yōkai evolve, exploring the question "What are yōkai?" and, more important, "Why are yōkai?" Ultimately, yōkai have no single definition or function—they are the spooky unexplainable things lurking on the edge of knowledge, and they are simultaneously the pictures—sometimes scary, sometimes cute or goofy—of what we imagine such things to look like. In the final analysis, defining yōkai is less interesting than the questions they raise and the discussions they inspire.

One question often asked about yōkai is whether people actually *believe* in them. This is tricky to answer, in part because it depends on what historical period, and which yōkai, we are discussing. Implicit in a question like this, however, is the assumption that there are only two possibilities—belief or doubt. One thing yōkai teach us is that between belief and doubt, between the literal and the metaphorical, lies a zone of ambiguity that is fertile ground for the imagination.

Humans seem to have a tremendous capacity to embrace different ideas, even ones that may seem contradictory. Any time we hear a story, read a novel, or watch a movie with fictional characters, we allow ourselves to "believe" in people and activities we know are not "real." But of course in one sense they *are* real: they make us laugh and cry, and they stay with us as memories, affecting the way we think and feel. We often express strong emotions about fictional characters—love and hate and everything in between.

When it comes to yōkai, too, different attitudes and different truths can interact productively—a process I call cognitive resonance. That is, the balance of seemingly contradictory ideas itself reflects a realistic and meaningful stance. One common Japanese phrase in the discussion of yōkai is *hanshin-hangi,* which means "half-belief/half-doubt." The appeal of this phrase is that it does not call for a decision one way or the other but combines two halves into a whole, a single attitude that recognizes that belief and doubt can live together harmoniously. Perhaps the question is not whether people believe in yōkai but why we require a yes-or-no answer in the first place.

Another yōkai-related question is whether Japan has more monsters and fantastic creatures than other countries do. Of course this depends on how we define such creatures. Moreover, to answer it thoroughly would require a tremendously extensive survey! Certainly, yōkai-like creatures and supernatural beings are found in cultures throughout the world—they are by no means unique to Japan—and they seem to be more prominent in some places than in others. In Ireland, for example, and certain European, African, and Native American cultures, such creatures still thrive in the cultural imagination and popular media. To a certain extent, I think, this stems from a deep association with local place—many such creatures, and the stories told about them, are linked to specific features of the landscape. Most important, they survive because people choose to continue to tell their stories, to document them, to re-create them, to keep them alive.

And this is certainly the case in Japan. In contemporary Japanese culture, yōkai may indeed be more prominent than monsters and spirits are in many other countries. If so, this is in part because of their deep connections to local places, to the landscape, and to folklore and history. And more important, it is because of the long and intimate relationship of local places, folklore, and history with art, literature, and popular culture. Having long ago been documented—made into objects, as Komatsu might put it—even old yōkai continue to have a presence in contemporary culture. This presence has been bolstered by key individuals who have breathed new life into yōkai at various times, reinvigorating them in the popular imagination.

I will also make the related argument that in Japan, perhaps more than in other countries, yōkai have long been the subject of serious academic study. Again, I don't think this has anything intrinsic to do with the nature of yōkai themselves or with some essential cultural attitude. Rather, it is because of specific historical circumstances through which certain intellectual leaders brought attention to the position of yōkai, gradually making viable their serious study.

The next chapter of this book takes a more detailed look at some of these people, and at the ways in which the representation of yōkai and the study of yōkai have evolved over the centuries. We can see how the theoretical concepts mentioned here play out against the backdrop of Japanese history and cultural change.

2 Shape-Shifting History

Most likely in every part of the globe, human beings have shaped mysterious and fearful phenomena into monsters and spirits as a way of making sense and meaning of their experiences. But the particular shapes such monsters and spirits assume are anything but universal. They are sculpted by the distinct cultures and societies in which they emerge, evolving through specific historical moments and with the changing desires and challenges of the people who tell their tales.

To understand the history of yōkai, then, we have to meet some of the individuals who have sought, documented, illustrated, explained, and discussed them over the centuries. That is, it is impossible to separate yōkai from their times and their texts, and from the people who have considered them. As otherworldly as yōkai may seem, they are also, of course, part of this world; throughout history both sword and pen have been invoked to eliminate them as a dangerous menace or, alternatively, to capture, preserve, and breathe life into them as a cherished part of heritage.

Yōkai have generally been overlooked in serious political, military, and social histories. To a certain extent this is because, like so many kinds of folklore, they are a taken-for-granted part of everyday life and rarely make it into official documents or registers. Moreover, when they did come to people's attention in the past, particularly during the modern period, it was only as unimportant relics or dangerous superstitions that were to be destroyed. All the more reason, then, to seek them out, because yōkai can in fact be found in all sorts of cultural records throughout Japanese history—in folklore, literature, encyclopedias, art, and even games. The yōkai in these places may point to overlooked ideas and changes and offer an unusual view of the wide sweep of Japanese history.

The pages that follow briefly trace the history of yōkai by introducing some of the big names—people both ancient and living who are associated with the world of yōkai. This includes a few legendary sorcerers and warriors famous for subduing yōkai, and it also includes artists, scholars, and writers who have illustrated and documented them.

Along the way, I also explore some major texts and trends in which yōkai have appeared. I focus mainly on written works, but even as they were being captured on paper, yōkai remained a feature of lived experience, part of beliefs, festivals, legends, and folktales throughout the country. These local versions, often passed along through oral tradition, very much influenced the textually captured versions, and vice versa. Most of my examples come from written sources simply because writing, as a technology for preserving thoughts, provides the easiest (though not necessarily the most complete) access to the past.

Some of the people and texts mentioned have already appeared in the preceding chapter, but here I situate them within a broader historical context. This brief outline, however, is by no means a thorough review of the role yōkai have played in Japan's complex history. For example, I only fleetingly touch on yōkai illustrations, since the visual culture and art history of yōkai deserve a whole separate book or series of books. But the pages that follow are intended to convey a broad sense of both changes and continuities in how people have imagined and understood yōkai through the centuries. The various sections in this chapter, therefore, introduce some of the highlights, the moments and places where yōkai appear most prominently, and where they clearly reflect the social, cultural, and intellectual circumstances of the moment.

HEROES OF MYTH AND LEGEND

Susa-no-O, Dragon Slayer

Other than wooden slips called *mokkan,* seals, and similar fragments of writing, the earliest known texts in Japan are the mythohistorical *Kojiki* (712) and *Nihonshoki* (720).[1] Although the word *yōkai* itself does not appear in these works, they do include some terrifying and monstrous creatures—as well as people, or gods, who subdue them. Perhaps the most famous is a deity named Susa-no-O, the mischievous younger brother of the sun goddess, Amaterasu. In one episode, Susa-no-O meets an old couple in despair because every year an "eight-tailed dragon," known as Yamata no Orochi, comes and devours one of their daughters. "His eyes are like red ground cherries," the father explains. "His one body has eight heads and eight tails. On his body grow moss and cypress and cryptomeria trees. His length is such that he spans eight valleys and eight mountain peaks. If you look at his belly, you see blood oozing all over it."

Susa-no-O asks for the hand of the remaining daughter and then orders wine to be made and a fence built. "Make eight doors in the fence," he tells them. "At each door, tie together eight platforms, and on each of these platforms place a wine barrel. Fill each barrel with the thick wine of eightfold brewings, and wait." Eventually, the huge serpent appears, and "putting one head into each of the barrels," drinks until drunk, and then falls asleep. Susa-no-O duly unsheathes his sword and "hack[s] the dragon to pieces." His own blade eventually breaks inside the tail of the creature and, digging around, he finds another sword, the spectacular Kusanagi, a legendary weapon that would eventually, along with a mirror and jewel (called a *magatama*), become part of the so-called imperial regalia of Japan.[2]

Susa-no-O's slaying of the Yamata no Orochi is a very early example of what would come to be known as a *yōkai taiji,* or yōkai conquest, a traditional narrative in which a (usually) human hero manages to vanquish or kill a dangerous yōkai. Such narratives resurface again and again in local folk culture as well as in written and theatrical venues.

Early Textual Sources

Along with the *Kojiki* and *Nihonshoki,* some of the earliest Japanese texts are regional gazetteers, known as *fudoki,* which contained all sorts of historical and geographical records as well as local legends, myths, folk-tales, rituals, and beliefs. Not surprisingly, they also document kami and demonic creatures, though it is important to interpret them with the particular historical and political circumstances in mind. For example, the *Hizen no kuni fudoki* (Fudoki from Hizen Province; Hizen was the region of present-day Saga and Nagasaki Prefectures) refers to a creature called a *tsuchigumo,* an "earth spider." This certainly sounds like a yōkai, and eventually it would become one. But in these early texts, *tsuchigumo* is actually used as a kind of ethnic slur in order to demonize, to make less than human, the native residents of the area that the Yamato people, the authors of the *Fudoki,* were trying to conquer.[3]

During the Heian, Kamakura, and Muromachi eras, we encounter many more written records. One of the richest resources from this time is a literary genre called *setsuwa.* Although opinions differ about how to actually define the term, setsuwa are generally explained as short prose narratives that were gathered and organized into collections. Some of these anecdotes and legends originally came from oral tradition. Many seem to express a moral of some sort and may have been used for didactic purposes. Indeed, some collections are clearly assembled to promote a specific set of Buddhist principles. Others seem to have been gathered by a fun-loving collector and contain humorous stories, satiric commentaries, and sometimes wondrously gory descriptions. Although there are numerous setsuwa collections, the most famous are *Nihon ryōiki* (Miraculous stories of karmic retribution of good and evil in Japan; ninth century; hereafter *Miraculous Stories*), *Konjaku monogatari shū* (Collection of tales of times now past; eleventh or twelfth century; hereafter *Tales of Times Now Past*), and *Tales from Uji.* No one is certain of the objectives of the compilers and editors of these works, but now these collections are rich storehouses of information about the beliefs, attitudes, and experiences of people of the past. As with all texts, literary and otherwise, they must be carefully interpreted and understood within the context of their production.[4]

From the Muromachi into the early Edo period (late fourteenth century through the end of the seventeenth century), there flourished a new literary genre known broadly as *otogizōshi,* or "companion books." Hundreds of otogizōshi are extant today, and more are being discovered all the time.

They come in a variety of formats but, on the whole, are relatively short, entertaining narratives that often include illustrations. Content varies greatly: there are stories about people from all walks of life, religious narratives, animal stories, travel adventures, and tales concerning various yōkai.

One famous early (fourteenth-century) otogizōshi is the *Tsuchigumo-zōshi*, which is in the form of a picture scroll and tells of the heroic conquest of the earth spider. In contrast to its appearance centuries earlier in the *Fudoki from Hizen Province*, the tsuchigumo in this scroll is a full-fledged yōkai, a gigantic spider-demon surrounded by its progeny of smaller spiderlike monsters, all fully illustrated in color.[5] The tsuchigumo is just one example of the way the "same" yōkai can appear differently at different times, invoked for diverse purposes in a wide range of media. Of course, it is always difficult to access the past, particularly intimate qualities of belief, through textual sources. But for exploring the development of yōkai and human interactions with yōkai, these texts are invaluable, and we know much of what follows because of setsuwa and otogizōshi.

Abe no Seimei, Sorcerer Extraordinaire

Susa-no-O is a mythological deity, but as far back as the Heian period, there were also humans who were very much involved with the spirit world. One of the most famous was Abe no Seimei, a historical figure who lived from 921 to 1005. Seimei was an *onmyōji*, a practitioner of Onmyōdō, a divinatory and geomancy practice with roots in Chinese yin-yang and five-element philosophies.[6] As mentioned earlier, it was the Onmyōryō, or the Bureau of Divination, that determined which nights the hyakkiyagyō were out. Technically this Bureau of Divination was divided into four sections, each with its own specialty: (1) divination, (2) calendar, (3) astronomy and meteorology, and (4) time measurement and scheduling.[7] In practice, all these were somewhat related, and the bureau was called on for a range of services, including interpreting the dreams of court nobility, performing purification ceremonies, calculating auspicious dates, and exorcising spirits when somebody was possessed.[8] The Abe family and the Kamo family held the directorship of the bureau during the Heian period.

Because of their influential and mystical role within the government during this period, Onmyōdō practitioners came to be portrayed as powerful wizards specializing in quelling yōkai, exorcizing bad spirits, and intoning secret spells in order to kill people. Historical evidence suggests that Abe no Seimei himself was nothing more than a "middle-ranking bureaucrat" who performed a variety of services for the court and eventually rose to become the highest-ranking and most prominent of the onmyōji. One scholar notes that, compared to the rise of other onmyōji, Seimei's rise was not particularly smooth; had he not lived such a long life, he might not even be remembered today.[9] Regardless of historical evidence (or its scarcity), however, Abe no Seimei came to be thought of as the embodiment of supernatural power and his life became enshrouded in legend. It was said, for example, that his father, Abe no Yasuna, saved the life of a fox, who returned the favor by transforming into a beautiful woman. Seimei (or Dōji as he was known as a child) was the result of their coupling—a sort of human-yōkai hybrid born with insight into both worlds.[10]

A legend recounted in the *Tales of Times Now Past* tells how a young Seimei was attending his teacher, Kamo no Tadayuki, as they traveled through the capital. Tadayuki had fallen asleep inside the carriage when Seimei spied a frightening group of oni (perhaps a hyakkiyagyō) moving in their direction. He woke up Tadayuki, who cast a spell over the travelers to hide them from the oni, and eventually the danger passed. After this incident, Tadayuki took Seimei under his wing because he was so impressed by the young man's special ability to see oni.[11]

The life of the adult Seimei is similarly embellished with legends, many of which celebrate his prowess as a wizard. One famous episode plays off his supposed rivalry with another onmyōji, Ashiya Dōman. In the story, Dōman hears of Seimei's abilities and challenges him to a contest, the loser of which must become the winner's disciple. On the emperor's orders, sixteen *daikōji*, a type of citrus fruit, are secretly put into a box, and the two wizards are challenged to reveal what is inside. Dōman stares at the box for a long time and then declares that it contains sixteen of the fruits. Next it is Seimei's turn, and he promptly declares that the box contains sixteen mice. The government ministers and nobility, who all favor Seimei, are disappointed by his incorrect answer and are reluctant to open the box. Finally, however, they remove the lid, only to discover that it does indeed contain sixteen mice. In other words, Seimei's power allowed him not just to see through a sealed box but also to change what it contained. As promised, Dōman submits to becoming Seimei's disciple.[12]

The image of Seimei and his exploits, therefore, has been shaped through legend and through numerous literary and dramatic portrayals. He makes a striking appearance, for example, in the Noh drama *Kanawa* (*The Iron Crown*). In the play, a man is haunted by nightmares; Seimei soon divines the cause of his malaise to be his wife, who is deeply resentful of his philandering. The wife has transformed herself into a demon who will, Seimei foresees, try to kill the husband that very evening. Through secret spells and rituals, Seimei manages to successfully transfer the wife's hatred to effigies of the husband and his new lover, thus saving the man's life (though, sadly, doing nothing to resolve the cause of the wife's resentment).[13]

Seimei and other onmyōji were also said to have at their command a magical familiar, or spirit servant, known as a *shikigami*. Often portrayed as a demonic, grotesque, oni-like figure, a shikigami was charged with doing the bidding of its master, whether the job was critically important or completely mundane. For example, rumor had it that the doors in Seimei's house would open by themselves because of the machinations of his shikigami. More significantly, shikigami served as bodyguards and magical protectors for their controllers; they could even be sent to inflict illness or kill an enemy. It was said that an onmyōji could actually create shikigami through magic; by using a complex series of spells and incantations, he could transform a piece of paper or wood into this potent spirit. In some cases, an onmyōji might also transform a defeated yōkai or oni into a shikigami.[14]

Legend has it that Seimei himself had twelve shikigami at his command. While they were usually invisible to the average person, at night you might catch a glimpse of them in his house. Seimei's wife found them frightening and unpleasant to look at, so she pleaded with her husband to remove them, and eventually Seimei put them in a stone box that he hid under a nearby bridge, called Ichijō-modori-bashi. As one scholar points out, a bridge is a particularly strategic place to stash one's familiars; not only does it represent a symbolic connection with the other world—a link between one realm and another—but it is also a place people pass over, often while having conversations and revealing potentially valuable information. All of which could be extremely handy for a diviner and wizard.[15]

The Ichijō-modori-bashi bridge is a real place in Kyoto and can still be visited today, but researchers have pointed out that "there is no mention in the historical record of Abe no Seimei employing shikigami, and virtually none even of shikigami themselves."[16] Indeed, historical evidence regarding shikigami is vague and varied. Like so much about Seimei, our understanding of these supernatural attendants is shaped by legend, literature, and drama, and even by later academic speculation. The fact that shikigami are so hard to pin down historically does not make them less interesting or valuable—as with all yōkai, their meaning at any given moment reflects the imaginations of the humans who conjure them up.

To a certain extent Seimei, Onmyōdō, and shikigami are popular today because they are one part of a general fascination with yōkai and the supernatural. Within this broader context, however, they seem to occupy a particularly glamorous position. To interject a brief personal anecdote: I first encountered Abe no Seimei in early 1999, when I was a graduate student trying to write a paper about *The Iron Crown*. I was eager to find out more about this mysterious sorcerer, so I scoured the Japanese collections at university libraries in the United States. Eventually I found a few relevant references here and there, usually in dusty old books that nobody had opened for years; but for the most part Seimei seemed an obscure, if intriguing, figure. My research did not get far. Later that year, however, I went to Japan. I walked into a Tokyo bookstore, and there was an entire display table covered with novels, manga, and research monographs about Seimei! I soon learned that Japan was in the midst of an Abe no Seimei boom.

In fact, Seimei had never completely disappeared from the popular imagination; throughout the Edo period his status as a hero became firmly entrenched through legend, fiction, and drama. But it wasn't until the Heisei period, particularly beginning in the 1990s, that he reemerged as a sexy star of modern literature and popular culture. This newfound popularity began with a series of romantic historical novels, titled *Onmyōji*, written by Yumemakura Baku (b. 1951) and featuring Seimei as a handsome young man, often accompanied by his nobleman friend, Minamoto no Hiromasa Ason (also a historical figure). The first book appeared in

1988 and was followed by numerous others, as well as an extremely popular manga series by Okano Reiko (b. 1960), a television series, and two feature-length films (2001 and 2003). In all these versions, the image of Seimei was "re-imagined as a *bishōnen*, a beautiful young man with huge eyes, flowing locks, and a sculpted face." This "extreme makeover," as one scholar puts it, transformed the Heian-period sorcerer into a delicate and handsome idol who conforms to the gaze of contemporary Japanese girls and young women, presumably the primary consumers of Seimei novels, manga, and films.[17]

During the 1990s and early 2000s, in response to Seimei's newfound popularity and the makeover of his image, dozens of Onmyōdō-related shrines throughout the country were rejuvenated. In Kyoto, for example, Seimei jinja (shrine) is relatively small and not centrally located, but it is now a popular pilgrimage site for Seimei fans. The shrine itself is crisply decked out with Onmyōdō symbolism—five-pointed stars, sun-moon motifs, yin-yang symbols—and sells all manner of charms and other official souvenirs. A shop right next to it has also tried to make the most of Seimei's popularity, selling Seimei and Onmyōdō T-shirts, key chains, cell phone straps, and other "unofficial" goods.[18] Akin to so many of the yōkai featured in this book, the Seimei of the past—of the Heian period, and even of Edo-period legend and literature—is very different from the Seimei of the early twenty-first century.

Minamoto no Yorimitsu, Legendary Warrior

Seimei's life overlapped historically with that of another hero of the yōkai world: Minamoto no Yorimitsu (948?–1021), commonly known as Raikō (the Sinified reading of Yorimitsu). Like Abe no Seimei, Raikō was a real person; he was a member of the Seiwa Genji, a branch of the Minamoto family renowned for its great warriors. And like Seimei, Raikō is most remembered today through the legends that grew up around him—in this case, legends about his prowess as a warrior and his ability to subdue yōkai with sword and cunning. Perhaps his most famous yōkai conquest is that of Shuten dōji, a great oni that terrified the capital. In some versions of this legend, Abe no Seimei is the diviner who reveals the location of the demon, so we get an instance of the two superheroes—one the brains, the other the brawn—working together to rid the capital of a troublesome monster.

Tales of Raikō are found in various sources, including the "Book of Swords" (Tsurugi no maki) section of *Heike monogatari* (*The Tale of the Heike*), various otogizōshi, Noh drama, and Kabuki. In addition to conquering Shuten dōji, Raikō is also the hero of the *Tsuchigumo-zōshi*, mentioned earlier. This picture-scroll narrative recounts a journey of Raikō and his faithful companion, Watanabe no Tsuna, one of four trusty retainers. Raikō and Tsuna come across a dilapidated old house, where they encounter all sorts of yōkai, including a 290-year-old woman, a nun with a gargantuan face, a sixty-meter-tall oni, a kitsune fox, and some random tsukumogami. In the end, they finally meet up with the gigantic earth spider, which Raikō duly beheads.[19]

Legends about Raikō nicely complement legends about Seimei. Raikō is the brawny, visceral warrior who conquers his enemies with his strength and his sword. Seimei, on the other hand, is the mystical, divining, intellectual counterpart who exerts power over others through knowledge, magic, and the strength of his secrets spells. Together these yōkai-hunting heroes neatly reflect the duality of event and object inherent in the very concept of yōkai: while Seimei divines the mysterious phenomenon, Raikō fights the weird body.

WEIRD TALES AND WEIRD TASTES

The Tokugawa, or Edo period, from around 1600 to 1868, was a time of great dynamism and change in Japan. Without oversimplifying a span of almost three centuries, we can say that during this period the disparate domains of the Japanese islands were, relatively speaking, united as one country through a complex system of oversight with a strong military government based in Edo (present-day Tokyo) and a weak but symbolically meaningful emperor in Kyoto. It was a period of comparative peace and rigid social order, often enforced by government suppression. Cities expanded rapidly: by 1700 the population of Edo was greater than that of either Paris or London at the time, making it one of the largest metropolitan centers in the world.[20]

As people converged from communities all over Japan, urban centers such as Edo and Osaka became dynamic sites of cultural exchange and creativity. The Edo period witnessed the rise of Kabuki drama and *ningyō jōruri* puppet theater (generally called *bunraku* today). Along with these dramatic arts, there developed a massive publishing industry that produced *ukiyoe* woodblock prints (the movie posters of their day) and printed thousands of relatively inexpensive books, many of which were filled with color and black-and-white images, making them the equivalent of today's manga and popular literature. Not surprisingly, yōkai also proliferated during this period of vibrant cultural activity, finding new homes in the world of commercial art, popular literature, and drama. At the same time, they remained part of local culture—still thriving in folktales and legends. As literary scholar Sumie Jones puts it, "One of the intersections between the high and the low was a taste for the weird."[21]

Spooky Tales: Hyaku-monogatari 百物語

One way in which yōkai from local rural communities made their way onto a more national (or regional) urban stage was through a practice called *hyaku-monogatari*. These were gatherings at which spooky stories, called *kaidan*, were exchanged one after another with the intent of inducing a supernatural experience. The procedure was simple: people would gather in a large room, sometimes in a temple or other semipublic venue, and tell short, spooky stories or anecdotes about ghosts, yōkai, or mysterious occurrences. After each brief tale, a lantern or candle would be extinguished. At the end of the final story, the room would be plunged into complete darkness. And then, it was said (or hoped or feared), a real yōkai would appear. Buddhist priest and author Asai Ryōi (d. 1691) explains, "It is said that when you collect and tell one hundred stories of scary or strange things that have been passed down since long ago, something scary or strange is certain to occur."[22]

The word *hyaku-monogatari* literally means "one hundred stories," but the number one hundred was not necessarily taken literally. In fact, most hyaku-monogatari collections include fewer than a hundred tales. In one sense, the implication was simply that this was a very large number.[23] The particular number one hundred (*hyaku*), however, also had symbolic implications for the mysterious. As mentioned earlier, *tsukumogami* refers to inanimate objects transformed into yōkai after reaching the magic age of one hundred. Similarly, one hundred was often cited as the age after which a normal fox, cat, or tanuki might turn into a yōkai. One hundred seems to have signified a transformative or liminal point— beyond the normal life span of an object or living thing but not so high as to be completely out of reach. One hundred was the number after which things might get a little unusual. The practice of hyaku-monogatari reflects this premise: after a certain point—after the one hundredth story—you were in a space in which the mundane and the normal could be transcended.

Hyaku-monogatari supposedly got its start as a test of bravery, a so-called *kimo-dameshi*, or "challenge of the liver," undertaken by samurai. Whether this is true or not, by the early part of the Edo period hyaku-monogatari gatherings seem to have become a popular form of entertainment and a lively venue for the performance and exchange of oral narratives. Some of these were based on local legends, others were personal experiences or memorates, some came from Chinese literature, and still others may have been invented expressly for the game.[24] Whatever the tales' origins, however, as people publicly shared and performed them, the images and attributes of individual yōkai were enhanced and developed, and these yōkai took on more concrete forms.

Given the vibrant literary and artistic world of the time, it is also not surprising that publishers soon began to gather and sell hyaku-monogatari collections.[25] The collections varied greatly in length and content. Some were dedicated not to telling mysterious tales but to explaining the reasons for such phenomena. This was the case most famously with *Kokon hyaku-monogatari hyōban* of 1686, which offered the interpretive wisdom, mostly based on yin-yang principles, of Yamaoka Genrin (1631–1672).

Although the oral practice of hyaku-monogatari started to go out of vogue around the mid-1700s, publication of written collections continued to flourish; in fact, the kaidan form also became part of high literature, most notably with the 1776 publication of Ueda Akinari's *Ugetsu monogatari* (*Tales of Moonlight and Rain*).[26] Though not explicitly a hyaku-monogatari text, this famous collection of nine spooky tales (some based on

Chinese stories) was considered a masterpiece of beautiful writing and eerie atmospherics and neatly reflected the popular fascination with the weird.

Picturing Yōkai: Emaki

So far, I have focused primarily on written records of yōkai and their subduers. But, particularly during the Muromachi period, yōkai started to proliferate in visual form as well, appearing primarily in *emaki* (picture scrolls or hand rolls): long, horizontal rolls of paper or silk that could be unfurled to show a series of events, often, though not always, with accompanying text. Many otogizōshi, such as the one concerning the tsuchigumo, were produced in this visual form.

But it was the first known *Hyakkiyagyō emaki* that really set the stage for a proliferation of yōkai illustrations. This picture scroll by Tosa Mitsunobu, often called the Shinjuanbon version, seems to have started (or at least been an early part of) a veritable hyakkiyagyō "boom," in which all sorts of different yōkai were pictured in numerous scrolls produced in a range of styles.[27] In most cases, these yōkai are portrayed with humor, a chaotic parade of wacky characters. In fact, the hyakkiyagyō became a sort of artistic genre that continued to be produced, often with clear allusion to earlier versions, throughout the Edo period and even into Meiji. The work of Kawanabe Kyōsai (1831–1889) stands out in particular as a brilliant late incarnation of this tradition.

Tosa Mitsunobu's Shinjuanbon version of the *Hyakkiyagyō emaki* does not tell a story as such, but the final scene shows the yōkai scattering—so there is a hint of a plot. A number of picture scrolls that were painted slightly later, during the Edo period, do not even bother with narrative at all; rather, they unroll to simply reveal one yōkai after another, individually depicted, and each one labeled with its name: *rokurokubi, yuki-onna, ubume*, and so on. Both these facts—that the yōkai are shown individually and that they are labeled—suggest that to a certain extent these scrolls may have been made for the purpose of recording information or perhaps even teaching, akin to children's books today. Unfortunately, we do not know the objectives of the artists; but we can think of these scrolls as an early artistic way of documenting yōkai, whether intentionally or not—a kind of "natural history record."[28]

If we look at some of these scrolls, such as *Bakemono zukushi* (artist unknown, date unknown) and *Hyakkai-zukan* (Sawaki Sūshi, 1737), we notice that they are populated with all sorts of yōkai; but in contrast to the Shinjuanbon *Hyakkiyagyō emaki*, they do not feature any household objects. These artists seem interested in documenting a range of folk beliefs beyond the tsukumogami; this would have included legends or descriptions they had heard about yuki-onna, kappa, or other yōkai that thrived in rural environments, as opposed to the urban settings where the artists themselves lived. Perhaps tsukumogami—household-object yōkai—were a sort of urban-consumer-society yōkai, whereas yuki-onna, kappa, and the others were more rural. Or perhaps these scrolls represent a visual supplement to some of the narratives recounted in hyaku-mono-gatari, an illustration of creatures described in oral tale-telling sessions. Although the number one hundred (hyaku) has numerous implications, it also certainly links together hyaku-monogatari and hyakkiyagyō, and it connects both to notions of the otherworld.[29] All this is speculative, but whatever they were intended for, ultimately these emaki demonstrate a taxonomic impulse to isolate and label the individual yōkai in the hyakkiyagyō parade.

Documenting Yōkai: Encyclopedias

This interest in identifying and naming reflects a broader zeitgeist, a kind of encyclopedic way of thinking about the world. Even while picture scrolls and spooky tale collections were produced and consumed as a form of entertainment, the Edo period was also a time of serious intellectual inquiry, informed especially by a strain of neo-Confucian philosophy known as Shushigaku. Based on the philosophy of Zhu Xi (1130–1200), Shushigaku promoted the "investigation of things" (*kakubutsu chichi*) in order to understand the structure of nature and the proper order of society; it was highly influential in intellectual and government circles, leading to the importation of all sorts of natural history texts and pharmacopoeias from China, and also to research and writing about Japanese plants, animals, and minerals (and all sorts of other things). One product of this broad interest in just about everything was a 105-volume encyclopedia called the *Wakan-sansaizue* (c. 1713; Japanese-Chinese collected illustrations of the three realms; hereafter *Three Realms*) compiled by an Osaka medical practitioner named Terajima Ryōan. The *Three Realms* drew on earlier Chinese sources (and images), especially a materia medica text called the *Bencao gangmu* (Japanese: *Honzō kōmoku*), but also presented original observations and indigenous Japanese learning.[30]

In certain sections of this massive compendium, yōkai appear right alongside other animals. In "fish types," for example, there is a short entry for *ningyo*, or "mermaid," that includes a matter-of-fact description of the creature's appearance and also casually mentions the handy fact that ningyo bones can be made into a poison with "wonderful effect."[31] In another section there is an array of strange beings all more or less anthropomorphic, including the monkeylike *enkō* and witchlike *yamauba*. Most descriptions include a straightforward presentation of physical characteristics, habits, and habitats, and they refer back to Chinese texts and earlier Japanese texts.

One of the entries, for the *kawatarō* (related to the kappa), is notable because Terajima makes no effort to connect it to previous Chinese sources; he simply includes a picture of the creature (a hairy, monkeylike figure walking upright) and explains that it likes to steal certain vegetables, challenge people to wrestle *sumō*, and pull cattle and horses into the water. In fact, one important dimension of the *Three Realms* is that it cites versions of yōkai from earlier texts, both Chinese and Japanese, but it also references oral and local folklore. Because the *Three Realms* is a serious academic work, written presumably for a scholarly readership, the incorporation of local beliefs like this helps to authenticate them as "facts" just as valid as data extracted from older documents.

The *Three Realms* also places yōkai right next to other creatures, such as rhinoceroses, that were not found in the wild in Japan. In a way this makes absolute sense: to an Edo-period reader in Japan, a rhinoceros would have been just as real or just as fantastic (if not more so) as a kawatarō or a ningyo. All these creatures fit neatly in a set of books that aimed to document all things, whether seen or unseen.

Toriyama Sekien and the Gazu Hyakkiyagyō *series*

During the first half of the Edo period, then, yōkai appeared in the oral and written tales of hyaku-monogatari, in playful picture scrolls, and also

in serious academic compendia such as the *Three Realms*. All these different forms come together in the work of a man named Toriyama Sekien
(1712–1788), an artist who had the most significant influence on how we
envision and understand yōkai to this day. Sekien was born in Edo and
was a follower of the Kanō school of painting. Not much is known about
his life, but there is speculation that he was a Buddhist priest and possibly
served the Tokugawa government.

Sekien is most remembered for his four sets of illustrated catalogs, produced between 1776 and 1784, that collectively document over two hundred
different yōkai: *Gazu hyakkiyagyō* (1776), *Konjaku gazu zoku hyakki*
(1779), *Konjaku hyakki shūi* (1781), *Hyakki tsurezure bukuro* (1784).[32] Both
in form and content, these books are a perfect combination of picture scroll
and encyclopedia. Some images are directly modeled on the yōkai in the
earlier picture scrolls, and in fact it has recently been discovered that Sekien
himself painted his own version of a *Hyakkiyagyō emaki*.[33] But what is
most significant about his illustrated catalogs is that they are *not* picture
scrolls. Like the *Three Realms* and other encyclopedic texts of the day, they
are bound in a *fukuro-toji* style with folded pages fastened with thread on
one side. In shape and style they are roughly similar to today's paperback
books, and they are read in the same fashion, by turning one page at a time.[34]

Each page of Sekien's catalogs features a separate entry, like you might
find in an encyclopedia, with a black-and-white line drawing of an individual yōkai and sometimes a description. The earliest set of catalogs,
Gazu hyakkiyagyō, contains three volumes and a total of fifty-one yōkai.
There is relatively little writing with each image; often the text notes only
a particular yōkai's name and maybe a variant name. The entry on kappa,
for example, states, "Kappa, also called Kawatarō." It is likely that in this
first catalog, Sekien was drawing the best-known yōkai, those creatures
that were already so deeply entrenched in the popular imagination that no
explanation was necessary. In his later catalogs, however, Sekien adds
more text to the images. In part, this may be because he is introducing less
established or regional yōkai, creatures that need some explanation. But
he also seems to be more playful in these later works, filling both text and
illustration with lively puns and image play.

Sekien was creating a comprehensive yōkai bestiary, but he also
seems to have been having fun. And as he produced additional catalog

sets over the next few years, his writing and his images became even more inventive. Some of his yōkai were adapted from the *Three Realms*, some were taken from picture scrolls, some from Chinese materials, some from local belief and legend, and more than a few were his own invention. According to one analysis of the more than two hundred distinct creatures illustrated by Sekien, most are derived from Japanese folklore, art, or literature; fourteen come directly from Chinese sources; and eighty-five may have been fabricated.[35]

Many common yōkai today may have started with Sekien, but even if he did not invent them from whole cloth, he certainly helped to popularize them. Through his books, creatures from China became Japanese yōkai, and local yōkai from all over Japan were presented to a mass readership. A yōkai from one small corner of the country might be combined with yōkai found in different regions, or under different names, to make a sort of generic yōkai shared by a larger, national folk group.

Today, the inventive aspect of Sekien's work, along with its wordplay and tongue-in-cheek quality, is difficult for readers to appreciate. Recognized less for their humor and levity, then, his catalogs are often treated as the quintessential record of the yōkai world. Even in his own day he influenced, either directly or indirectly, a number of important artists. He taught Kitagawa Utamaro (1753–1806) and Utagawa Toyoharu (1735–1814); Utagawa would become the founder of the Utagawa line of painters, which included Utagawa Kuniyoshi (1797–1861), who in turn taught Tsukioka Yoshitoshi (1839–1892) and Kawanabe Kyōsai (1831–1889).[36] Although their styles varied, and differed greatly from Sekien's, all these artists would eventually become known in part for portraying yōkai and for illustrating supernatural narratives. Sekien's own works today are still referenced for their encyclopedic value, and his images and descriptions continue to inspire numerous contemporary manga artists and others.

Yōkai as Characters: Kibyōshi

By extracting yōkai from other texts and from local legends, Sekien helped disconnect them from their particular places of origin and from the narratives in which they played a part. This made them more generic and more versatile, employable in all sorts of new places. And in fact, during the latter part of the Edo period, yōkai haunted literature, art, and popular culture, everything from woodblock prints to Kabuki to *rakugo* storytelling. They especially thrived in a lighthearted genre of illustrated books known as *kibyōshi*, or "yellow covers," produced mainly between 1775 and 1806. Kibyōshi were a kind of *kusazōshi* (picture book), a popular form of comic book or graphic literature that came in a variety of styles—including red books, black books, and blue books. As the name implies, kibyōshi had yellow covers (actually they started out blue-green but faded to yellow); a single kibyōshi narrative might consist of two or three separate volumes, each one only about ten pages long. Every page contained a detailed line drawing, and the space around the image was crammed with text—the books are often thought of as an early-modern version of manga. Of all the popular books of this time, the kibyōshi were considered the most sophisticated and the most satiric. In fact, one reason their production came to an end in 1806 may have been because the authorities did not take kindly to their critical humor.[37]

It was in part to facilitate this satire that kibyōshi drew on yōkai as rich stock characters; a particular yōkai might stand in for an individual, a whole class, or a particular type of person. These texts, therefore, provide a glimpse into the Edo-period popular imagination. An example of how yōkai were used is *Bakemono no yomeiri* (*The Monster Takes a Bride*, 1807), by Jippensha Ikku (1765–1831). During the eighteenth century there were picture books that depicted the marriage of two people (and the uniting of their families) through careful illustrations of various wedding rituals. Such books may have been simultaneously entertaining and used as manuals for prospective brides. The kibyōshi version parodies these books by adopting the same format but portraying all the characters as yōkai, with ritual behavior appropriate only to the yōkai world. Tsukumogami-style lanterns, each hopping on a single leg, help light the way, for example, and one yōkai remarks that a storm is brewing—perfect weather for a wedding.[38] It is a comical portrayal without much of a plot to speak of. But by showing human behavior through the topsy-turvy world of yōkai, the author helps to defamiliarize, to make strange, a whole range of wedding customs and social standards that otherwise might go unquestioned.

For the most part, yōkai in kibyōshi were anything but scary; they were goofy and comical, their language full of puns and topical references. This was an urban genre with a mass readership; like the encyclopedias and Sekien's catalogs, they must have spread a kind of shared understanding about yōkai to people from all over Japan. That is, they would have made distinctions between yōkai from different regions less pronounced.

Another important effect of kibyōshi is that they transformed yōkai into "characters." Removed from its connection to a particular legend or belief, a given yōkai could become an iconic image—like an advertising mascot—independent from text or tale. It was in the kibyōshi, for example, that an eerily cute tofu-carrying urchin called *tōfu-kozō* prospered, and where a romantic relationship between long-necked *mikoshi-nyūdō* and long-necked rokurokubi bloomed.[39]

I have only scratched the surface of the Edo-period relationship with yōkai. The humorous and cute characters of the kibyōshi were dynamic and innovative and became memorable icons that still influence our image of yōkai today. The last one hundred years of the Edo period also witnessed a variety of other playful uses of yōkai: they appeared in board games (*sugoroku*), shooting galleries, spectacle shows (misemono), and even a popular card game known as *yōkai karuta,* which is remarkably similar to contemporary Pokémon.[40]

But these playful and ironic images of yōkai did not kill off the frightening folk creatures from which they developed. For example, the Kabuki play *Tōkaidō Yotsuya kaidan* (1825) by Tsuruya Nanboku IV (1755–1829) thrilled Edo audiences with its portrayal of the vengeful ghost of Oiwa-san, a story based on "real" local ghost stories. It was an exceedingly popular fictional entertainment—but in order to avoid being cursed, the actors made sure to pay respect to the grave of the real woman on whom the Oiwa-san character was based.[41]

Similarly, yōkai were still a subject of fascination for intellectuals as well. Famous *kokugaku* (national studies) scholar Hirata Atsutane (1776–1843), for example, interviewed individuals who had been carried away by tengu or had had other supernatural experiences. He documented a report by a man who claimed to understand the chatter of birds, and by another who could recall his former life.[42] Even as yōkai were the subject of fun and games, they were also a matter for serious inquiry. Atsutane's investigations of the otherworld foreshadowed the folkloric study of yōkai that would begin as Japan started to modernize in the years to come.

MODERN DISCIPLINES

During the Meiji period (1868–1912), Japan began a vigorous push toward what it called "civilization and enlightenment" (*bunmei kaika*). In a short time, the nation experienced rapid and momentous changes. The capital was officially moved to Edo, which was renamed Tokyo. Knowledge was actively sought from abroad by inviting foreigners to come teach and by sending promising young scholars to study in Europe and the United States. Meanwhile, the educational system at home was revamped. And so was the military, as the nation began a series of wars and colonial incursions abroad (that would eventually culminate in Japan's involvement in World War II). Social structures, such as the system that designated samurai as an elite class, were abolished. And government policies to rationalize and organize belief systems were implemented, leading, for example, to the forced merger of local shrines throughout the nation. In cultural circles, too, change was rapid and radical, even on the level of language and literature, as evidenced by the *genbun'itchi* movement that strove to unite spoken and written Japanese.

Inoue Enryō and the Invention of Yōkaigaku

Within this radical restructuring of society and culture, what happened to yōkai? Simply put, during the Meiji period a number of Japanese scholars and ideologues, under the influence of Western scientific knowledge and attitudes, tried to demystify mysterious phenomena. In particular, a charismatic Buddhist philosopher and educator named Inoue Enryō (1858–1919) created the discipline of *yōkaigaku* (yōkai-ology, or "monsterology") with the objective of rationally explaining away supernatural beliefs so that Japan could become a modern nation-state.[43] Enryō himself was a dynamic character, clearly a man on a mission, who was so obsessed with collecting and explaining supernatural phenomena that he was nicknamed Professor Yōkai (Yōkai Hakase).

Enryō (or Kishimaru, as he was known as a child) was born in 1858 in Echigo (present-day Niigata Prefecture), where his father was a Buddhist priest at a small temple. A lot of energy was invested in young Kishimaru's education; he studied *kangaku* (Chinese learning) as well as Western and Japanese natural history and sciences, a mixture that would greatly influence his own philosophical interests and the later development of yōkaigaku. He also trained in the Buddhist priesthood, taking the name Enryō when he was ordained.[44]

In 1881 Enryō entered the Department of Literature and Philosophy at the University of Tokyo. He studied Chinese and Indian philosophies along with Western philosophy, particularly the work of Spencer, Hegel, and Kant. He also took courses in various sciences, history, and literature and was a founding member of the Tetsugakkai (Society of Philosophy), an organization that is still active today. When Enryō completed his degree in 1885, he was the first Buddhist priest to graduate from the university and the first graduate to specialize in philosophy.[45]

Enryō believed that by drawing on Western philosophy, Buddhism could be modernized and reformed. He also felt it was important for people from all walks of life—not just those with the chance to study at the University of Tokyo—to be exposed to Western philosophy. And with these objectives, he founded his own academy; opened in 1887 and called Tetsugakkan, the school would eventually develop into Tōyō University, which today has over thirty thousand students.

Clearly Enryō was passionate about philosophy, Buddhism, and education. So maybe it is not surprising that he also had an abiding interest in getting to the bottom of the mysteries of the world around him, such as yōkai, and a deep desire to tell people of his discoveries. Even in 1886, as plans were taking shape for Tetsugakkan, Enryō and some friends formed an organization called the Fushigi kenkyūkai, literally the Mystery Research Society. The group seems to have been inspired by the British Society for Psychical Research, which itself had been founded in 1882—and is still active today.[46] The Mystery Research Society actually met only three times, but Enryō had already embarked on his yōkai research, publishing an appeal for information on "strange dreams, ghosts, kitsune and tanuki, tengu, inugami, shamanism, possession, physiognomy, prophecy, etc.," in order to analyze such phenomena from a psychological perspective and "consider and report on the facts of yōkai from each region."[47]

Throughout his life, Enryō traveled around Japan lecturing about yōkai and collecting information on beliefs and customs. Additionally, he seems to have created a network of likeminded colleagues and followers throughout the country who would keep him informed about local yōkai in their regions. Before his death (while lecturing in China) in 1919, Enryō wrote thousands of pages on the subject. His early magnum opus, *Yōkaigaku kōgi* (Lectures on yōkaigaku), was first published in 1893–1894 and is over two thousand pages long. He explains that this new academic discipline, "yōkaigaku," is a form of enlightenment every bit as profound as all the modern technologies that were changing Japan: "If through this [discipline of yōkaigaku], the light of a new heaven opens inside the hearts of the citizens, then is it too much to say that these achievements are just as important as the installation of railroads and telegraphs? Herein lies the necessity of the research and explanations of yōkaigaku."[48]

At first glance it seems that Enryō insisted that mysterious phenomena could not exist, that science and psychology could ultimately explain everything. But his thinking was actually more subtle than this, and his categorization of strange phenomena was complex. He divided yōkai into two broad categories: *kakai* (false or provisional mystery) and *shinkai* (true mystery). His goal was not to dismiss all mystery but to systematically filter out *meishin* (superstitions), *gokai* (mistaken mystery), *gikai* (artificial mystery), and all sorts of other false mysteries that were deceiving the Japanese people and inhibiting their enlightenment. After all the false mysteries had been weeded out, one would be able to identify "true mystery." The ultimate goal of Enryō's yōkaigaku was to locate this true mystery, the shinkai: the secret thing at the core of existence.

In service of this objective, Enryō collected massive amounts of data on yōkai from all over the country. Despite his expressed desire to debunk mysterious creatures and phenomena, he certainly seems to have enjoyed telling people about them. It was through his work as a public intellectual, who lectured continuously and wrote numerous newspaper articles, that the word *yōkai* became part of the popular vocabulary. And the mountain of data Enryō collected still provides invaluable information for scholars today.

Lafcadio Hearn and Spooky Translation

In 1891, when Inoue Enryō was in his early thirties and already deeply immersed in his yōkai research, he traveled to the small city of Matsue in Shimane Prefecture. There he spent the morning of May 30 engrossed in conversation with a forty-year-old English teacher recently arrived from America.[49] There is no record of what the two discussed, so we cannot know if they talked about yōkai. But it is certainly intriguing that the two men actually met: the English teacher, Lafcadio Hearn (1850–1904), would go on to become one of the most important foreign-language interpreters of Japanese culture. Among other things, he would write extensively on the supernatural, folklore, religion, and yōkai. Perhaps most famous among his many works is a book called *Kwaidan,* an early, romanized rendering of the word we have already seen as *kaidan,* or "spooky tales." Although Hearn's contribution to the understanding of yōkai is rarely noted in books on the subject, it is important to include this enigmatic Greek-Irish-American-Japanese writer here as a key figure in the modern history of yōkai studies. Not only did he eloquently record some important narratives, but also his passion for the strange and supernatural, and the deeper cultural insights they could provide, prefigured the work of Japanese scholars who would come after him.

Hearn led a complex life. He was born in 1850 on the Greek island of Lafkada (hence the name), the second child of a passionate affair between an Irish officer in the British Army and a local Greek woman. Several months later, his father was transferred to the West Indies, and his mother took baby Patrick Lafcadio Hearn to Ireland. She returned to Greece after two years, leaving the boy with a wealthy great aunt (on the Hearn side). In his teens, young Paddy was sent to a Catholic boarding school in England. In an accident at school, his left eye was blinded and slightly disfigured (it is in order to hide this disfigurement that Hearn is always turned to the side in photographs). Meanwhile, his great aunt lost her fortune, and the family fell into poverty.

When he was nineteen, Paddy went off to America and ended up in Cincinnati, where he quickly managed to become a successful newspaper journalist. He especially made a name for himself reporting on the seamier side of life—murders, slaughterhouses, garbage dumps, corruption, and the poor districts of the city. In his twenties, he moved to New Orleans, where he continued his successful journalism career, but this time dropping the "Patrick" in favor of his more exotic-sounding middle name, "Lafcadio." He wrote a novel, *Chita*, and received a commission to travel to the West Indies (especially Martinique), where he wrote another novel as well as a successful collection of nonfiction essays titled *Two Years in the French West Indies*. In all these places, Hearn—with his awkward appearance, his one good eye, his restless spirit, and an abiding interest in folklore, religion, and occult practices—always lived on the edge of the mainstream but wrote about people and places and his own experiences in a thoughtful, accessible prose style.

In 1890, Hearn was commissioned to travel to Japan. The changes of the Meiji period were rapid and revolutionary, and he found himself profoundly interested in both the disappearing ways of the old Japan and the new emerging culture. In his first year in the country, while teaching English in Matsue, he married a woman named Koizumi Setsu. When he became a Japanese citizen in 1896, he changed his own name to Koizumi Yakumo, taking the family name Koizumi from his wife. Yakumo literally means "eight clouds" and can be understood more as "abundant clouds," or possibly "sacred clouds." It is the first line of the earliest known Japanese poem, appearing in the same passage of the *Kojiki* in which Susa-no-O slays the Yamata no Orochi, and it is also a poetic reference to Izumo, near Matsue, where Hearn met his wife.

Hearn subsequently lived in Kumamoto City for three years, went to Kobe to work as a journalist again, and then moved on to Tokyo to take a position as professor of English literature at Tokyo Imperial University. Until his death of a heart condition in 1904, he published numerous books and essays on Japan, creating a body of work that, according to one biographer, "is among the best ever written on that country, and is of continuing relevance."[50] Hearn was a master of the essay form and wrote about everything from Buddhism to proverbs to incense to insects (he loved insects: ants, crickets, silkworms, and even mosquitoes). He also had a deep interest in spooky tales, and much of his work includes translated or rewritten versions of legends and literary ghost stories. Even his book titles, such as *Glimpses of Unfamiliar Japan* (1894), *In Ghostly Japan* (1899), and *Shadowings* (1900), reflect this interest in the otherworld.

Published in 1904, the year of his death, *Kwaidan* is particularly full of spooky stories and includes such yōkai as rokurokubi, *mujina,* and yuki-onna.

Hearn probably never mastered Japanese well enough to collect and translate these tales by himself. In his early years in the country, he relied on a translator or his wife to collect stories orally, and in later years he would carefully work through written texts, retelling them in his clear English prose.[51] While his interests tended toward local legends, folktales, and beliefs, ultimately Hearn was not an ethnographer but a creative writer; his objective was not to scientifically record narratives but to re-create them in a literary format. And perhaps his skillful prose is one reason many of these stories, particularly the ones in *Kwaidan*, are still well known in Japan today, and still readily available in translation more than a century after they were written.[52]

Hearn's importance to the history of yōkai studies is twofold. First, he put great value on certain aspects of Japanese culture—yōkai and kaidan—at the very moment Enryō and others were working to banish them as incompatible with modernity. In some cases, his embrace of everything "traditional" could be problematically nationalist, especially as Japan was in the process of building its military and embarking on colonialist invasions. In fact, the publisher's introduction to *Kwaidan* notes that even as the book appeared, Japan and Russia were at war, and the publication of the volume "happens, by delicate irony, to fall in the very month when the world is waiting with tense expectation for news of the latest exploits of Japanese battleships."[53] In the Japanese context of modernization and Westernization, Hearn's interest in the strange and overlooked aspects of Japanese culture was particularly meaningful: in part because he was a respected teacher from abroad, his recognition of the value of yōkai traditions brought them new attention and reconsideration. It also helped that he was a good storyteller, and that his skillful retellings were soon translated back into Japanese, where they "became a much-loved part of the modern literary canon, familiar to every schoolchild."[54]

Secondly, Hearn was a romantic and a nostalgic. Unlike Inoue Enryō, he did not dismiss yōkai as impediments to progress; he celebrated them as an intrinsic and meaningful part of Japanese culture—a culture that he saw changing in front of his very eyes. He felt there was value in collecting and understanding them for the insight they might offer into fading beliefs and shifting worldviews and what it means (or meant) to be Japanese. This attitude prefigured the approaches that would be taken by a number of important Japanese scholars in subsequent years.

Ema Tsutomu and the Changing History of Yōkai

One of these scholars, Ema Tsutomu (1884–1979), wrote a book called *Nihon yōkai-henge shi* (Japanese history of yōkai-henge) in 1923. Ema was not an expert on yōkai, but he was the leading scholar of a field called *fūzokushi-gaku,* which was concerned with the history of customs and manners. Ema recognized the importance of yōkai in shaping and reflecting the broader history of the Japanese people. He was not interested in documenting yōkai in order to debunk them; rather, his objective was to "look at how humans interacted with them in the past[,] . . . the way our ancestors saw yōkai-henge, how they understood them, and how they dealt with them."[55]

Ema's point is that yōkai, whether you believe in them or not, have always been part of the human world and, therefore, have to be taken seriously. His own analysis examines a range of sources (including many of those already mentioned) and divides the history of Japan into several different epochs. One of his arguments is that there is a distinction between *yōkai* and *henge. Henge* was sometimes used interchangeably with yōkai, but Ema suggests that the two words have different emphases, with *henge* being more closely associated with the notion of changeability. "If I were to give the definitions of both words," he explains, "I would say *yōkai* is an ungraspable mysterious nondescript, whereas *henge* is something that has externally changed its identity."[56]

Ema creates a complicated typology of both yōkai and henge, classifying them by their ability to shape-shift, by the forms they generally take, and by when and where they appear. Most of them, he says, emerge in the evening and, depending on particular type, may inhabit mountains, shrines, houses, or the ocean. Although he finds mysterious creatures to be important during all periods of Japanese history—"since the beginning of time in Japan, our ancestors have had a close relationship with yōkai-henge"—he also suggests that attitudes changed with the Meiji period.

Whereas in the past people were afraid of yōkai, he explains, now yōkai are afraid of humans.[57]

Ema's distinction between yōkai and henge, his specific typology, and his historical analysis do not seem to have greatly influenced subsequent scholars. But his general attitude toward yōkai is significant: for Ema, yōkai are encoded with critical data from the cultures and times in which they thrived, and they can tell us about the values and beliefs of the people who created them. Unlike Inoue Enryō, Ema did not worry about whether yōkai exist or not. And in distinction to Lafcadio Hearn, he did not set out to salvage them or cherish the eerie aesthetics of yōkai narratives. Rather, he simply argued that yōkai are an integral part of Japanese history, and therefore we should study them.

Yanagita Kunio and the Folkloristics of Yōkai

This general attitude is paralleled in the cultural approach assumed by Yanagita Kunio (1875–1962). Yanagita was one of modern Japan's most influential thinkers, best known as the founder of *minzokugaku,* an academic study translatable into English as "folklore studies," "native ethnology," or "Japanese folkloristics." Largely because of Yanagita's own interests, even today minzokugaku is the academic discipline in Japan most closely associated with the study of yōkai.

Yanagita himself began exploring yōkai early in his career. His most famous book, *Tōno monogatari* (Tales of Tōno), contains several references to kappa and *zashiki-warashi,* for example, and recounts a number of ghostly occurrences. He would go on to write about yōkai in numerous short essays, often as part of his exploration of other issues and themes. For Yanagita, research into yōkai represented a way to think broadly about Japanese folklore and folklife. Although he never devised an explicit methodology for interpreting yōkai, we can extract three general theoretical directions from his essays: (1) an acceptance of ambiguity, (2) collection and categorization, and (3) a theory of degradation.[58]

The "acceptance of ambiguity" means that Yanagita was not concerned about whether yōkai actually exist or not; like Ema, he figured that if people believed in their existence or told stories about them at some point, we should study them. Generally speaking, this attitude is now a given in folklore studies, in Japan and elsewhere, in which belief systems are not refuted but observed and interpreted. During the early twentieth century, however, Yanagita's promotion of this approach stood in distinct contrast to Enryō's method and set the tone for future studies of yōkai and, more generally, for the development of Japanese folkloristics as a discipline that sought to explain the interiority of people's lives.

As we have seen, "collection and categorization" of yōkai started at least as early as the Edo period, so Yanagita's interest here was nothing new. Yanagita's own collection of data on yōkai entailed fieldwork (talking with people in various regions) as well as scouring documents and other written sources. In many essays, he provides examples of yōkai and reasserts the need for further collection. Over several months in 1938 and 1939 he published a glossary of yōkai called "Yōkai meii" (Yōkai glossary) listing seventy-nine different yōkai. Most of the information was garnered from local gazetteers and folklore collections; each entry contains a short description of the yōkai in question.[59]

Yanagita's most notorious contribution to the classification of yōkai is his distinction between yūrei (ghosts) and bakemono (or obake), introduced earlier. In short, he claims that bakemono "generally appear in set locations," haunting a particular *place*, in contrast to yūrei, which haunt a particular *person*. Yūrei come out only late at night, but bakemono prefer the "dim light of dusk or dawn," finding this border zone between light and dark the most productive for their purposes: "In order for people to see them, and be frightened by them, emerging in the pitch darkness after even the plants have fallen asleep is, to say the least, just not good business practice." Although many people have found exceptions to his rules, Yanagita's distinctions here are often cited in books about yōkai and have been important in stimulating conversation on the topic.[60]

The third aspect of Yanagita's approach to yōkai is his "theory of degradation." In 1917 Yanagita wrote, "When old beliefs were oppressed and made to surrender to new beliefs, all the [old] deities [kami-sama] were degraded [*reiraku*] and became yōkai. That is to say, yōkai are unauthorized deities."[61] His point is that yōkai were deities who had fallen in status; they were no longer sacred but still possessed some of their old supernatural powers. Yanagita repeated this idea in a number of different essays throughout his career, using the *devolution* of yōkai for measuring the *evolution* of humans. As human beings progress and move into a modern way of life, he suggested, supernatural beings gradually degenerate from kami, objects of serious belief, to yōkai, which are sometimes even comical. To a certain extent, this attitude reflects Yanagita's general approach to folklore and history; he saw many present customs as "survivals," or relics, of an older, bigger system of belief that had faded over time and was disappearing even more rapidly with the changes of the twentieth century.

Yanagita's attitude toward yōkai, and to the beliefs of the "folk," continues to influence scholars and writers today. As with other aspects of daily life that would become the subject of his folkloristics, Yanagita understood that it was not up to researchers to decide whether yōkai had an objective existence or not; if yōkai were part of the life of the people, then they existed as a meaningful and *real* part of Japanese culture and they should be studied as such.[62] By taking yōkai seriously and giving them an important (if not central) role in the development of an entirely new academic discipline, Yanagita signaled to generations that followed that any study of culture could not ignore its monsters.

POSTWAR ANIMATION AND THE YŌKAI BOOM

Animating Nostalgia: Mizuki Shigeru

Yanagita recorded yōkai as a critical part of the Japanese cultural imagination even as the nation was embarking on the terrible calamity of the Fifteen-Year War (1931–1945).[63] During the second half of the twentieth century, while Japan recovered from the devastation of war and entered a period of rapid economic expansion and industrial growth, yōkai took on yet another meaningful role. Yanagita had collected them as relics from a disappearing Japan; now they became infused with nostalgia as icons from a more innocent, prewar Japan that had already disappeared.

The individual most responsible for making yōkai relevant during this period was the manga and anime artist Mizuki Shigeru (b. 1922). Unlike Yanagita, Mizuki is not generally characterized as a scholar; he is a creative illustrator and storyteller who skillfully mixes history and folklore with invention and imagination to produce compelling narratives and memorable characters. Mizuki was deeply influenced by Yanagita, Sekien, and other scholars and artists who came before him, but ultimately it is Mizuki's manga and anime that most transformed the elusive yōkai of folklore into the concrete yōkai characters of contemporary popular culture and mass media.

Mizuki's most significant manga series, which has been around for half a century now, is called *Gegege no Kitarō* (Spooky Kitarō); not only are the characters from this series famous throughout Japan today but also Mizuki himself is a well-known personality. In 2008, his wife, Mura Nunoe (b. 1932), published an autobiographical account of their life together called *Gegege no nyōbo* (Wife of Gegege), which was made into a successful morning television series in 2010 and a feature-length movie (dir. Suzuki Takuji). Since the 1990s, Mizuki's rural hometown of Sakaiminato in Tottori Prefecture has been developed as a tourist attraction featuring a museum dedicated to Mizuki's work, along with the Mizuki Shigeru Road, a shopping street lined with more than 130 bronze yōkai figures. In short, Mizuki is a nationally known personality, and his yōkai characters animate contemporary Japan.

Mizuki was born Mura Shigeru in 1922. Although his family was from Sakaiminato, he was actually born in the city of Osaka, where his father was working, and moved to Sakaiminato with his mother one month later.[64] He has written nostalgically of his childhood in this small port town, and particularly about an old woman named Nonnonbā (Granny Nonnon) who looked after him when his parents were busy. According to Mizuki's memoirs, Nonnonbā was knowledgeable about the yōkai world, and it was through her that he was first trained in the mysterious things residing around him.

Mizuki came of age during World War II and saw combat with the Japanese infantry near Rabaul in Papua New Guinea, where he lost his left arm. He has written movingly of his time in the military, of his struggles as a bumbling soldier and of his near-death through injury and illness in the tropics. While he seems to have despised most of his superior officers, he portrays the natives of Rabaul with great affection, as true friends who cared for him when he was ill and suffering.

After returning to Japan, Mizuki studied at Musashino Art School and worked as an illustrator for *kamishibai* (picture-card shows) from 1950 to

1957; between 1957 and 1965, he wrote and illustrated *kashi-hon* manga, cheaply produced manga available for a small rental fee at shops throughout Japan.[65] His first critical success came with the 1965 magazine publication of "Terebi-kun" (Television boy), the story of a boy who enters into televisions to participate in the world beyond the screen. "Terebi-kun" received the Sixth Kōdansha Jidō Manga Award and propelled Mizuki into the more lucrative world of magazine manga publishing.[66]

It was as a kamishibai artist in 1954 that he first created Kitarō, the charming boy yōkai who would become his signature character. The original production was called *Hakaba Kitarō* (Graveyard Kitarō), a title that Mizuki retained, with small variations, until his successful 1968 series, *Hakaba no Kitarō* (Kitarō of the graveyard), was to be made into an anime for television. The sponsors of the television version were concerned that having *graveyard* in the title would not be good for business, so Mizuki changed it to *Gegege no Kitarō*, a title derived from his own nickname as a child—Gege, or Gegeru (a mispronunciation of Shigeru).[67] *Gegege no Kitarō* became the title of the anime first and, subsequently, the title of the manga; in a sense this moment also marks the invasion of the postwar Japanese media world by Mizuki's yōkai.

The black-and-white anime ran until 1969, followed by successive series in color: 1971–1972, 1985–1988, 1996–1998, and 2007–2009. There have also been a live action film (2007; dir. Motoki Katsuhide), video games, and even a new TV anime series based on an early version of *Hakaba Kitarō*. Through this skillful promulgation in a wide range of media, Mizuki's distinctive yōkai characters have become part of the popular imagination of children and adults in late twentieth- and early twenty-first-century Japan.

Because of this dynamic media mix, and with so many different episodes and versions, *Gegege no Kitarō* narratives cannot be summarized concisely, but they generally involve the adventures of Kitarō and a cohort of yōkai friends. Kitarō himself is the progeny of a ghost family: an otherwise normal-looking boy, he wears magic geta sandals and a protective black-and-yellow *chanchanko* vest, and there is always a shock of hair covering the left side of his face. *Kitarō* is written with the character for oni (*ki*), a not-so-subtle reminder of his origins and affiliations.

Kitarō is frequently accompanied by another character, Medama-oyaji (Papa Eyeball), a disembodied eyeball with arms, legs, and squeaky voice (even though he has no mouth), who represents the remains of Kitarō's dead father and is often pictured perched on Kitarō's head or shoulder.[68] Many of the episodes in the series involve Kitarō, Medama-oyaji, and other regular yōkai characters teaming up to fight for the survival of good yōkai and good humans against evil yōkai and evil humans. Mizuki also celebrates the ambiguous nature of yōkai; one of the other regular characters, for example, is the ne'er-do-well Nezumi-otoko (Ratman), a mischievous trickster figure who is both friend and foe of the boy hero.

Kitarō, Medama-oyaji, and Nezumi-otoko are Mizuki's original creations. But Mizuki is also a scholar of yōkai folklore and history, and many of his characters are adapted from the work of Sekien, Yanagita, and others. For example, one famous character in Kitarō's yōkai gang is Nurikabe, or "Plaster Wall," mentioned earlier, which Mizuki extracted directly from an entry in Yanagita's "Yōkai Glossary." By illustrating a wall with arms, legs, and eyes, he transforms what Yanagita described as a vague phenomenon into a solid, free-standing character. Similarly, Sunakake-babā, the Sand-Throwing Granny, was also a relatively obscure yōkai whom Mizuki lifted from "Yōkai Glossary" and made into a star.

Mizuki's narratives are full of other yōkai mined from folklore and previous texts. Moreover, in addition to his narrative manga, he has also published numerous illustrated catalogs consciously reminiscent of the Edo-period bestiaries of Toriyama Sekien. Indeed, in many ways Mizuki might be considered a modern-day Sekien, using the popular media of his day not only to document yōkai but also to invent new ones. And just as Sekien's eighteenth-century images exerted enormous influence on the understanding of yōkai in succeeding years, so Mizuki's images powerfully shape the popular imagination of contemporary Japan. Although Mizuki has published many other yōkai-related manga, such as *Kappa no Sanpei* (Sanpei the kappa) and *Akuma-kun* (Devil boy), he is still most famous for *Gegege no Kitarō*: the manga, the numerous anime series, and all sorts of spin-off goods and products, from key chains and cell phone straps, to plastic figurines, clothing, and even canned coffee.

Mizuki's hometown of Sakaiminato, with its yōkai statues and Mizuki museum, has become a Mecca for yōkai lovers from all over the country—tens of thousands visit each year. You can find tourists of all ages clustered next to each small bronze statue along Mizuki Shigeru Road. Grandparents stoop to carefully read the engraved nameplate, parents chat nostalgically, and children excitedly shout out the name of each yōkai character the moment they recognize it. For children in particular, these yōkai are contemporary celebrities, stars of TV and film and video games. For older visitors, they inspire nostalgic memories of their own childhoods—when they heard tales of yōkai, perhaps, or more likely when they first encountered Mizuki's manga and anime. Recalling his own excitement when visiting the road, eclectic writer and scholar Aramata Hiroshi (b. 1947) explained, "Even if my head has been corrupted by old books and cigarettes, my heart, it seems, is still a child's."[69]

In fact, this is the power of Mizuki's yōkai—they emit a potent nostalgia for a time that is now gone (if it ever existed in the first place). Yōkai narratives and beliefs may have been extracted from village life, debunked by Inoue Enryō, or put into the pages of library books by Yanagita Kunio, but Mizuki's work makes them seem alive again. And as living characters in his manga and anime, they re-create a lost time when they were also alive in everyday life—or at least, in an imagined everyday life of the past, one that is created by the longings of everyday life in the present.

There is no denying the real sense of nostalgia invoked by his characters, but we should remember that Mizuki himself and his production company (Mizuki Production) are also extremely skilled at using media to promote his creations. Many of Mizuki's yōkai characters may have folkloric precedents, but they are ultimately a distinctive brand, trademarked, copyrighted, and marketed with great skill. Mizuki is a documenter of yōkai but also a producer and popularizer of his own yōkai vision. In contemporary Japan, his images are so deeply ingrained in popular culture that you would be hard-pressed to find a child or adult unfamiliar with them. It is likely that without Mizuki's prolific work over the last half a century, many older yōkai of folklore would have been forgotten or relegated to library books and museum shelves. So even as he inflects them with his own particular spin, Mizuki has kept these creatures alive in the cultural imagination.

Urbanizing Yōkai: Miyata Noboru

Just as Mizuki, a creative artist, was in part inspired by Yanagita's work on yōkai, so too were professional scholars, especially those affiliated with Yanagita's own discipline of folkloristics. For the most part these researchers adhered to Yanagita's theoretical framework. But in 1985, a folklorist named Miyata Noboru (1936–2000) published a book titled *Yōkai no minzokugaku* (The folklore of yōkai), which used the concepts of borders (*kyōkai*) and the city (*toshi*) as "keys to break open the deadlock."[70] This new perspective was important because it helped rescue folkloric yōkai from being written off as nostalgic rural icons from the past, and brought them into contemporary culture so they could be understood once more as an aspect of the lived experiences of real people.

For example, in discussing the Kuchi-sake-onna, the female yōkai protagonist of urban legends that had circulated wildly throughout Japan in 1979, Miyata links her appearance in modern urban and suburban settings to earlier, more rural yōkai, such as *yamamba*, a mountain-dwelling witchlike woman (sometimes called *yamauba*). He demonstrates continuity not just with the image of the yōkai itself but also with emotional, geographic, and social factors that give birth to yōkai. Similarly, he seeks to connect random urban crimes that were occurring in Tokyo to the Edo-period yōkai phenomenon known as *kamikiri* (hair-cutter), in which a person would suddenly discover that her hair had been sheared off.

Miyata's focus on place ("the topology of yōkai," as he puts it) also builds on earlier suggestions by Yanagita that yōkai haunt the borderlands. But Miyata pushes these ideas further, exploring examples of strange occurrence at crossroads, on bridges, and in the no-man's-land outside the safe space of everyday life. The city, of course, is filled with these uneasy, dangerous places that belong to nobody. In effect, Miyata developed a field of urban folklore studies that does not deny connections to the past or to rural areas, but which also recognizes that "folklore involving mysterious phenomena is constantly being exchanged within the glittering spaces of large modern urban centers."[71]

A New Yōkaigaku: Komatsu Kazuhiko

At the same time Miyata was exploring strange phenomena in the city, folklorist and anthropologist Komatsu Kazuhiko (b. 1947) was beginning to develop a new yōkaigaku. Like Miyata, Komatsu observed the way in which borders played a role in determining who was human and who was an outsider. In a seminal 1985 book titled *Ijin-ron* (Theories of the stranger), he examines so-called *ijin-goroshi* (stranger-killing) legends, in which a wandering beggar or mendicant priest is murdered while passing through a village. Sometimes, through the phenomenon of communal illusion (*kyōdō gensō*), the crime is hidden under a thick layer of legends—often concerning yōkai and yūrei. Although this book does not focus on yōkai per se, in the last chapter Komatsu looks toward a new theory that would explore links between yōkai and concepts of otherness, suggesting that sometimes yōkai can be interpreted as folkloricized versions of outsiders (including outcastes/outcasts).[72]

Whether this social model of yōkai actually represents the beginnings of a new yōkai theory or simply a new perspective on previous approaches, it signaled Komatsu's own deepening interest in exploring yōkai in fresh ways. One of his important early contributions, for example, revisits the difference between yōkai and kami. He updates Yanagita's "degradation theory" by stressing the fact that both yōkai and kami possess supernatural powers. What determines whether they are kami or yōkai is whether or not humans worship them—so the movement can go both ways, from kami to yōkai or from yōkai to kami, depending on the needs of the society in question. To understand yōkai, then, you have to understand the people for whom they are important, and this requires a broad, multidisciplinary, humanistic approach.

Komatsu presents these ideas as part of a reevaluation of yōkai studies in his 1994 book, *Yōkaigaku shinkō* (New thoughts on yōkaigaku); more than a century after Inoue Enryō coined the term, Komatsu proposes a new yōkai-ology:

The new yōkaigaku is a discipline that researches the yōkai that humans imagine (create), that is, yōkai as cultural phenomena. Just as with animals, plants, and minerals, the form and attributes of yōkai existence cannot be studied without considering their relationship with human beings; they always reside within this relationship with humans, within the world of human imagination. Accordingly, the study of yōkai is nothing other than the study of the people who have engendered yōkai. In short, yōkaigaku is "yōkai culture studies [*yōkai bunka-gaku*]," a "human-ology [*ningengaku*]" that seeks to comprehend human beings through yōkai.[73]

As part of developing this new yōkaigaku, Komatsu—under the auspices of the International Research Center for Japanese Studies (known as Nichibunken), a national research institute located in Kyoto—organized a series of interdisciplinary research workshops to study yōkai from a variety of perspectives. Participants included scholars of literature, folklore, history, art, anthropology, sociology, and religion, as well as museum curators, photographers, and novelists. All together, these various workshops met some sixty-two times from 1997 to 2013, leading to the publication of dozens of books and articles and the creation of three public databases of yōkai research material and images through an ongoing "yōkai project."

Komatsu himself first became interested in yōkai in graduate school while exploring setsuwa and picture scrolls in which references were made to mono-no-ke, spirit possession, Onmyōdō, and *shugendō* (aesthetic religious) practices for warding off demons and illness. He also learned about a community in the mountains of the island of Shikoku that still practiced rituals of this nature as part of a religious system called Izanagi-ryū.[74] During his initial fieldwork in that community, he felt a sense of strangeness, as if he were simultaneously in the Heian period and the present. So his initial interest in yōkai was spurred by this exciting mixture of past and present, and methodologically he felt it was important to combine archival and historical research with ethnographic fieldwork. He felt there was a conception of something between what is visible and what is invisible that played a distinctive role in Japanese culture and could not easily be classified under a particular academic subject heading; this "mystical thinking" (*shimpi-shisō*) spanned literature, art, history, and religion and was part of people's everyday lives. His classification of yōkai, then, is purposely inclusive and "provisional" in order to encompass the "complexity" of the way yōkai are written about, spoken about, and illustrated.

He suggests that what we find surprising about yōkai should *not* be surprising—those things that seem strange to us now can be understood through carefully examining the ideas and practices of the past and tracing how things came to be the way they are. That is, yōkai are a window into something else—into popular thought and Japanese culture. Ultimately, Komatsu stresses, defining yōkai is not important; rather, we should learn to read through the "yōkai-ish thing," using it as a lens with which to explore "what is on the other side," the "message" of the text or belief in which yōkai appear. This is a way for people to get a deeper grasp of Japanese culture—and to achieve a different perspective on their own culture, whether Japanese or Western.[75]

Komatsu and many of the other people involved in the study of yōkai produce work that is highly accessible and well read by the general public. In fact, Komatsu purposely chooses to write some of his texts so that they can be understood by high-school-age readers.[76] Any major bookstore in Japan today has a few shelves devoted to Japanese folklore, and there is usually a subsection specifically dedicated to yōkai. Sometimes there is even a smaller subsection devoted to Komatsu's writing and edited volumes.

In 2012, Komatsu became director of the International Research Center for Japanese Studies. In one sense, his appointment to the helm of a major government-funded research center suggests that yōkai are no longer a marginalized topic of study; their value for understanding Japanese culture is, as it were, authorized by the government. On the other hand, the fact that their value for understanding "Japanese culture" has been authorized in this way places them at the center of sometimes problematic discussions of what it means to be Japanese. Nichibunken itself was established in the 1980s under the directorship of Umehara Takeshi (b. 1925), a philosopher notorious for his Japan-first "nativist" ideology, and Nichibunken has sometimes been accused of promoting Nihonjinron, discourses on the uniqueness of Japan.[77]

A great deal has changed since Umehara's tenure, and the research institute has come to be known for its interdisciplinary scholars and for hosting foreign researchers, many of whom come from other Asian countries, such as China, Korea, and Vietnam. Komatsu's own research, and the work of his yōkai workshops, is never explicitly nationalist. Having acknowledged that, however, we should remember that the study of yōkai, because it is so deeply intertwined with discourses of Japanese history and culture, and because it has now been "sanctioned" by the government, can easily slip into commentary on the uniqueness of Japan. Particularly as they become recognized in other countries as a distinct product of Japanese culture, yōkai are dangerously poised to be part of essentialist or orientalist discussions about "weird," "wacky," or "inscrutable" Japan. And that is why, hopefully, the serious study of yōkai can get us beyond such positions—by understanding where they come from, we can see that yōkai are not, after all, so surprising.

As I have suggested from the outset, Japanese yōkai are specific to Japan—that is, they are molded by the particular history and culture of the group of islands that is now called "Nihon" (Japan). To be sure, then, yōkai do tell us something about the "Japanese" experience, but they also tell us a lot more: about how people understand their world, about artistic and narrative expression, about the transmission of knowledge from one generation to the next, about science and religion, and on and on. Komatsu may have first come across what he calls "mystic thinking" in Japanese texts, but as the history of monsters and the supernatural in other countries also reminds us, such thinking is clearly not limited to Japan. Ideally, the study of yōkai gestures to something beyond Japan—to the study of human culture—and the new yōkaigaku can work to transcend the language of essentialism.

Best-Selling Yōkai: Kyōgoku Natsuhiko

Although Komatsu's books are well read, he is still working within an academic environment. The current star of the creative yōkai world (other than Mizuki Shigeru, who remains exceedingly popular) is the best-selling novelist Kyōgoku Natsuhiko (b. 1963). Kyōgoku grew up with the manga and anime of Mizuki, whom he credits as a direct influence on his own career. He is also a serious researcher and has worked with Komatsu and other scholars (he participated in Komatsu's yōkai workshops).

Kyōgoku is almost supernaturally prolific. Since his debut novel in 1994, he has written dozens of books and hundreds of short stories and essays. Many of his novels are so long they are easily spotted in the paperback section of a bookstore: bricklike books dwarfing their neighbors. His fiction has been adapted for television, film, manga, and anime. He also publishes research articles, edits academic volumes on yōkai, lectures widely throughout Japan, and appears annually in forums and panel discussions, where he always draws a huge crowd. He is a celebrity in both the literary and yōkai worlds, and his work brings these two worlds together.

Born in Hokkaido, Kyōgoku attended the Kuwazawa Design School in Tokyo, worked for a while at an advertising agency, and set up on his own as a designer. Legend has it that one day, with no warning, he simply brought a massive manuscript to the Kōdansha publishing house; the resulting book was *Ubume no natsu* (*The Summer of the Ubume*), a runaway best seller. Set in 1950s Tokyo, *The Summer of the Ubume* is a mystery story told in the first person by tabloid writer and novelist Sekiguchi Tatsumi, and it features a cantankerous but brilliant used-book dealer named Chūzenji Akihiko, generally called by the name of his shop, Kyōgoku-dō. The complex narrative surrounds the yōkai ubume; in the process the book mentions Sekien, Enryō, and Yanagita, and it explores questions of belief and psychology. Parts of the novel read like an introduction to yōkaigaku. All the characters are quirky, and the unlikely hero, Kyōgoku-dō, seems like an odd mixture of Inoue Enryō and Abe no Seimei, cloyingly scientistic but simultaneously privy to the mysteries of the otherworld (and the human mind).

The Summer of the Ubume is the first work in Kyōgoku's "Hyakkiyagyō series" of novels, each of which features many of the same characters found in the others and draws on a Sekien yōkai for title and motif. The theme of each story reflects the nature of the particular yōkai, resulting in a unique blend of the mystical atmospherics of yōkai fiction and the rational deductive methods of a modern detective novel. Kyōgoku's writing is famous for its sophisticated use of difficult kanji, and the books themselves are known for their high production values and stylish design.

Kyōgoku has also written numerous short stories, often set in the Edo period and presented under various different "hyaku-monogatari" titles. *Nochi no kōsetsu hyaku-monogatari* (Subsequent hyaku-monogatari rumors) won the prestigious Naoki Prize for popular fiction in 2003. Moreover, Kyōgoku is extremely adept at crossing into other media; his second novel in the Hyakkiyagyō series, for example, *Mōryō no hako* (The box of the mōryō, 1995), was made into a manga, anime, and a live action film.

Along with yōkai researchers Tada Katsumi and Murakami Kenji, Kyōgoku has published an informal roundtable discussion called *Yōkai baka* (Yōkai crazy, 2001). With Aramata Hiroshi and Mizuki Shigeru, he is one of the driving forces behind a triannual journal called *Kai* (The strange) that began publication in 1997 and advertises itself as the only magazine in the world completely dedicated to yōkai. It publishes scholarly articles (by

Komatsu, among others), as well as roundtable discussions, manga, analyses of Sekien's images, short fiction, and photographs.[78]

Kyōgoku has expressed deep admiration for Mizuki Shigeru, and even jokingly claims to "want to become like that old man in forty years."[79] And indeed, like his mentor, Kyōgoku is a celebrity, known not only for his creative genius and prolificacy but also for his personal style. Unlike most contemporary writers, for example, he often appears in public wearing a traditional Japanese kimono. And, mysteriously, he always wears black, fingerless gloves.

Boom

Since the 1980s, Japan has experienced a "yōkai boom." Although it is impossible to quantify what actually makes something a *boom*, it seems that the combination of manga, anime, research, fiction, film, and other manifestations of yōkai and yōkai-related material in popular culture reached a tipping point of sorts: suddenly, in the 1980s, yōkai became visible and commercially profitable. The continued production of yōkai manga, anime, and video games suggests that they still are. At the same time, serious research into yōkai also continues. Occasionally an undiscovered text will come to light—an otogizōshi or kibyōshi—and experts such as Tokuda Kazuo or Adam Kabat will explore what they reveal about how people once understood yōkai. Komatsu's work in particular has spawned a whole new generation of researchers—people such as Kagawa Masanobu, Yasui Manami, and Iikura Yoshiyuki—who continue to expand the boundaries of the new yōkaigaku.

For the sake of brevity, my historical summary here has focused primarily on people and texts related to yōkai per se, but other fields are closely associated. For example, recent Japanese horror movies, known as J-horror, draw on many folk ideas and images, often developing them in modern settings with contemporary technology. And the internationally recognized anime of Studio Ghibli are steeped in yōkai lore and traditional imagery and ideas. Takahata Isao's *Heisei tanuki gassen: Pompoko* (*Pom Poko*, 1994) draws directly on tanuki legends as well as famous hyakki-yagyō images. And Miyazaki Hayao's films, from *Tonari no totoro* (*My Neighbor Totoro*, 1988) to *Mononoke hime* (*Princess Mononoke*, 1997) and

Figure 2. Big names of yōkai studies. *Back row from left to right:* Inoue
Enryō, Mizuki Shigeru, and Ema Tsutomu. *Front row from left to right:*
Lafcadio Hearn (Koizumi Yakumo), Komatsu Kazuhiko, Yanagita Kunio, and
Kyōgoku Natsuhiko. Original illustrations by Shinonome Kijin.

Sen to chihiro no kamikakushi (*Spirited Away,* 2001), are creatively
inspired by the yōkai world. And this is to say nothing of Pokémon,
Yu-Gi-Oh! and the explosively popular Yōkai Watch, which are all directly
and indirectly related to yōkai folklore.

If all of this is part of the so-called boom, then it has been going on so
long now that perhaps it is not really appropriate to call it a boom. Rather,
it is simply that yōkai, in many different shapes and in a huge range of
media, are an indelible feature of contemporary Japanese cultural life
and—given their proven ability to adapt to new forms of expression—will
remain that way for years to come.

3 Yōkai Practice/Yōkai Theory

By tracing how yōkai have been portrayed, illustrated, and analyzed at different times in Japanese history, we can see that they are a permanent (though ever-changing) feature of the cultural landscape. And if Japan is currently experiencing a yōkai boom, it is only because in recent years Mizuki, Komatsu, Kyōgoku, and others have brought this feature to the attention of a large number of people. In other words, the boom is about awareness. Now that people notice that yōkai have long been part of their lives—in legends or literature or art or games—they feel a greater affinity for them and are more interested in thinking about what they mean. In places where a local yōkai legend may have been all but forgotten, efforts are made to revitalize it. Scholars spend time looking for yōkai-related texts and images and exploring new approaches for analyzing them. And certainly commercial businesses such as publishers, filmmakers, and toy companies are well aware of the profit potential of anything having to do with yōkai.

In a sense, then, yōkai can be thought of as part of contemporary commercial and folkloric practice. When I use the word *practice* here, I mean yōkai are not just found in historical texts, old images, folktales, and legends from the past, or even in manga, anime, and films today, but rather they play an intimate and informal role in everyday lives—at least for some people. Yōkai of *practice* are not simply objects or creatures or phenomena but a broad and exciting theme around which people gather.

The idea of practice has a long history in anthropological and sociological theory, but what I stress here is that the practice of yōkai entails people not simply accepting yōkai as they are handed down but actively engaging with them, changing them, and making them their own. By thinking in terms of practice, we explore how people express agency and creativity within existing rules and structures. We see close up the folkloric creativity mentioned earlier, the negotiation between conservative tradition and innovative change, between communal and individual voices. This is particularly evident when we visit a "folk group" deeply immersed in the practice of yōkai: we see how people can be meaningfully connected to each other through their interests, and how yōkai can be, in a sense, a concrete part of life.

At the same time, yōkai always also raise abstract questions. In the final pages of this chapter, I further develop some of the ideas we have seen throughout and explore more conceptual ways that yōkai reflect and inform our cognitive and social structures. Of course, there is no grand unified theory of yōkai, but thinking about them in the abstract can inspire theoretical and philosophical speculation about the ways we experience and make sense of the world. And the abstract and the concrete, the theory and the practice, are never far apart.

YŌKAI CULTURE NETWORK

Long ago, folklorist Alan Dundes argued that a folk group can be any group of people with a shared interest or some other linking factor, such as an association with a common idea, place, or even language. In Japan today, the word *yōkai,* along with the various associations that go with it, serves as just this sort of linking factor, providing a bond for an otherwise diverse set of people. Members of this extended community may not actually know each other and may never even meet—but nonetheless, they are connected by a common interest in yōkai. This folk group would certainly include all the people mentioned in the previous chapters—the scholars, writers, and artists, as well as all the people who read and view their work.

Such a group, however, would be so extensive as to be almost meaning-less, or at least not a manageable size for exploring the way people associate with ideas and each other. It is more productive to think of people (and ideas) as being connected through a kind of network. I call this the yōkai culture network. The YCN has no center; it is a kind of "rhizome," a concept originally used in botany but developed by philosophers Gilles Deleuze and Félix Guattari to refer to systems that are interconnected and nonhierarchical. The structure of relations in such a system is not treelike, with a trunk and branches, but more like a web of tangled roots and vines. As Deleuze and Guattari explain, "Any point of a rhizome can be connected to anything other, and must be."[1]

Within the YCN, however, we do find a few particularly dynamic points of intersection—let's call them nodes or hubs—around which certain people and activities tend to cluster. We can think of each one of these nodes as a kind of community of practice, each with a slightly different focus, from which influences and ideas radiate. There are at least four of these: the local, the academic, the commercial, and the vernacular. These nodes are all equally important—they are connected and symbiotic. By briefly examining them, we can explore what yōkai mean to different people in different places and positions; we can also see how they mutually influence each other and how individuals fit into different parts of the broader network. After a brief tour of each node, I will zero in particularly on the vernacular.

Local: Heritage and Connection

The *local* here refers to the many manifestations of yōkai found in specific places throughout Japan. This may be the oldest node of yōkai culture, and it is often the impetus for the development of the others. It includes, for example, legends of tengu living on a particular mountain, or tales of tree spirits haunting a dark forest, or ghost or poltergeist phenomena associated with a particular building in a city. In some cases, a yōkai may be known only to a few hundred people living in a corner of one small village or neighborhood. In short, the *local* suggests a direct connection with location, with place. If we think of practice as the way in which people engage with and use yōkai, then local practice is characterized by people interacting with the legends, beliefs, folktales, and so on that are part of their own geographical community.

But even though the local is defined by its affiliation with a particular place, the way people interact with their own local yōkai can be determined by outside factors, such as the academic and the commercial. For example, in the city of Tōno, in Iwate Prefecture, there have long been stories of kappa. But after Yanagita Kunio wrote *The Tales of Tōno* in 1910, the local kappa there became part of the academic world and now reside not only in the *kappa-buchi* (kappa pond) there but also in research books—including this one. They are simultaneously part of the commercial world, used to advertise Tōno; the kappa pond is a tourist attraction now, and even the police box at the Tōno train station is shaped like a winking kappa, a gesture of friendly welcome to visitors from out of town.[2]

Mizuki Shigeru's hometown of Sakaiminato provides another example. Certainly there were once local yōkai legends and beliefs there, but now (at least to the casual visitor) they have been overwritten by the connection with Mizuki, and the town is full of references to yōkai from his manga—that is, from all over the country. For many of the residents of Sakaiminato, then, local engagement with yōkai means a kind of commercial engagement with Mizuki's yōkai and their fans.

There are many other examples, most of which do not demonstrate such a direct influence from academic or commercial interests. In some places, a local yōkai legend may be learned at school, for instance, as part of the study of local or regional history. Or it may be the focus of a shrine ritual or festival. Sometimes a legend may be the catalyst for local engagement with the wider world. For example, the Japanese Oni Exchange Museum (Nihon no oni no kōryū hakubutsukan) is located in a rural part of Kyoto Prefecture famous as the site of the Shuten dōji oni legend. The museum celebrates the local relationship with the legend but also introduces oni-related lore and material from all over Japan.

Similarly, but on an even smaller scale, in rural Fukuoka Prefecture, in Ukiha City near the Chikugo River—famous for kappa—there is a shop that makes and sells traditional style Japanese sweets, many of which have a kappa theme. It turns out that the owner has long been fascinated by kappa lore and for decades now has collected ceramic figurines and other kappa-related goods from all over Japan. The store itself is decorated with these items, and the second floor—which the owner may allow interested visitors to view—is like a private museum dedicated solely to kappa.

It is hard to draw any general conclusions about the local. But in many cases, the local practice of yōkai is characterized by a sense of tradition and history and community. Whatever the local yōkai legend is—indeed, no matter how gruesome or unattractive—it suggests continuity with residents in the past. On the local level, yōkai are a form of heritage, often a source of pride, and sometimes a resource for commercial prosperity. They provide a cherished connection with the past that people living in the present feel compelled to hand down to future generations.

Academic: Lens into Another World

There is no need for me to write much about the academic node of the YCN here, because so much of the information in the previous chapters emerges from this particular form of practice. Suffice it to say that even though only a few scholars, such as Komatsu, have actually built their academic careers around yōkai, many scholars in a variety of disciplines touch on yōkai in their research. Similarly, archivists and museum curators, such as Yumoto Kōichi and Kagawa Masanobu, have an abiding interest in yōkai culture in general and its material aspects more specifically. It seems that at least once a year somewhere in Japan there is a major museum exhibition of yōkai art and artifacts. The academic node focuses on collection, interpretation, writing, and display; for people involved in this form of engagement, yōkai provide a lens into bigger issues—literature, history, art, and religion, as well as concepts of nation and "Japanese culture."

Commercial: The Yōkai Industrial Complex

Since at least the 1970s and 1980s, a plethora of books, manga, anime, video games, and films have creatively played with traditional and historical images of yōkai, recontextualizing them and repurposing them for all sorts of uses. In the previous chapter, I reviewed some of the largest actors in this commercial node of the YCN, but what I stress here is simply that there is clearly money to be made from yōkai. Mizuki's manga and anime are at the heart of this; their success proved that yōkai can be profitable. While not quite the Disney of Japan, Mizuki Production is instrumental in publishing Mizuki's work and licensing his images to toy companies, game makers, and other manufacturers. Among the Mizuki goods for sale on the Mizuki Production website are yōkai candles, Papa Eyeball figurines, Nurikabe bags, Kitarō calendars, Mizuki yōkai stickers, bookmarks, coffee mugs, folders, DVDs, games, and a whole range of smartphone apps.[3]

Mizuki is the seminal figure in this commercial node, but many other individuals and manufacturers produce yōkai-related materials for profit, starting with the range of products (books, DVDs, etc.) generated by best-selling author Kyōgoku Natsuhiko. Numerous manga artists incorporate yōkai in their work, and even some researchers, such as Murakami Kenji and Tada Katsumi, make a living through a mix of writing and lecturing on yōkai. Many of them contribute to the journal *Kai*, with its blend of manga, fiction, and academic research and commentary. Another more recent journal, *Yū* (written *Yoo* on the cover), is similar to *Kai* but focuses more on ghost tales and horror stories than on yōkai themselves.

All these products attest to the fact that yōkai have commercial allure. Some individuals, like Kyōgoku, Tada, and Murakami, are simultaneously active researchers and creative producers of new ideas. Others are less caught up in the creative side of the practice and more involved in actually manufacturing the items themselves—whether in paper or plastic or celluloid or digital form. But all these people and products are part of what we might call the yōkai industrial complex, in which commercial producers draw on traditional yōkai imagery and historical background to create attractive yōkai-related goods. The yōkai industrial complex provides a structure not only for creating products but also for promoting and selling them. Negatively viewed, it is a system that corrupts the "authenticity" and "folkloric" value of yōkai, removing them from their local or personal context and transforming them into commodities from which only a few individuals and businesses profit. It makes the public property that is a folkloric yōkai into a private commercial possession. On the other hand, such commercial production is one way in which yōkai stay relevant and viable and ever changing. It is a circular process: yōkai keep businesses afloat and people employed, and the yōkai industrial complex in turn ensures that yōkai continue to play a role in the cultural imagination of consumers.

Vernacular: Subculture of Yōkai Aficionados

In addition to the mass producers of these widely distributed goods, there is also an overlapping group of people who participate in the production of yōkai items. These individuals grew up with Mizuki's images and now Kyōgoku's novels; not satisfied with simply consuming, however, they have entered the fray as independent producers themselves. Some are yōkai *otaku*, profoundly inspired by manga and anime and possessing an almost encyclopedic knowledge of yōkai. Others are more enamored with older or localized yōkai manifestations, and have traveled (or read) widely in search of yōkai folklore. I call this the vernacular node, to stress its informal, unofficial nature. In a sense, this is a sort of subculture of yōkai aficionados, a grassroots community of yōkai producers focusing on hand-crafting and very small print runs.

One member of this community, for example, is the illustrator of most of the pictures in this book—Shinonome Kijin—who has a full-time job completely unrelated to yōkai (he is a schoolteacher). In his spare time, however, Shinonome not only draws yōkai in a wide variety of styles but also writes short texts introducing yōkai and their history. The brief, inexpensive booklets he produces are lovingly and meticulously crafted. One or two have been published by commercial presses, but for the most part Shinonome puts them together himself and sells them independently at manga- and yōkai-related gatherings.

This node of the network is restrained by neither the rules of academia nor the demands of a highly commercialized market economy. The members of this small community are, as they sometimes call themselves, *yōkai-zuki*, literally "lovers of yōkai" or yōkai aficionados; they are well versed in folklore and history but also engage imaginatively, inventively, with yōkai culture. By briefly visiting a "yōkai event" run by one such group of yōkai aficionados, we get a sense of the dynamism of this group of people and the diverse ways they articulate their creativity through yōkai. It becomes evident that within the vernacular community of the YCN, yōkai provide a kind of language, a form of communication through which individuals express artistry and humor.

In February 2013, Shinonome Kijin invited me to attend an event at which he would be selling some of his works. The gathering was held from noon to 5:30 P.M. in a creative studio in the basement of a building in the Takadanobaba district of Tokyo, a lively area near Waseda University, full of bars, restaurants, used bookstores, and other shops catering to a young, creative crowd. The venue consisted of two large rooms with about twenty-five tables displaying all sorts of yōkai items for sale. This was the second such gathering for this group, the first one having occurred several months earlier; both were organized by Nurarihyon Uchida (an alias), who was dressed in costume and makeup to look like the yōkai *nurarihyon*, a creature of obscure origins that has come to be considered a yōkai leader. Nurarihyon Uchida describes himself as a "yōkai navigator," "yōkai performer," and writer. At the event, he was flanked by four women dressed as kitsune and tengu, complete with feathery wings, in rather revealing costumes. Such cosplay is a common element of this vernacular yōkai community, especially since many members are interested in manga and anime. Uchida explained to me that organizing these gatherings was easy for him because about two-thirds of the participants were his friends; they were already part of a community linked by their interests, associating in similar events, or communicating through Internet forums and social-networking sites. Many of them, like Uchida himself or my friend Shinonome Kijin, are known primarily by their pen names or other aliases. Most participants were between the ages of twenty and fifty, and about 60 percent were male.

A wide range of wares was on display. One participant sat behind a table full of plastic yōkai figurines, some his own design and others modeled on Mizuki images (with legal permission, he explained). Right nearby, another participant exhibited—in stark contrast to these colorful plastic items—a variety of handmade objects modeled to look like mummified yōkai, or mummified parts of yōkai, such as a kappa's arm, complete with its own wooden case. There were also various yōkai body parts in specimen bottles. (Special orders are accepted.) At the next table a vendor was displaying tengu-themed items, including small plastic tengu heads that could be attached to the wall in such a way that the tengu's notoriously long nose would serve as a hook or a coat peg. And another artist had created small wood-framed paper lanterns, each one illustrated carefully with a line drawing in the style of Toriyama Sekien.

Several people, such as Shinonome, were selling manga they had drawn themselves—some had a handcrafted pen-and-ink appearance, while others were printed in brilliant color on glossy paper. One woman was selling original yōkai-themed short stories; each booklet, between twenty and forty pages, cost no more than five hundred yen. At another table, a man calling himself Schumann Shigeoka had humorously rewritten the lyrics of famous popular songs, giving them all yōkai themes. In the introduction to his twenty-three-page illustrated booklet, he explains that "the lyrics have been changed so that only yōkai aficionados can understand them. Please use them at gatherings of yōkai aficionados." The songs themselves are lighthearted and creative, each page illustrated with a relevant yōkai and brief explanation.[4]

Consider both the enthusiasm and imagination that go into the production of so many of these items, as well as the fact that these artists and authors are producing their work for members of their own community. Shigeoka's comment that his lyrics are only for yōkai aficionados applies to his own changed songs and to many of the other items for sale. This sort of creative in-group communication is, in fact, one of the ways folklore has been defined—"artistic communication in small groups."[5]

Another example of this form of practice is evident in a collection of "yōkai photographs." Each entry in the booklet starts with a picture drawn by an artist to replicate a well-known illustration of a particular yōkai. For example, one page has a small, hand-drawn copy of Toriyama Sekien's image of *akaname*. Above this is another picture, this one a copy of Mizuki's version of akaname (which is itself based on Sekien's image). Finally, on the facing page is a photograph of the yōkai aficionado artists themselves posing to replicate, cheaply and very tongue in cheek, the Mizuki image. In short, every entry demonstrates the derivative nature of each succeeding image. Like a visual version of the old game of telephone, the portrayal of the yōkai is transmitted up through the ages—from Sekien to Mizuki to the present artists—until it becomes a photograph, which ironically seems the least "real" of them all.[6]

This is a profound form of play: the images are copies, of course, but they are also originals—part of the constant process of replication and innovation that is the very essence of folklore, with its different versions and variants transmitted through time and space. Such playfulness, however, can work only if the members of the yōkai network feel an affinity with each other not only across the present (synchronic) moment but also through the historic (diachronic). That is, just as these artists are communicating with each other across space in the present, they are also connecting to their predecessors, whether living people they have never met, like Mizuki, or long-dead historical figures like Sekien. The yōkai network is an "imagined community" linking both the living and the dead through a common interest in yōkai.[7]

The gathering of yōkai aficionados was not simply a marketplace for yōkai-themed creations. There was also a performance. At six that evening, some forty people paid one thousand yen each (about ten U.S. dollars) for admission to a panel discussion, emceed by Nurarihyon Uchida and featuring manga artists Shinonome Kijin and Schumann Shigeoka, a figurine maker, a cosplayer, and a paper-cutting artist. The event was called "Yōkai-tachi no iru tokoro" (Where the yōkai are) and began with Uchida asking each member of the group which yōkai he or she was currently most excited about.[8] The discussion was wide-ranging and humorous, with participants presenting new versions of old yōkai, complete with PowerPoint slides of their illustrations, and also introducing little-known yōkai from the Edo period. As with the items for sale earlier, the performance demonstrated a dynamic engagement with yōkai as living, changing things with as much meaning in the present as they had had in the past.

The second part of the event was a contest of images and wit, in which Uchida challenged the panel to create illustrations in response to questions, such as "What is the cutest yōkai?" and "What is the difference between a yōkai aficionado and a normal person?" While participants spoke with knowledge about and respect for yōkai images from the past, they also demonstrated dexterity and imagination in converting these images for the present, complete with references to contemporary popular culture. As an observer, I was reminded of the playfulness of the Edo-period kibyōshi artists and others who had treated yōkai as mutable figures to express both personal creativity and social satire. To current-day yōkai aficionados, the pantheon of known yōkai provides endless source material for creating innovative and topical characters.

Concluding at eight o'clock, this event was followed by a reception, complete with sake from all over Japan, the label of each bottle containing a yōkai motif of some sort. Meanwhile, at a venue a few train stops away, another group of yōkai aficionados was gathering for an annual party.

These were people from the more commercial node of yōkai culture: they included publishers and commercially successful manga artists, the novelist Kyōgoku Natsuhiko, the editors of *Kai* and *Yū*, and researchers Tada Katsumi and Murakami Kenji (who organizes the event every year). Altogether some forty-six participants attended the raucous party at an all-you-can-eat-and-drink Chinese restaurant. Some participants from the earlier, vernacular yōkai event also joined this one, arriving a little late; in other words, the two nodes within the network are not mutually exclusive. After three hours at the Chinese restaurant, about twenty stalwarts rented a private room in a karaoke bar, where they hung out until sunrise, drinking, talking, and singing songs, including the yōkai-themed parodies from Schumann Shigeoka's collection.

I linger on the events of that day because so often folklore is relegated to the past, or it is thought of as something untainted by commercial interests and contemporary media or, similarly, as something "authentic" in danger of disappearing. But when I arrived home after a long night spent talking and drinking (and singing) with members of the yōkai community, it was clear to me that yōkai as a folk practice, as part of a constant process of tradition and change—a process of both preservation and innovation— is very much alive today. Its vernacular and commercial practitioners, whether they make manga, or CDs of yōkai-themed songs, or models of mummified kappa, are deeply aware of the history of yōkai (as outlined by the academic practitioners) and are also profoundly interested in the continued meaning of yōkai on the local level. At the same time, however, they do not feel restricted by these approaches, and they themselves engage creatively with yōkai, reinventing them, animating them, infusing them with contemporary relevance.

My own research has brought me into most frequent contact with the academic node of the YCN: I have met scholars who seek the meanings of yōkai in artistic forms and literary texts. I have also worked in villages and cities with local people who are very knowledgeable about their own yōkai beliefs and legends, and who develop these for festivals and community celebrations. While the particular objectives of people clustered around each node of the network may be different, such differences are less interesting than the convergences. If the study of yōkai is, as Komatsu puts it, a kind of human-ology, then yōkai are a window into a world of personal obsession, community concern, commercial production, and folkloric tradition. The model of the YCN gives us insight into human connections as well as cultural and economic structures. In a hundred years, I suspect, scholars will look back on this particular period in the same way we look back at the late Edo period—as a time when the practice of yōkai was thriving, a moment of great creativity fueled by new media technologies, changing social relations, and a vibrant network of imaginative individuals linked by a concept.

ZONE OF UNCERTAINTY

I hope it is clear by now that yōkai existed in the past but are also very much alive today. As we have seen, if we keep the word *yōkai* relatively loose in definition and open-ended in usage, it can encompass an exciting diversity of phenomena. At this juncture I wish I could offer a single yōkai theory to bring all this diversity together in a meaningful way, some sort of key to crack the "yōkai code." But such a gesture, unfortunately, would not do justice to the complexity of yōkai culture.

That said, however, this culture is not without its governing principles. In the next few pages I briefly explore some of the ideas, orientations, and keywords that can be extracted and abstracted from the historical instances and concrete examples we have looked at already, and from the entries on actual yōkai in the bestiary section of the book, which follows. In some cases, the discussion here simply pushes a little harder on ideas introduced earlier, but these are, in my view, critical concepts that inform the way yōkai work and the functions they serve. These are the abstract theoretical points that emerge from the concrete practice of yōkai. With that in mind, each one of the short sections that follows is an arrow pointing in a direction for further exploration.

Empathy

I have already discussed how yōkai reflect a generally animistic worldview—the idea that all things possess a spirit, a soul, a life force of some sort. As one scholar of Western monsters puts it, "Animism can be defined as the belief that there are many kinds of persons in this world, only some of whom are human."[9] By interpreting the environment in this way, we can understand how trees and stones become the dwelling places of kami. With such an approach we can also imagine why an old musical instrument that once sounded beautiful, or an old broom that was once indispensable for keeping your home clean, is so much more than just a disposable material object. It is this feeling that gives life to tsukumogami.

This feeling also allows us to see the invisible: the rattling window in the dead of night is the work of yanari intent on disturbing our sleep. We attribute the cause of the rattling to a consciousness similar to our own, something or someone with desires and a will and the ability to make decisions. While such a worldview may be key to the emergence of yōkai, it is certainly exclusive neither to Japan nor even to explicitly "animistic" cultures; witness, for example, the popularity and emotive resonance of movies such as the *Toy Story* series and *Wall-E*, which concern the feelings of nonliving things.

A keyword here is *empathy*. Empathy is notoriously difficult to define but is often characterized as the ability to understand (or at least imagine you understand) the feelings of another. Taken one step further, we can think of it as the attribution of feelings, of intentionality and agency, to somebody/something else, to an *other*—even to an object or phenomenon. As one scholar puts it, "It is part of our constant, everyday humdrum cognitive functioning that we interpret all sorts of cues in our environment, not just events but also the way things are, as the result of some agent's actions."[10] In a sense then, yōkai are artifacts of an energetic expression of empathy—the discovery of intention and subjectivity in the events of the outside world, a projection of our own abilities to think and act onto something else.

Antiempathy

But even as empathy allows us to attribute will and intentions to things in the world around us, it does not quite allow us to transcend the differences between those things and ourselves. There is still a gap between self and other. And this is one reason yōkai are often frightening or grotesque—because even though they may emerge from a feeling of empathy, it is ultimately our inability to fully empathize with them, to imagine leaving our own bodies and entering into theirs, that keeps them strange.

One of Japan's most important modern writers, Abe Kōbō (1924–1993), wrote an essay on why he and a lot of other people are afraid of snakes. He explains that snakes are beyond just "scary." There is something deeply unnerving about them; they provoke a loathing that is qualitatively different from the fear we have of other wild beasts. This is not, he says, because they were dangerous to our tree-dwelling ancestors and this sense of danger has come down to us through our genes. Rather our fear stems from the fact that snakes have no legs, and when we look at one slithering out of a small hole in the ground, we have an experience very different from the experience of watching an animal like a dog or cat. Somehow we can imagine ourselves in the place of a dog or cat (we know what it is like to walk on our hands and knees). But a snake is too alien for us to "personify" in this way; it is simply "close to impossible to imagine its everyday life from the inside."[11] The same problem occurs when a creature has too many legs—as in the case of a *mukade* (centipede)—because it, too, moves so differently from us. We cannot identify with it; we can't empathize.

Abe does not mention yōkai specifically, but we can see the same dynamic at work. It is not surprising that gigantic snakes as well as mukade are also considered yōkai, or that spiders like the tsuchigumo become symbols of dangerous, monstrous otherness. We understand that a spider is a living thing, but with only four limbs of our own we find it difficult to imagine what it is like to propel ourselves forward on eight. Think of the 1998 movie *A Bug's Life*. The filmmakers wisely chose to draw most of the major insect protagonists with two legs and two arms rather than six legs, a move that made them seem somehow more human, allowing the viewer to identify with them.

My point is that yōkai operate in a tricky middle zone that tests our powers of empathy. They emerge from an instinct to imagine life and agency in other things; but at the same time, they remain alien and creepy because of our inability to fully empathize with them. They unsettle us because they don't "make sense" intellectually or emotionally: they are the familiar and the unfamiliar merged together in an uncanny assembly.[12]

The bestiary in the next section of this book contains a number of yōkai sutured together from pieces of animals—the legs of a tiger, the head of a

monkey, the wings of a bird, and so on. These are chimeras, hybrids, neither one animal nor another: they are uncanny exactly because of their
simultaneous resemblance to animals we know and the unfamiliarity of
their combination. The same goes for a creature like the *nekomata*, a cat
that looks like a run-of-the-mill feline except for its forked tail—and that
forked tail makes all the difference. There are also all sorts of humanlike
creatures with exaggerated features, such as a long neck (e.g., mikoshi-
nyūdō and rokurokubi) or a long tongue (e.g., akaname, *tenjōname*). One
frequent trait of yōkai (and monsters from many other cultures) is asym-
metry: many of them have only one eye (e.g., *hitotsume-kozō*) or hop
around on a single leg (e.g., *kasa-bake*). This imbalance, too, contributes
to a sense of simultaneous familiarity and distance.

Interstitial

For several decades now, theorists of robotics have explored the idea that
"as a robot's appearance becomes more human-like it is perceived as
familiar to a viewer, until finer nuances from human norms cause them
[*sic*] to appear strange, evoking a negative effect for the viewer."[13] In other
words, when something looks *almost-but-not-quite* human, it repulses us.
In 1970, roboticist Mori Masahiro famously named this gap between the
familiar and the unfamiliar the "uncanny valley."[14] Mori and others are
concerned with robots designed to look human, but I suggest that many
yōkai also reside somewhere in this uncanny valley. Again, take the tsukumogami: familiar household objects that suddenly have arms and legs,
making them uncomfortably unfamiliar. Or a kappa, green and amphibious like a frog, but with a shell like a turtle and the ability to walk upright
like a monkey: a combination of perfectly natural traits combined in an
unnatural, unfamiliar way. Or consider a shape-shifter like a tanuki or
kitsune. One creepy thing about shape-shifters is that, despite their familiar appearance, they are never fully what they appear to be—a fact occasionally revealed by a tail emerging from their human clothing. They are
literally *between*—not really humans but not really furry little mammals
either.

    There are many words we might use to describe this common yōkai trait:
in-between, hybrid, ambiguous, liminal, but let me suggest *interstitial.* The

quality of being interstitial relates to gaps, the zones of uncertainty between zones of certainty. Similarly, *interstitial* can refer to an assembling of different and perhaps seemingly incompatible elements into a new whole. The interstitial is not an empty and meaningless space but just the opposite: a site of communication, combination, and contact. The zone of uncertainty is the space where meanings are made.

Space and Time

The notion of the interstitial also helps us explore questions of where and when yōkai appear. Although answers depend on the particular yōkai, we can make a few generalizations. Yōkai tend to appear between and at the edge. I remember the first time I heard of a *kamaitachi*, a "sickle weasel," from a Japanese friend who had learned of this yōkai as a child. When I asked her where it lived, she explained mysteriously that it resided in the "spaces between the hours."

Yōkai love bridges, tunnels, intersections, crossroads, and borders. These are spaces where control and ownership is unclear. Governing authority is undetermined. A bridge is neither land nor water, neither this side of the river nor that. A tunnel is a dark narrow portal through which you are transported almost magically into a world different from the one you just left. And a crossroads is a point where one can go different ways, a space that demands a decision, and where what you decide has consequences. All these interstitial spaces are dangerous exactly because they are zones of uncertainty. They are spaces of change and potential, of passage from one realm into another. Sometimes this passage is literal, as in the passage from one side of the river to the other or from one town into another, but such movement easily dovetails with the figurative: such places of passage can also become, as it were, portals to the otherworld of yōkai.

Similarly, yōkai may appear at different times of day, but in general they seem to be most active during the twilight hours: the vague, hazy, gray period between the light of day and the dark of night. Yanagita Kunio highlighted this in several essays focusing on the words *tasogare* and *kawatare*, which mean "twilight." He says that these words originally meant something like "who are you?" or "who is that face?" They were uttered at dusk, when you could no longer recognize the person walking in your direction. Depending on the response, you could determine whether the figure coming toward you was a villager, an outsider, or perhaps a yōkai.[15] In zoological terms, yōkai would be known as "crepuscular," a word used in distinction to *diurnal* or *nocturnal* and indicating a predilection not for brightness or darkness but for the interstitial moments of twilight.

Again, yōkai emerge from spaces and times between existing structures, between here and there, between day and night, when nothing is quite certain. In the philosophical study of logic, the "law of the excluded middle" suggests that for any proposition there are only two possible choices: *true* or *not true*. The middle is excluded. But, of course, the interstitial space-time in which yōkai thrive is this excluded middle—wherein lies the possibility of a third, previously unimagined, choice. This excluded middle is a zone of uncertainty not because of the negative value associated with uncertainty but because of its potential. Certainty can delimit vision and hinder change. Uncertainty requires us to see things in fresh ways and find things we otherwise would not look for.

Variation and Abundance

If these are some of the principles by which human beings interact with yōkai, perhaps it is not surprising that the yōkai world is one of variation and abundance. Variation is intrinsic to any folkloric phenomenon, and yōkai are no exception. Their diversity is dazzling. They originate from both native and foreign sources, are constructed from a mixture of past histories and present concerns, from communal beliefs and individual creativity, visual imagery, narrative innovation, wordplay, and commercial inspiration. Not only are there thousands of local yōkai that live only in particular small communities or are known by only a single group of people, but even a yōkai such as the kappa goes by dozens of different names (raising the question, of course, of how we decide what a kappa actually is).

Because of this diversity and variation, the sheer number of yōkai is overwhelming—the recurrence of the number one hundred reflects this abundance. It is exciting, and frightening, to know that there are always more yōkai out there. And if yōkai are often a combination of traits of other things (animals, people, etc.), then of course such combinations are infinite—and relatively easy to imagine. While this book tends to concentrate on yōkai within a folkloric context, yōkai have many different origins, some of which we can never know and others which we can clearly attribute to a particular individual. It is no coincidence that a game like Pokémon, whether consciously or not, develops this notion of abundance to invent hundreds of new monsters.

Encyclopedic

But how do we get a handle on this variation and abundance? One way that has been predominant since at least the early Edo period is what I call the encyclopedic mode. As we have seen, some early Japanese encyclopedias, such as the *Three Realms,* included yōkai in their pages. And even though works such as those by Toriyama Sekien are not "real" encyclopedias, they operate in the same fashion, extracting yōkai from their stories, from the particular space-time contexts they haunt, so that they can be ordered and organized. This encyclopedic mode for thinking about yōkai (and other things) emphasizes: (1) the presentation of inclusive knowledge about a subject, (2) the compression of this knowledge into self-contained units, and (3) the organization of these units.

This is exactly what Sekien did with his catalogs. It is what Yanagita did with his "Yōkai Glossary." And it is still done today: many books about yōkai contain some form of listing and explanation, and some, including many by Mizuki Shigeru, are full-fledged encyclopedias. This desire for order seems to be a governing principle of how we approach the world of yōkai. Perhaps it is precisely because they reside in the zone of uncertainty that we call out for something certain about them.

Ludic

It is also clear that even though yōkai may be strange and interstitial, they are not always scary: they are also about play, or the "ludic mode." In fact yōkai are often produced through playfulness. Many of Sekien's yōkai, for example, were consciously created from wordplay, and his images are full of visual puns. (Because he puts his newly invented yōkai in an encyclopedic format, however, they *seem* as if they have been around for a very long time.) Even a practice such as hyaku-monogatari was a form of recreation and entertainment, to say nothing of kibyōshi and, of course, manga and anime and video games today. For all the spookiness they may educe, yōkai are also *fun*. And this levity is one key to their longevity and versatility: if the zone of uncertainty allows limitless possibilities and unbridled imagination, then it is a space of experimentation and play and ultimately of creation. The ludic mode often coincides neatly with the encyclopedic mode; again, Sekien is one example, but think also about the games of Pokémon and Yu-Gi-Oh! and the way each card contains a compact unit of information, like an encyclopedia entry.[16]

Media Mix/Multiplatform

We should also remember that franchises such as Pokémon or Yu-Gi-Oh! are "media mix," a term suggesting that narratives and individual characters—such as, for example, Pikachu—are equally at home on trading cards, on television screens, in comic books, in electronic games, or even in three-dimensional performative forms such as cosplay. All these different expressions contribute to our image of Pikachu. As one scholar puts it, the media mix creates "a synergistic relationship between multiple media formats."[17] It allows for a multiplatform mode of expression, in which the "same" character can perform on many different stages, none of them necessarily more authentic or original than the next.

I am talking here about contemporary media, but notions of media mix, multiplatformativity, and intertextuality are also helpful for thinking about much older forms of expression. As we have already seen, questions of authenticity and origins are less important for the yōkai of folklore than the fact that they are at home in a wide range of environments and media. Even some of our oldest-recorded yōkai move from one platform to another. A tengu, for example, might be the protagonist of a Kamakura-period setsuwa, be portrayed visually in a Muromachi-period picture scroll, be discussed orally in a local legend, and appear in a video game or anime series. We cannot say that any of these is the "true" or "original" tengu. They are versions of each other—the same but different—and it is the tengu's ability to thrive within diverse genres and media environments, to perform simultaneously on multiple platforms, that makes it such a vital yōkai even today. It has been noted about anime that "media mix must presuppose or must create a situation where characters can move beyond one media format and beyond one narrative context."[18] These same ideas about transferability also apply to the yōkai of tradition.

Characters

We have already explored the way yōkai *phenomena* change into yōkai *things,* morphing from events or occurrences into beings or creatures. Because of this process, today those things we usually call yōkai are no longer scary phenomena but instead named creatures that may refer to scary phenomena. Remember how a feeling of powerlessness to move forward morphed into a yōkai called a nurikabe with eyes and arms and legs? Similarly when the local river floods or a child drowns, the culprit is not the weather or the water but a creature identified as a kappa. Labeling and naming are at the heart of this process. "For something to become a yōkai, it needs to be named," Shinonome Kijin explains. "Because without a name, it is just a scary story [kaidan]."[19]

Naming is part of the encyclopedic process, a way to identify something with concision and accuracy. It is also part of a process of *character creation,* by which I mean the way specific versions of tanuki and kappa, the kind found in legends and folktales, are combined into generic versions of the creatures and then eventually transformed into, for example, PR mascots for a credit card (DC Card). As advertising icons, tanuki and kappa are cute and cuddly, akin to commercial characters such as Sanrio's Kero Kero Keroppi or most famously, Hello Kitty. The mascot-ified tanuki and kappa are still indexable as traditional yōkai, but as representatives for a credit card company they presumably are no longer associated with causing mischief or drowning children!

Such yōkai characters appear nationwide in advertisements, manga, anime, and video games; they also serve as icons in any number of local communities. The neighborhood of Kappabashi in Tokyo, for example, employs a kappa as its symbol. The much smaller town of Satsuma-Sendai in southern Kyushu also uses a kappa—called by its local name *garappa*—as a mascot figure. And Hachiōji City recently created a cute, red-faced, geta-wearing boy tengu as its "tourism character."[20] For decades now tengu, oni, and all sorts of other yōkai have been enlisted in communities throughout Japan as mascots for village revitalization (*mura-okoshi*).

But since the first decade of the twenty-first century, there has also been another trend in character creation. Although these newly created characters are not necessarily yōkai, the creation process is related. Hundreds of communities and institutions (including museums, private companies, and even Tokyo Tower) have developed what they call *yuru-kyara:* a word derived from "loose [*yurui*] mascot character." These are often made into big, soft, lumbering, cutesified figures—think of those puffy big-headed Mickey Mouse characters prancing around Disneyland—and used for PR and advertising.[21]

Inspirations for yuru-kyara mascots vary and include (but are not limited to) animals, local products, physical objects, and historical figures. Occasionally they are directly inspired by yōkai, especially when there happens to be a famous local legend or relevant belief. More often, however, yuru-kyara are created anew by imaginatively assembling representative characteristics of the community or region. In the town of Imabari in Shikoku, for example, the mascot (named Barysan) looks like a gigantic yellow chick with a towel around its waist and a tiara on its head. All these elements have meaning: the area is famous for its grilled chicken (*yakitori*) and its towel industry, and the tiara is shaped like the bridge that connects Shikoku and Honshu. In a sense, these characteristics are filed away in the shared "encyclopedia" of the local community and can be selected and skillfully assembled into a new creation.

The ancient capital of Nara, famous for its Buddhist temples and free-roaming deer, designed a character named Sento-kun: a young Buddha-shaped boy dressed in religious clothing, with deer antlers emerging from his gigantic bald head. This particular mascot caused some controversy among religious practitioners, as well as among members of the general public who thought it looked just plain ugly or, as it were, monstrous. But my point here is that the creation of these yuru-kyara mascots is much like the creation of yōkai; local features and characteristics are stitched together to create a hybrid creature or being to represent the community.

This idea of selecting from an existing set of characteristics recalls a notion by the popular-culture theorist Azuma Hiroki, that of a conceptual "database." Azuma suggests that consumers of manga and anime interact with products and information through "database consumption"; rather than thinking in terms of narrative, they focus on settings, characters, and component parts.[22] Clearly, a similar process of picking and choosing elements to construct an appropriate new character occurs when a yuru-kyara is created, just as it might (and does) when a new yōkai comes into being. Such characters are portable and identifiable across different contexts and different media—just like yōkai who thrive and multiply and mutate across diverse platforms. Of course, unlike the animals, objects, or folkloric yōkai on which they may be based, yuru-kyara are not necessarily in the public domain—as individual or commercial inventions, they are subject to copyright laws and conventions. While some of the more popular characters allow for "looseness" in this regard, many are "tightly" controlled and can be used only for certain approved products and venues.[23]

Creation

I started this book with a discussion of how yōkai emerge as people grapple with mysterious experiences, putting names and faces on occurrences or feelings that are otherwise indescribable. But from at least Sekien's time onward, we see a complementary process of creation occurring. Just like the yuru-kyara devised all over Japan today, many of the yōkai Sekien invented did not come into being through attempts to describe mysterious phenomena. Rather they were drawn from relevant elements and existing motifs and put together in an interesting and often ingenious fashion. I am not saying that new yōkai characters do not serve a function; I am only noting that their inception is different and, in a sense, more playful. It derives not from the challenge of grappling with the incomprehensible in the world around us but from the challenge of making something new and sending it out into that world.

But even freshly minted yōkai have something to say. In a recent experiment, a Japanese university professor gave her students twenty minutes to come up with a "new yōkai"—to name it, describe its characteristics, and draw it. The results were varied, of course, but many of the invented creatures related directly to the concerns of student life. Several students, for example, created yōkai who mischievously alter the flow of time in order to make people late for class. Many students built their yōkai around wordplay and puns. One particularly resonant example was called *hitoma*, which can variously be interpreted as "one space," "human gap," or even "human demon." It refers to the single open seat one often finds on a crowded train or subway, a seat that mysteriously nobody seems willing to sit in. The student drew this yōkai as a foreboding dark shadow, an eerie inky aura, occupying the "empty" seat.[24]

This sort of newly created yōkai, whether it goes on to circulate as a "real" belief or not, reflects associated processes of play and naming. More important, even though the hitoma did not emerge from a profound need, its genesis still reflects the same process of creation we have seen before. It expresses a subtle phenomenon—the oddly untaken seat on a crowded train—for which no word previously existed. Even when yōkai are purposely created (for a class assignment no less!), they remain effective vehicles for articulating thoughts for which we do not already have vocabulary.

Global

With all this in mind, let me reiterate here the danger of treating yōkai as a key to some essential secret of the "Japanese people" or "Japanese psyche." To be sure, those things we call yōkai usually reside within the broad geographic region known as Japan, but this region has over 120,000,000 individuals who, like people everywhere, hold diverse beliefs and values. How is it possible to speak collectively of "the Japanese"? Throughout this book I try to avoid such language—and such traps of thinking—because if yōkai teach us anything about "the Japanese," it is that monolithic terms like this are all but meaningless. As I have stressed repeatedly, yōkai are characterized by diversity, abundance, regional variation, and multiple origins; only in this sense, perhaps, can we say they represent the Japanese people!

I emphasize this here because people sometimes tend to exoticize "Japan." Distinctive aspects of culture and aesthetics—such as ninjas, geishas, samurai, tea ceremonies, even television game shows—are portrayed in Western media as enigmatic or wacky. Yōkai certainly fall into this category, particularly as part of a discourse on "weird Japan," in which unusual-seeming aspects of culture are highlighted as somehow indicative of a generally bizarre "foreignness" that cannot be penetrated by non-Japanese. No surprise, perhaps, that several English-language websites feature tongue-in-cheek postings on "bizarre Japanese mythological creatures."[25]

Whether the tone of this exoticization is celebratory or mocking, it tends to position "the Japanese" and their "beliefs" as special or unique. Sometimes such characterizations of uniqueness are embraced by Japanese politicians, cultural commentators, and scholars who promote concepts of Nihonjinron or suggest a kind of dangerously nationalist Japanese exceptionalism.[26]

I am wary of the fact that yōkai can be used as examples of a particular Japanese spirit or way of interpreting the world. This book was written in part to show that the mysterious creatures of Japanese folklore are, when we have a sense of their history and cultural context, not so mysterious after all. Once we know a little of the context, they start to make sense. Does Japan have more (or stranger) monsters than other cultures? There is no simple answer to this question except, perhaps, "It's complicated." Yōkai have as much to do with indigenous kami beliefs as they do with an exchange of ideas (and languages) with other cultures, especially those found in China and the Korean peninsula. And the continued proliferation of yōkai today is energized not so much by intractable and ancient cultural beliefs as it is by a vibrant and cutting-edge media industry. Moreover, as I have discussed, we can pinpoint several prominent (human) individuals throughout history who have kept yōkai alive and abundant in the popular imagination.

Given all this, it is important to think a little about the broader picture. Even though yōkai are associated with Japanese culture, they have always also been part of *world* culture. The fears and desires and creativity that go into their creation are human traits found all over the globe. Certain individual yōkai have parallels in the monsters of other cultures, but even yōkai that are native or unique to Japan are also shaped by influences from other places. Just as the history of Japanese religion or aesthetics or philosophy is a history of exchange, so too is the history of yōkai. It is no coincidence that almost every entry on a yōkai-like creature in the *Three Realms* references earlier Chinese texts. And many of those Chinese texts look back toward other parts of the world. Like all folklore, yōkai travel across time and space.

But of course the world is even more closely connected today, and ideas and images travel even more easily (and faster). Not surprisingly, yōkai flourish in contemporary media, proliferating on the Internet and in anime and in computer games. Part of this has to do with transnational commercial interests: the anime of Studio Ghibli, for example, and translations such as *Nura: Rise of the Yōkai Clan,* and blockbuster films such as *The Great Yōkai War* are moneymakers that draw on the cultural capital of the Japanese supernatural.

Perhaps even more interesting, however, is the informal, vernacular creativity that yōkai generate. There are numerous role-playing games based on them, and even public art shows of "original" yōkai. A quick glance at DeviantART.com reveals thousands of yōkai images from artists all around the world, and recently an American artist published a book called *The Night Parade of One Hundred Demons,* based on the idea of hyakkiyagyō and financed by raising more than eighteen thousand dollars through Kickstarter in 2011 (even though the goal was only two thousand dollars!). The second volume raised more than twenty-seven thousand dollars in 2013.[27] Clearly a lot of people are interested in yōkai, and clearly, also, yōkai are part of global culture. It is questionable whether we should even call them *Japanese.*

But what does it mean when yōkai cross into new places? In postwar Japan, yōkai became nostalgic icons of an imagined, more innocent time. For people in countries far from Japan, perhaps they work in a similarly nostalgic way today, but by reflecting a desire for an imagined place called "Japan," an "otherworld" where mysterious or "bizarre" creatures still lurk. Whatever the case, wherever yōkai travel, they speak to a desire of some sort. They *mean* something. Which brings me back, finally, to the idea of language.

Language of Yōkai Redux

Earlier in this book, I suggested that yōkai begin where language ends. I will amend that thought now. Certainly the process of yōkai creation starts with the need to express something for which there are no words; it emerges from an aporia, a hole in language. But gradually, abstract phenomena become concrete creatures. Similarly, somebody might set out to invent a yōkai, giving it a name and describing its shape and features and behavior. In either case, named and identified, these creatures/beings/things can now, like words, be put in their appropriate place in a dictionary and listed alongside other yōkai. They are figures of speech.

When I was a child growing up in New York City, one of my closest friends was from Japan. I remember sitting next to him one day in first grade as the two of us happily drew pictures of "monsters." I don't recall the details, except that we engaged in a friendly competition to create stranger and stranger creatures, and that we laughed until the teacher told us to be quiet. But most important, I recall that this experience made our friendship stronger. Looking back now, I realize that by adding bits and pieces to each other's pictures and by coming up with new combinations and novel shapes, we were using monsters to communicate in a way that transcended the words we had at our disposal.

In a sense, then, the creation of yōkai is the creation of language: with grammar, vocabulary, and even local dialects. Like all languages, this one is constantly adding new words to respond to emerging needs, to express new ideas, or to say old things in fresh ways. It is constantly changing as different people learn to speak it. Ultimately, the language of yōkai allows us to talk about the most intimate of beliefs, about fears and desires, and about the mundane and the silly. Where once yōkai emerged to fill the holes in language, to describe the unexplainable, now we also seek ways to describe yōkai in their many different manifestations. And as we learn the language of yōkai, deciphering the various signs out of which it is constructed and adding new words to it, we hear the voices of people who lived in the otherworld of the past and we project our own voices into the otherworld of the future.

PART II   Yōkai Codex

Books are bound, literally: pages are put into a particular order and sewn together or cemented along the spine so that they cannot be removed or reordered. And in contrast to a picture scroll, an individual page of a book, and the words and images imprinted on it, can be accessed at any time without having to review what comes before it. That is, even though the pages are in a sequence, they can be opened and read at random. A book like this is called a codex, simply defined as "a collection of sheets of any material, folded double and fastened together at the back or spine, and usually protected by covers."[1] During the Edo period the codex became the most popular written medium for a flourishing urban and literate culture.

As far as we know, Toriyama Sekien was the first person to put yōkai into the pages of a book like this—to extract mysterious creatures and phenomena from folklore, literature, and earlier picture scrolls and bind them together in codex form. Because Sekien's catalogs are similar in format to the encyclopedias and almanacs of the time, they had the effect of appearing to be an authoritative take on yōkai. Even today, despite the fact that we know Sekien invented many of his yōkai, and that many of his entries were intended to be tongue in cheek, his catalogs are still the go-to guides for exploring the Edo-period yōkai world.

So what does it mean to put a yōkai in a book? One effect is that it preserves a creature long after its living relevance may have disappeared. To a certain extent, documenting a yōkai freezes it in place, stabilizing it in a certain form with a certain set of behaviors, changing the course of its evolution, and making it generally more accessible to people. In Japan, the yōkai "of the book" are the yōkai that people know. But of course, only a very limited number of yōkai can fit within the covers of a book. So what of all the yōkai that are not recorded? One of the yōkai in the pages that follow is a local kappa-like creature called a *gamishiro* that I came across during my fieldwork in Kagoshima. I have not been able to find it in any "authoritative" book or dictionary of yōkai, and these days very few young people in the community have even heard of it. So what of the thousands of yōkai like this throughout Japan that have never been captured on paper?

This section, the final and longest of my own book of yōkai, does not necessarily answer these questions, but it implicitly explores them. I begin with the simple premise that, as much as we take this sort of thing for granted in our daily lives, the ordering and accessing of knowledge is always a historical and subjective undertaking that reflects and affects our cognitive approaches to everything we encounter around us. In the pages that follow, I briefly discuss the encyclopedic mode and the taxonomy of yōkai. Then, in the remainder of the book, I present my own version of an encyclopedic text, a bestiary in which I list and describe and sometimes illustrate a select portion of the expansive pantheon of yōkai.

4 The Order of Yōkai

OF FISH AND YŌKAI

The ocean is full of fish. When you look at the opaque surface of the water, you can't see them, but you know they're down there, everything from gargantuan silver-sided tuna to wormlike fingerlings to deep-sea dwellers moving like ghosts in the cold darkness. There are blue-bodied sharks and shimmering schools of tropical fish, red and yellow and luminous indigo, flitting this way and that with the slightest current. And there are slithering eels and flat, gliding rays, some of which can make electricity, and hagfish that secrete gallons of gooey slime when you touch them.

This is to say nothing of squid and octopi, and shellfish, and shrimp, and lobsters, and sea urchins, and sea cucumbers, and plankton, and animals that are not "fish" but which also live in the ocean, such as whales and dolphins and sea turtles. The numbers and variety are overwhelming. How can we sort this all out? How do we make sense of this morass of shapes and sizes and colors, of these creatures, with their different habitats and special characteristics, hidden in another world beneath the surface of the water?

I start here with questions about fish because, it turns out, there are actually quite a few similarities between fish and yōkai. Not only do fish possess all sorts of different characteristics—some of which, like the hagfish's ability to produce slime, seem downright supernatural—but also this chaotic, jumbled abundance of fish presents similar challenges to anybody trying to organize them into an accessible body of knowledge. Whether you are creating a compendium of information or are just curious about what kind of fish you caught, there are different ways of knowing. Humans master and organize knowledge through a variety of methods.

When I started working on this book in 2012, I was also doing research on folklore, rituals, and everyday life on an island in the south of Japan (Shimo-Koshikijima in Kagoshima Prefecture). As part of learning about daily life, I helped out on a fishing boat a few days a week. Early in the morning, just as the sun was rising, we would haul up nets set just a little offshore. It was the season for horse mackerel (*aji* or *ma-aji*), so on good days we caught a lot of them, but we also caught lots of mackerel (*saba*), yellowtail (*buri*), and various types of bream (*tai*). Those were the most common fish, but really you never knew what you would find in the nets. Sometimes there were tiny squid or mahi-mahi (*shiira*), and once we even caught a moray eel (*utsubo*). I was new to this, so I was constantly pestering my coworkers to explain what each kind of fish was called, when it was in season, and how it was best eaten (as sashimi, for example, or dried and salted). This is a kind of knowledge—what the Japanese call *chie*—that is learned by word of mouth and years of experience.

But this information was sometimes confusing. For example, along with the yellowtail, we often also caught a similar fish that my colleagues on the boat called *hirasu*. If you look up *hirasu* in a common Japanese dictionary, you won't find it. It turns out that *hirasu* is a local name for a fish technically called *hiramasa*, which can be translated into English as "yellowtail amberjack." So my first lesson here was that each fish has a different local name, to say nothing of the different local ways of preparing it for dinner.

Moreover, this yellowtail amberjack looks so similar to the yellowtail that I couldn't tell the difference—though of course all the experienced fishermen could. And while these two fish may look very similar, I was told that, at certain times of the year, the yellowtail amberjack actually tastes much better than the yellowtail and therefore is more desirable and sells for a higher price at the market. So my other lesson here was that differences, no matter how subtle, can be meaningful.

The fishermen have acquired all this knowledge, this *chie*, through years and years of working in the same environment and talking with their seniors and their colleagues. But I was way behind and wanted to catch up, so I bought a pocket fish dictionary; every entry contained a photograph of a fish, its "official" name, regional variant names, description, habitat, and the best ways to eat it. The book had a thorough index, with both official and regional names, and it was organized into categories, such as fish caught from boats, from sandy beaches, and in freshwater.[1]

All this might seem completely natural, because we have grown up with dictionaries and encyclopedias and databases; websites such as Wikipedia are all about organizing, synthesizing, and making information accessible. But of course, creating a fish dictionary like this is really a difficult and profound process. All this information about sea creatures has been neatly ordered and made accessible, folded into a convenient and portable packet. This work of carving order out of chaos is by no means a natural process. The divisions between types of fish, the naming of these creatures, distinctions between them, data on where they live and what they eat, even information about how tasty they are, come from years of observation and research and generations of shared wisdom. And only then did the author of this particular book have to decide exactly what information to include in each entry and how to organize the entries. This process of naming and grouping, of ordering, listing, and describing, is a concrete way to make sense of the worlds we contend with every day.

Which brings me back to yōkai. As I argue in the first part of this book, yōkai are a way to carve something sensible, believable perhaps, out of the chaos of the world around us. A particular yōkai can be the metaphoric embodiment of a vague fear or mysterious phenomenon, like mists of anxiety merging into a sentient, tangible shape with a name and a personality. It is not surprising, then, that there are numerous yōkai dictionaries and encyclopedias on the market, and several websites dedicated to just this process of naming, categorizing, and documenting yōkai. Just like my fish dictionary, many of these encyclopedias contain illustrations (though usually *not* photographs), descriptions of habits and habitats, and lists of regional names and related phenomena.

TAXONOMY

Everything I describe here is part of the process of taxonomy, how things are arranged and ordered. *Taxonomy* most often refers to the naming and classifying of natural phenomena such as animals and plants, but it can also be applied more generally to any kind of object or even to ideas or abstract concepts. In contemporary scientific culture, the taxonomy of animals generally follows an accepted set of principles set out in the *International Code of Zoological Nomenclature*, which is an attempt to systematize the "confusion of names that occurred in the zoological litera-ture of the early part of the 19th century."[2] Of course, any taxonomy, even one with an international code, grows out of years of work and interpreta-tion by people looking for commonalities and differences between the things under investigation.

In the case of yōkai, there is no universal classification code or nomen-clature. But certainly a lot of attempts have been made, some more serious than others, to organize them into a coherent, useful, and accessible sys-tem. Each particular taxonomic effort reflects the concerns and technol-ogy of the historical moment in which it emerged. In Japan, we can roughly trace these attempts to some early documents imported from China. One of the oldest of these is the *Shanhaijing* (*Guideways through Mountains and Seas; J. Sangaikyō*), probably written during the Warring States Period (475–221 B.C.E.), and brought to Japan by the tenth century. This text is a geographical compendium, a kind of atlas with descriptions of strange places and their unusual inhabitants. Organized by location, a geography such as this represents one way in which yōkai and other mys-terious things could be, in a sense, put in their proper places. *Guideways through Mountains and Seas* does not focus specifically on each yōkai, but rather it focuses on the distant places where odd beings happened to reside. Still, it was a great influence on early Japanese texts and picture scrolls, many of which include the yōkai it identified.[3]

As discussed earlier, the Edo period in particular witnessed the devel-opment of an encyclopedic mode of expression through which the world was divided into component parts and organized in a comprehensible way. During this time, Japanese cities were becoming bigger and bigger, literacy rates were rising, and a lively commercial book industry was developing.[4] Along with fiction and other works for entertainment, there were all sorts of almanacs, farming manuals, travel guides, dictionaries, and compendia. All these books, in the words of historian Mary Elizabeth Berry, made up a "library of public information" that served "to examine and order the verifiable facts of contemporary experience for an open audience of consumers."[5]

Information about yōkai was part of this "library." Extracted from stories and beliefs, yōkai were identified as individual units: artists started painting them in picture scrolls as separate creatures, each labeled with a name. And then Toriyama Sekien came along and put them in a series of books, just like in a real encyclopedia, each creature with its own separate page, name, and commentary. Since that time, there have been dozens of compendia of yōkai. Some of them are serious and scholarly, others are creative and illustrated, some are for kids, and still others are firmly tongue in cheek. Even in English now, there are books about yōkai that take the form of an encyclopedia—or a "field guide" or "survival guide."[6]

And more recently, of course, there are also databases—the digital version of the encyclopedic mode. Some of these, like the ones produced by Nichibunken, are professionally curated—even government funded. Others, like the *Gensō dōbutsu no jiten* (Dictionary of fantastic animals), which is in Japanese but is not limited to Japanese yōkai, are created by knowledgeable enthusiasts.[7] Because of their abundance and diversity, yōkai lend themselves to this sort of encyclopedic cataloging.

Databases may be particularly handy for accessing information on yōkai, because their contents can be searched through keywords. In fact, one of the biggest challenges for anybody putting together a taxonomy is to decide what principles should be used in the ordering process. With animals and plants, the most common forms of classification come from the Linnaean system, which organizes the natural world into ranks of species, genus, family, and so on. In determining how to label a particular plant or animal, biologists and taxonomists use a variety of criteria to establish similarities and differences between specimens. Such determinations are based on everything from physical appearance and biological makeup to habitat and other factors.

So how would you do this with yōkai? You could say that, for example, a *kawatarō* is the name of a species; the genus is *kappa;* and the family is *water-dwelling creatures.* But of course, this gets much more confusing with, for example, a yōkai like the *makura-gaeshi* (pillow-shifter), whose identity is commonly described in terms of behavior (i.e., flipping people's pillows) rather than physical appearance. Also, of course, we know that yōkai descriptions and images change through time—so you would have to choose a manifestation at one particular moment for your classification. In short, it would be an interesting exercise to arrange yōkai by means of a Linnaean system—but certainly a challenging one.

So how *have* yōkai been ordered? Usually, it seems, pretty randomly. Sekien breaks up his own books into several sections, but his criteria for organizing are not clear. In his first book, *Gazu hyakkiyagyō,* some of the yōkai do seem to be placed in relation to each other: for example, two yōkai associated with rivers, *kawauso* and kappa, are on facing pages, as are *yamabiko* and tengu, both associated with mountains. But as he produced more and more yōkai, and their descriptions became increasingly complex, such connections became harder to pin down.

More recent attempts also demonstrate the difficulty of figuring out a logical system. Mizuki has produced numerous encyclopedias and seems to have tried a variety of methods. In one case, for example, he divides his yōkai into broad categories that may seem somewhat systematic but which are ultimately subjective: "Yōkai I Have Met," "Celebrity Yōkai," and "Ghosts and Tsukumogami Types." In other books, he lists them in the order of the Japanese syllabary. Murakami Kenji, too, in his massive yōkai dictionary, follows a syllabary-based index, a handy system if you happen to know the name of the yōkai you are searching for. Another method, which emphasizes the diversity of yōkai throughout the country, is to list them by region, as Chiba Mikio does. This may make it difficult to find immediate connections between "species," and it also raises questions not only of how to divide yōkai but also of how to divide regions of the country. Yet another strategy, this one employed by Itō Ryōhei, is to create categories based on place of appearance, such as: "Yōkai of the Rivers and Bogs," "Yōkai of the Ocean," "Yōkai of the Slopes, Roads, and Mountain Passes," and "House Yōkai." This method differs from a Linnaean system in that it does not privilege shape or body type and instead emphasizes the human relationship with yōkai. And most recently, there is now a 680-page dictionary with over thirteen hundred entries compiled by more than a hundred researchers, based on the material recorded in the Nichibunken yōkai databases. The editors have included different indices so yōkai can be searched through type and location, without omitting regional names or squelching their abundance and diversity.[8]

A COMPLETELY INCOMPLETE BESTIARY

In short, creating a taxonomy of yōkai is not a simple task; it often takes a whole committee of researchers and, ultimately, can never be completely complete. But by grappling with how best to compartmentalize and order these diverse beings, we discover both connections and contradictions and better understand their complexity. The rest of this book is my own small attempt, embarked upon with all this in mind, to present yōkai in an encyclopedic format. Such an undertaking is made all the more complicated in English because, of course, many readers may not have a background in Japanese and so will be unable to look up yōkai names alphabetically. And unfortunately, there are no standardized English translations, even for the most common of yōkai (except perhaps for the kitsune, or fox). So in creating this compendium here, I have had to make some difficult decisions about naming, ordering, and which yōkai to include.

Inclusiveness

The first principle of the encyclopedic mode is to strive for *inclusive knowledge* about a subject, and the pages that follow include dozens of individual yōkai, with dozens more mentioned in passing. But this only scratches the surface. As I have stressed, yōkai are characterized by abundance and infinite variety. Since the space of this book is not infinite, however, many fine yōkai had to be left out, and I apologize if the particular one you were looking for does not appear.

I have of course included the big five: kappa, tengu, kitsune, tanuki, and oni. These are not only found locally throughout Japan but also seem to be the most documented in folklore, literature, and even secondary sources. I have also included a lot of other major yōkai, particularly those that are well distributed throughout the country and generally known by

Japanese people today, such as yamamba, *nopperabō,* and rokurokubi. At the same time, I have put in a few very local and all-but-forgotten phenomena, such as *bābū* and gamishiro. There are urban yōkai and rural yōkai, age-old yōkai and recent ones. I have tried to choose a representative sampling of different types, but of course, the result remains incomplete. There is just no way to record them all. Nor, ultimately, would you want to: this inconclusiveness, the knowledge that there are always more out there, may be one of the elements that keep them interesting.

Units

The second principle of the encyclopedic mode entails the compression of knowledge into self-contained units. For each entry, I provide a Japanese name, sometimes more than one, and, when appropriate, an English translation. In general, each entry outlines the history or context of the particular yōkai, noting some regional variations with regard to nomenclature, beliefs, legends, habitat, and attributes. Some entries are illustrated, either with original images made for this book or ones borrowed from historical texts. (I do not include kanji in the entry itself, but at the end of the codex there is a list of all the yōkai included; that list contains kanji when it is unusual or helpful for understanding the character of the yōkai in question. Otherwise, assume the name is most commonly written in hiragana or katakana.)

Overall, I strive to provide a sense of each yōkai in its context and complexity as the product of a process of storytelling, popular beliefs, and creative innovation. Because of this, I try to avoid simple characterizations and generalizations. I emphasize variation and inconclusiveness even if it means sacrificing concise narratives or neat definitions.

Especially for the more prominent or well-documented creatures, entries are detailed and include representative tales and where they come from. One goal is to demonstrate that knowledge about yōkai is not set in stone: it differs from place to place, from person to person, and is constantly in flux. (In the language of semiotics, we might say that a particular signifier can point to many different signifieds.) Ideally, each entry would be a self-contained unit, but of course, yōkai are tied to each other, and tied to other ideas, so the borders between entries are porous.

I have also tried to carefully note where I get my data. Because yōkai are developed through generations of storytelling, and through layer upon layer of retellings and reimaginings, information about them can sometimes feel ungrounded, free floating, unsourced. This is all part of the dynamic folkloric process, the way material is exchanged and changed and infused with meaning in the present tense. One of my goals as a scholar of yōkai, however, is to present this material, in all its complexity, with as much documentation and grounding as possible. Readers can take it from there.

Organization

As noted, there is no perfect way to organize a text like this, and my own structure is certainly not based on an "objective" rationale. Instead I embrace the fact that an author's subjectivity always informs the content and organization of what is written. Rather than use body shape or behavior as governing factors for organizing groups of yōkai, I have chosen to separate them here into "contact zones," the places in which humans and yōkai might come in contact with each other.[9] These are spaces where two worlds intersect—those zones of uncertainty discussed earlier.

I begin with the zones most distant from the places where people usually live, and follow a trajectory inward. The first zone is the *Wilds:* mountains and forests in which human intruders are rare. Next comes *Water:* ocean and ponds and rivers, which are often murky and hard to fathom. Such places can be like little regions of mysterious nature located right inside the most developed parts of human culture. And then there is the *Countryside:* where humans and the natural world are in constant contact. Next is *Village and City:* places of human habitation that are open and porous to outside incursion. And finally, we enter the *Home:* where humans and yōkai may live side by side, this world and the otherworld overlapping in the most intimate of spaces. Of course, these groupings are anything but rigid, and many of the yōkai described here cross from one zone to another. But in this organization there is a sense of movement from the distant and external to the close-at-hand and personal: from that mysterious thing way out there in the wilds, to this mysterious thing right here at home.

For convenience, at the end of the codex there is an alphabetical listing of every yōkai mentioned—including those only alluded to in passing within an entry for another creature. As limited as this list may be, at the very least it underscores the abundance and variety touched upon in the following pages.

The codex can be used as a reference to look up individual yōkai. Or the entries in it can be read straight through, one by one, as you might read the chapters of a novel. I call it a *bestiary* because it collects all sorts of beasts in one place. Medieval bestiaries in Europe were often infused with symbolism—each animal, real or imaginary, also indicating something beyond itself and sometimes representing a moral of some sort. The yōkai here may not articulate specific morals, but they are symbolically charged. Yōkai are real and, at the same time, imagined; they are literal and figurative, simultaneously themselves and metaphors. Each yōkai recorded here, and its connections with the others, is open to individual interpretation. Read with this in mind, individual entries may reveal hidden meanings; and read together one after another, they may also tell a larger story.

5 Wilds

All the yōkai in this chapter are associated in one way or another with natural landscapes, especially forests and mountains. They are creatures or phenomena that humans may encounter when they venture into the woods or walk along a mountain pass. A lone traveler in a distant part of the forest, for example, may bump into a nurikabe or mikoshi-nyūdō. Some of these yōkai—such as tengu and yamamba—live in the mountains but also may descend specifically to visit the habitations of humans. Wherever they are encountered, however, all these yōkai possess a certain wildness: they are undomesticated expressions of nature, denizens of a wild territory beyond human agency.

KODAMA

Tree Spirit

Trees are prominent features of the landscape throughout Japan; large, unusual, or old trees are often considered sacred. In shrines throughout the country it is common to see a *shimenawa* rope draped around the trunk of an ancient tree, indicating a divine connection. Belief systems

木
魅

Figure 3. Kodama. Original illustration by Shinonome Kijin.

associated with trees are complex, and they vary depending on the region and the particular tree.

The *kodama*, which means "tree spirit," is not set in behavior or appearance. Toriyama Sekien uses a kodama as the opening image in his first catalog of yōkai, completed in 1776—making it the first yōkai in his famous series. The picture shows an old man and woman who seem to have emerged out of a crooked old pine tree. The entry itself is unusual because it is spread across two pages, rare for Sekien, and because it is the only entry in the entire volume that includes commentary. The caption simply reads, "It is said that when a tree reaches the age of one hundred, it has a kami that will show its form."[1] In more recent iconography, the kodama appears in Miyazaki Hayao's anime *Mononoke hime* (*Princess Mononoke;* 1997) as a multitude of cute ball-like creatures that make a clicking sound; this imagery, one scholar suggests, may be based on the *ninmenju*, another kind of arboreal yōkai.[2]

In Japanese, the word *kodama* also means "echo." This usage may be directly linked to the yōkai kodama—from a belief that an echo is the spirit of the woods responding to a call.[3] Another yōkai, the yamabiko, is also associated with "echo." Given that an echo is an animated voice that seems to emerge from the forest or the mountains, the echo-yōkai connection is not surprising. In contemporary Japan, the word *kodama* is now closely associated with the Kodama Shinkansen (bullet train), presumably named for the echo rather than the yōkai.

ONI

Demon or Ogre

A ubiquitous character in Japanese folklore, religion, and popular culture, the oni may be variously translated into English as "demon," "devil," or "ogre." Found in written documents as far back as the eighth century, oni feature in numerous folktales and legends and, more recently, in manga, anime, and film. Historically there is a wide variety of oni images, but in contemporary Japanese culture oni are commonly imagined as large, powerful, frightening, humanlike male figures with red, blue, black, or yellow faces, clawed hands, and sharp, protruding fangs. They have horns, carry an iron staff or club, and wear a loincloth (*fundoshi*) made of tiger skin. While many of these details vary, the horns—whether a single protrusion or two or more—are the creature's most definitive feature in the modern Japanese imagination.[4]

Although there is some variation, the oni is generally portrayed in narratives and ritual contexts as a nasty otherworldly being who threatens humans; he is a person-shaped antiperson, encapsulating everything that imperils humans and human society. As one scholar notes tersely, "The oni is a presence that excludes human nature [*ningensei*]."[5] There are also numerous examples of humorous, stupid, innocuous, and even benevolent oni, but these are the anomalies, the ones that stand out because the "premise" is that the oni's general intentions are negative; oni are "constructed as antisociety and antimoral."[6]

The word *oni* is found in the earliest-known Japanese texts, including the *Kojiki, Nihonshoki,* and various fudoki (local gazetteers). Although the pronunciation—oni—seems to be a Japanese construction, the kanji currently associated with it is inconsistent in these early texts and became established only during the Heian period. (At that time, the reading *ki* also came to be used in compound words.)

The earliest images of oni (or figures that would come to be associated with oni) are seen in Buddhist depictions of hell, such as the late-twelfth-century *Jigoku zōshi* (Hell scrolls).[7] As the image developed it was probably also influenced by early pictures of Raijin (the thunder deity), as found in, for example, the thirteenth-century illustrated *Kitanotenjin engi emaki*. Portrayal of the oni as a fierce, demonic, violent horned figure has remained remarkably consistent since these early illustrations. Similarly, its characterization as a "frightening presence" has been constant since its earliest mention in writing.[8] Whatever the absolute origins of the oni concept and image, influences on the development of the figure have varied and include Chinese, native Japanese, Buddhist, and Onmyōdō sources.[9]

Historically, oni were conflated with yōkai more generally—invoked as generic signifiers for all sorts of frightening or unknown monsters. For example, the medieval-period expression *hyakkiyagyō* contains the kanji for *oni* (pronounced *ki*) and translates as "night procession of one hundred oni." But in most cases, the oni in the procession are interchangeable with yōkai more generally; that is, they are not only anthropomorphic demonlike creatures but also monstrous beings of all shapes and sizes.

Through time, however, the oni eventually developed into a specific figure (a single type of yōkai) characterized by a number of traits that appear again and again in visualizations and descriptions. These include a fierce countenance, a large muscular body stripped to the waist, a nasty temper, an association with lightning, and a penchant for eating people. In many images, oni have only three fingers on each hand and three toes on each foot, all of them with sharp, clawlike nails. Sometimes oni are portrayed with a third eye in the middle of the forehead. As mentioned earlier, they commonly have ox horns on their heads and wear tiger-pelt loincloths. These features suggest an association with the north-east direction, known in Japanese as *ushitora*, literally "ox-tiger," a direction linked with the *kimon*, or "oni-gate," through which misfortune was said to enter a household or community.[10]

The specific visual imagery associated with the oni may have taken shape in response to vague fears and invisible dangers. That is, the image of the oni serves as a floating signifier applicable to any number of threats to human society. One interpretation of the oni's origins, for example, is that the word signified an epidemic; the physical body of the oni thus became a visible image of the invisible yet terrifying spread of disease.

Similarly, oni can be interpreted historically as visualizations of *otherness* and the dangers associated with it. Almost human in form, but at the same time imperiling all that is human, oni represent everything foreign and mysterious that threatens the status quo. Varying interpretations suggest that these humanlike supernatural beings may reflect fear of historically marginalized populations, such as *shugendō* religious practitioners, who were "outsiders" living in the mountains and engaging in mysterious practices. Similarly, oni may have been associated with communities of blacksmiths, metalworkers, and miners who lived on the outskirts of villages and were believed to possess—along with their ability, literally, to shape metal—supernatural powers for safe childbirth. As a kind of antihegemonic cultural metaphor, then, the presumably negative and destructive oni can also assume a positive and creative role as antiestablishment rebel or underdog, the marginalized or disenfranchised Other who challenges the entrenched sociopolitical order and becomes a driving force in shaping history.[11]

This transgressive but ambiguous role is evident in one of the most famous oni legends, the story of Shuten dōji, literally, "Sake-Drinking Boy." As with all folk narratives, there is more than one version, but the oldest extant written account is the so-called Ōeyama text (early fourteenth century) in which the demonic protagonist resides on Mount Ōe, on the edge of the Heian capital, present-day Kyoto. In the story, the time period is not specified, but references to real people hint that it probably took place around the late tenth or early eleventh century.

The capital is plagued by demons abducting young women, including the daughter of an important government official. Eventually, a divination is performed and it is determined that the demon culprits reside on Mount Ōe. The emperor orders the great warrior Minamoto no Yorimitsu (Raikō) and his lieutenants to subdue the demons.

Raikō and his men pray to various Buddhist deities, and then, disguised as mountain ascetics, they head into the hills in search of the oni's hideout. Along the way, they meet three old men who explain that the lead oni, Shuten dōji, is particularly fond of alcohol; the old men give Raikō and his entourage a container of magical sake that is poisonous to oni but beneficial to humans. It turns out that these men are actually deities, incarnations of the very gods to whom Raikō and his men had prayed. After pointing the warriors in the direction of the oni's lair, the deities disappear into thin air.

Traveling upstream, the warriors meet a young woman who provides them with more information, explaining that Shuten dōji "has light-red skin and is tall with disheveled short hair. He has a human appearance during the day, but at night he transforms into a ten-foot-tall demon whose countenance is truly horrible. He always drinks sake. Once he becomes intoxicated, he forgets everything." The warriors eventually come to the iron palace in which the oni and his demon army live. Through a mixture of good fortune and cunning, Raikō and his men end up eating and drinking with Shuten dōji and his henchmen, sharing the magical liquor, until all the oni become drunk and disoriented and, eventually, pass out. In repose, Shuten dōji himself expands to twice his size: "His horns were now protruding through the spiked red bristles on his scalp, his beard had become wildly shaggy, and his eyebrows were overgrown. His limbs had become heavy and thick, like those of a bear."

With the assistance of the three deities, who appear again just when they are needed, Raikō cuts off Shuten dōji's head—which at first continues to attack and bite even after being separated from its body. And then, in a dramatic battle, the warriors dispatch all the other oni. Entering deeper into the compound, the men discover a scene of horror, replete with skeletons, pickled human flesh, and a woman with severed limbs but still alive, who they vow to come back for later. Raikō and his men then lead the young, abducted women to safety, reuniting them with their families in the capital, where Raikō himself is celebrated as a heroic warrior.

In this extended and theatrical narrative, Shuten dōji and his fellow oni are vicious and unpleasant to be sure, but they can also be read in a more sympathetic light. They are, after all, somewhat hospitable and good-natured when banqueting with the warriors, they fight honorably and well, and ultimately, they fall victim to the warriors' deception. Indeed, as Shuten dōji himself exclaims before his head is cut off, "How sad, you priests! You said you do not lie. There is nothing false in the words of demons."[12] In one sense, they might be seen as antiestablishment rebels— no coincidence, perhaps, that the women they kidnap all seem to be the daughters of government officials. Shuten dōji himself can certainly be interpreted in terms of otherness: a being unable to live within society and driven into an isolated existence literally on the margins of the seat of power (the capital).[13]

While the Shuten dōji story is considered a classic literary text, many legends and folktales concerning oni were passed down orally in local communities and reflect a much more popular approach, in which oni are outwitted or subdued not by great warriors but by cunning common folk. A tale collected in Yamanashi Prefecture, for example, tells of an excruciatingly poor mother who can no longer afford to feed her three sons, and who reluctantly abandons them in the forest. The children seek shelter in a hut, but the old woman living there tells them that the house belongs to an oni, who will soon be coming home. Sure enough, a moment later they hear him coming, and the old woman quickly hides the boys in a storage pit. Sensitive to the odor of human flesh, the oni is immediately suspicious; the old woman explains that three boys had come, but had left as soon as they heard he was coming. The oni proceeds to put on his magic boots, which allow him to travel many miles with each step, and dashes out to look for them. Try as he might, however, he cannot find them anywhere, and eventually he concludes that he has gone too far. Deciding to wait for them to come his way, he lies down to take a nap.

Meanwhile, the old woman instructs the boys to escape out the back door, and they run off. Eventually, they hear a sound like the thunder god and realize they have come to the place where the giant oni lies fast asleep, snoring. The youngest brother decides to steal the oni's magical boots, which he manages to do—very carefully—while the slumbering demon mumbles something about mice. The boy gives the boots to the oldest brother, who puts them on, ties his brothers to his back, and flies away with them. Without his boots, the oni cannot catch them, and the brothers soon escape to the safety of human habitations, where "they worked very hard and helped their mother."[14] The tale is lighthearted, to be sure, and it features an oni who eats flesh but is at the same time a bit goofy, as in the typical "numbskull" tales found in folklore of cultures around the world. But as with the Shuten dōji legend, it is also a tale of conquest and escape from mortal harm.

The most famous of all Japanese folktales, the story of Momotarō (Peach Boy), presents a similar situation, in which oni are defeated. In this case, a boy born from a peach and raised by an old couple decides to travel to Oni Island (Oni-ga-shima) to conquer its demonic inhabitants. His parents supply him with energy-giving *kibi-dango* (millet dumplings), and he sets off on his quest, acquiring along the way a loyal entourage made up of a dog, pheasant, and monkey. Upon arriving at Oni Island, the small band of warriors, fortified by Japan's finest millet dumplings, easily defeat the oni, making them pledge never to be bad again and receiving all sorts of treasure.[15]

The tale of an exceedingly courageous boy defeating a band of terrifying demons is a gratifying story in which the underdog wins and good triumphs over evil. Because of this relatively simple structure, the narrative lends itself to allegorical interpretation and manipulation; it is not surprising that this tale in particular was adapted for early-twentieth-century textbooks and for propaganda during Japan's colonial period and the Pacific War, when the allied troops were portrayed as the dangerous demonic Other. In one 1942 film, Oni Island is identified as Hawaii.[16]

Female Oni

The oni I have described here are primarily male figures; this is the imagery commonly associated with them in Japan today. But historically, as the embodiment of anger and resentment, oni have also often assumed female form. In fact, perhaps the earliest known oni-like figures are the Yomotsu-shikome, the "hags of Yomi," who appear in the *Kojiki* and *Nihonshoki*. These demonic women chase Izanagi from the underworld after he has glimpsed his deceased wife, Izanami, as a rotting corpse in which "maggots were squirming and roaring."[17]

While the word *oni* is not actually used for these hags of Yomi, it does appear during the medieval period, in a tale from a Buddhist setsuwa collection called *Kankyo no tomo* (A companion in solitude), believed to have been compiled in 1222 by the priest Keisei Shōnin.[18] The tale relates an event that "took place not too long ago in the province of Mino." A young woman is neglected by her lover from a distant province. She quietly gives up eating and takes to her bed, until "one day she took some millet jelly from a container lying nearby. She tied her hair up into five knots and smeared some jelly on them; she then let them dry so they would look like horns. Then, putting on a red skirt, she quietly ran away that evening."

After some thirty years, word spreads that there is a demon living in an old temple, who has been wreaking havoc in several villages. Finally, the villagers burn the temple, and from the flames runs "a creature with five horns, wearing a red skirt, bent at the hips and looking indescribably frightening." The oni identifies herself, confessing that she had indeed murdered the man who had deserted her. "After that," she continues, "no matter how much I tried, I could not regain my former physical self." In a sense, by not only taking on the superficial form of a demon but also actually acting demonically—that is, committing murder—she has transformed herself irrevocably into a demon whose very existence "is extremely painful." In tears, she eventually leaps into the fire and dies. The tale is one of pathos and sadness and, as one scholar puts it, "reveals an understanding of the *oni* as ultimately lonely and pitiful, and with human pain despite her transformation."[19]

This particular Buddhist tale seems to be related to a number of later, similar narratives, including one found in a version of *The Tale of the*

Heike (fourteenth century) and the Noh play *The Iron Crown* (fifteenth century). In all these cases the woman's transformation into an oni comes about as a result of inordinate passion and jealousy. Her internal state of mind, one of anger and resentment, causes her body to change—often through purposeful and sustained effort—into the body of a demon. It is a profound and presumably permanent transformation that makes visible an invisible emotion—in this case, rage. As pitiable and *human* as this emotion may be, it is expressed by the oni's deeply *antihuman* behavior.

Oni in Festival and Ritual

Oni are a lively presence in contemporary Japanese ritual and festival life. Particularly on New Year's Eve, or a date known as *Koshōgatsu* (Little New Year) observed around January 15, oni-like figures feature in local observances in a number of small communities, especially in the Tohoku region. The most famous version of this ritual is called Namahage and takes place on the Oga Peninsula of Akita Prefecture. Young men from the local community dress in straw raincoats and demon masks and tromp through the snow from house to house, receiving offerings of food and drink from the residents and chasing and scaring the kids of the household. The origins of Namahage and similar rituals, including summer rituals observed in the Ryukyu Islands of Okinawa Prefecture, are unknown, and there is much debate about whether the frightening figures are oni, kami, or some other presence. Whatever the case, however, it is clear that the current incarnation of these figures has been deeply influenced by oni iconography and behavior.[20]

A much more common and widespread oni-related ritual is the Setsubun holiday observed in early February. Strictly speaking, *setsubun* refers to a "joint" in the year when one season changes into another, so there are four Setsubun annually; in Japan, however, the only one still observed to any extent is in February, the day before *risshun*, or the first day of spring (according to the old calendrical system). So Setsubun is much like New Year's Eve, a dividing point between the old year and the new and therefore a ritually meaningful moment of transition. This is a crack in the flow of time, a potentially dangerous bridge between one period and another, during which both good and bad spirits might enter.

Accordingly, a custom found throughout Japan is to scatter beans around the house or throw them out windows and doors, shouting, "Out with oni; in with good fortune" (*Oni wa soto; fuku wa uchi*). The actual practice varies with region and family tradition, but the notion of simultaneously inviting in good fortune and banishing bad (i.e., oni) is generally consistent. So too is the power of beans (usually roasted soybeans); during this time throughout Japan, supermarkets and convenience stores sell small packets of beans expressly for banishing oni.[21]

The origins of the Setsubun ritual are likely a combination of Buddhist, Onmyōdō, and popular religious practices. The expulsion of oni is related to a purification ceremony called *tsuina*, probably of Onmyōdō origins, which was enacted to cleanse the palace before the emperor's appearance on the eve of the new year. The practice entails banishing bad spirits and warding off evil for the coming year through a variety of symbolic gestures, such as shooting arrows in four directions and striking a shield with a staff.

In the modern era, tsuina has been revived at various shrines and temples. Currently, every year at the Yoshida Shrine in Kyoto, for example, tens of thousands of people gather to witness a tsuina ceremony featuring three large (and somewhat comical-looking) red, blue, and yellow oni, who dance and roar at the crowd but eventually leave weakened and cowed, having been conquered by the ritual. The Rozan Temple in Kyoto also holds a similar ritual presentation to banish disease and bad fortune, in which red, green-blue, and black oni perform a slow dance of intimidation and eventually depart, defeated and submissive. After they leave, temple officials throw lucky beans to the throngs of visitors.

Similar ceremonies involving humans wearing oni costumes are enacted throughout Japan on Setsubun. This visualization—the transformation of the invisible vapors of pestilence, famine, and all sorts of bad fortune into a visible, embodied form—is critical to the oni's pervasiveness in Japan. While the medieval version of the tsuina ritual most likely only suggested oni (that is, the oni themselves were never visible), the oni of the modern Yoshida Shrine ritual have horns and wear tiger-skin loincloths, at once reflecting and contributing to the oni image in the contemporary imagination. Catching a glimpse of an oni is one of the most exciting aspects of the experience; people stand in place for hours before the ritual begins, children sit on parents' shoulders, and amateur photographers with massive

Figure 4. Oni. Original illustration by Shinonome Kijin.

telephoto lenses position themselves atop stepladders throughout the shrine grounds. Interestingly, when the tsuina ceremony was first reintroduced at the Yoshida Shrine in the twentieth century, it garnered little public attention. Only later, when the shrine staff decided to make the oni visible, did tourists flock to see it.[22]

Komatsu Kazuhiko writes that in his own family version of Setsubun, he used to put on a paper oni mask and run through the house while his wife and daughter threw beans at him. Rather than aiming at an imagined but invisible oni, he notes, his family found it was "much more fun and easily understandable" to throw beans at an oni they could actually see.[23] This simple family anecdote reflects the same logic found in making oni visible at public events, such as those enacted at Yoshida Shrine and Rozan Temple. It also reflects the process by which generations of artists have illustrated oni, and storytellers have described them, making the dangerous, threatening, fearsome things around us into visible embodied beings—and accordingly subject to efforts to control them.

In one form or another, then, oni play a role in thousands of folktales, legends, festivals, and customs throughout Japan. While it would be dangerous to generalize, we can certainly say that many of these—from the Shuten dōji narrative, to Momotarō, to the enactment at Yoshida Shrine—involve the triumph of human over oni. Sometimes this triumph is accomplished by courage and strength, sometimes by cunning or deceit, and sometimes by dumb luck, but if oni are the Other of the human, embodying the fears and dangers of worldly existence, then their defeat—in narrative and ritual—reflects a symbolic triumph of human order over chaos. At the same time, the oni's failure makes the creature seem somewhat comical and even loveable. In contemporary Japan, the negative, terrifying image of the oni coexists happily with a more cheerful, amiable image found in media of all sorts and used as an advertising icon for a wide range of products.

YAMABIKO

Mountain Echo

The yamabiko is said to be responsible for the echo that answers when you shout into the mountains. The word *yamabiko* actually means "echo," and

幽谷響

Figure 5. Yamabiko. Original illustration by Shinonome Kijin.

it is unclear whether the word came before the yōkai, or the yōkai led to the creation of the word. Toriyama Sekien portrays the yamabiko as a floppy-looking, monkeylike creature sitting atop a high stony peak. The kanji characters are not the standard ones associated with the word or the reading; rather they might be translated literally as "spirit of the valley reverberation." Similar yamabiko are pictured in several Edo-period picture scrolls, so it is likely that it was a well-known yōkai at the time.[24]

Yamabiko is also the name of a Shinkansen train running between Tokyo and the Tohoku region. Presumably, like the Kodama Shinkansen, which similarly means *echo* and similarly references a yōkai, the Yamabiko Shinkansen was named for the echo and not the yōkai.

TSUCHIGUMO

Earth Spider

The word *tsuchigumo,* literally "earth spider," appears in the *Kojiki* and *Nihonshoki* as well as in various fudoki, such as the *Fudoki of Hizen Province*. In these mythohistorical texts, *tsuchigumo* seems to have been used as a derogatory and demonizing label for the indigenous inhabitants of Japan. That is, the people writing the texts used the term to negatively describe the natives they were conquering; they portrayed them as having short bodies and long arms and legs, and as living in holes in the ground.

Over time, the image of the tsuchigumo shifted, and it developed into a murderous yōkai not directly connected with these indigenous people. From the Kamakura period onward, the tsuchigumo appeared in texts and legends in which it was subdued by the gallantry of a human hero—most famously the well-known demon-slayer Raikō.[25] The fourteenth-century *Tsuchigumo-zōshi,* for example, tells how Raikō and his warrior companion Watanabe no Tsuna kill a tsuchigumo, which is illustrated as a zoologically realistic but gigantic spider surrounded by a host of smaller spiders. They cut off the tsuchigumo's head and slice open its belly, out of which pours 1,990 skulls of its victims.[26] Stories concerning Raikō and the tsuchigumo have been made into a Noh play and a Kabuki drama, both called *Tsuchigumo*.

During the late Edo period, the great ukiyoe-woodblock-print artist Utagawa Kuniyoshi (1797–1861) drew on the popular knowledge of the tsuchigumo to create a famous triptych titled *Minamoto Raikō kōkan tsuchigumo saku yōkai no zu* (1843). Raikō is shown asleep in the tsuchigumo's den, surrounded by hundreds of yōkai in a hyakkiyagyō-style display of variety and abundance. Though the artist's intentions are unknown, the painting was interpreted at the time as a satire against the Tokugawa government, particularly in response to the unpopular Tempo Reforms of

Figure 6. Raikō beheading the tsuchigumo. From the *Tsuchigumo-zōshi* (Edo period; artist unknown). Courtesy of International Research Center for Japanese Studies.

1841–1843. Viewers of the painting associated specific yōkai with specific individuals; the spider's lair itself may have been a reference to the sticky web of Tokugawa rule.[27] In their earliest appearance in ancient texts, tsuchigumo were invoked for their metaphoric power to demonize the people being conquered; in Kuniyoshi's triptych, they are still used metaphorically, but this time by the folk to demonize the rulers.

TENGU

Mountain Goblin

One of the best known of all yōkai, the tengu has played a long and varied role in Japanese history, religion, literature, and folklore. Often characterized as a "mountain goblin," tengu tend to have birdlike characteristics and superlative martial arts skills and are often associated with Buddhism and mountain ascetic practices. Even today, there are mountain shrines and festivals that honor tengu.

There are two types of tengu. The first is the *karasu tengu*, literally a "crow tengu," which is a birdlike creature with wings, beaked mouth, and the ability to fly. Despite the word *crow*, karasu tengu are often portrayed as birds of prey, particularly *tonbi* (kites). During the Edo period, the ka-rasu tengu was gradually supplanted by a more humanlike creature—tall, dressed like a Buddhist monk or other religious practitioner, and featur-ing a long, bulbous, red nose. This long-nosed tengu is the version most commonly depicted in Japanese culture today. In some cases, karasu tengu are portrayed as lieutenants to this distinguished, long-nosed figure.

Tengu literally means "celestial dog" or "heavenly hound" (Ch. *tian gou*), and the same combination of kanji is found in various early Chinese texts, where it refers to a comet or star or possibly an "enormous dog-shaped meteor."[28] In Japan, the word is first found in the *Nihonshoki,* in an entry for the year 637, in which it is recorded that "a great star floated from East to West, and there was a noise like that of thunder." A monk explains that this is not a shooting star but rather a "Celestial Dog, the sound of whose barking is like thunder."[29] Despite the continued use of the "dog" kanji, however, subsequent references to tengu in Japan never actually describe it as looking or acting doglike; rather it is almost always depicted as anthropomorphic or avian (or a mixture of both).

It is impossible to unpack the exact process by which a word meaning "heavenly hound" and indicating an astronomical occurrence gradually came to signify a long-nosed monk with wings, but it is clear that this transmogrification reflects a mixture of historical, religious, and popular influences. For example, the avian image of the tengu may be associated in some way with the Garuda, a deific bird figure that features prominently in both Hindu and Buddhist beliefs, and which most likely entered Japan through China—along with Buddhism itself. But just as Buddhism has gone through many changes in its long journey across continents, so too tengu, and the meanings and images associated with them, have altered with different historical circumstances.

During the Heian period, tengu were thought of as mysterious forces residing in the mountains. Similar to mono-no-ke, they were amorphous malignant spirits that could cause illness or war or torment an individ-ual.[30] There are few records of what they might have looked like during this time: generally they were invisible, but on occasion one might appear as a bird or monk.

It wasn't until the Kamakura period that tengu really started to acquire more established characteristics. Considered after-death incarnations of emperors or dead warriors, they would appear as malevolent birdlike creatures, monks, or *yamabushi* (mountain ascetics), descending from the mountains to torment the powers that be. In the *Taiheiki* (Chronicle of great peace; late fourteenth century), for example, twelfth-century emperor Sutoku, who was banished to a remote province, is described as a kite plotting with a troop of demons and tengu how best to disrupt humanity.[31] It was also during this time that tengu took on a more profound relationship with Buddhism; in particular they were associated with the concept of *ma*, or evil—that which hinders a person on the path toward enlightenment.[32]

Some of the setsuwa collected in the late Heian-period *Tales of Times Now Past* tell of tengu who possess (and teach) supernatural powers called *gejutsu* (outside technique): non-Buddhist magic that was deceptive and could be used for nefarious purposes. Although tengu might appear as accomplished monks, in reality their powers were false and would not lead to enlightenment. But tengu, like so many yōkai, are ambiguous. In one tale, for instance, a mountain ascetic is called upon to heal an ailing emperor. The ascetic demonstrates amazing magical powers, rapidly curing the emperor. But the emperor's priests, having studied the way of the Buddha, are suspicious of the ascetic's uncanny abilities and set about directing incantations toward him: "Suddenly the ascetic hurtled out through his curtains and crashed to the floor, where he lay sprawled on his back. 'Help!' he shrieked. 'Good sirs, save me, please! All these years on Kōzen I've worshipped the tengu and prayed to them to make me famous. And it worked, you know, because I *was* called here to the palace! But what an awful mistake it was! I've learned my lesson now, yes I have! Please save me, oh please!'"[33] Although the ascetic had followed the false path of the tengu in order to become famous, his curing of the emperor appears genuine. While the tengu's power may not be in accord with Buddhism and may never lead to enlightenment, in this example at least it nonetheless proves effective (and beneficial).

There developed at this time a concept called Tengu-dō, the Way of Tengu, or the Realm of Tengu, which was "a realm reserved for Buddhist practitioners who had failed to overcome the temptations of evil."[34] A text called *Hirasan kojin reitaku*, for example, records a fascinating dialogue between a monk and a tengu. The tengu, speaking through a young woman he has possessed, tells the monk about the otherworldly realm of the Tengu-dō and its inhabitants (including some former emperors). In fine zoological detail, he also describes tengu themselves as being the size of ten-year-old children, having human bodies and heads, short tails, bird legs, and wings about a yard long.[35] In disputes between different Buddhist temples and sects, sometimes one faction would negatively represent the priests of another by conflating them with tengu. Portraying a monk of an opposing temple as a tengu was a way to demonize (tengu-ize?) him and imply that his teachings were dangerous or deceptive.[36]

Tengu, Yoshitsune, and the Arts of the Warrior

At the same time, we can also imagine how tengu might become potent symbols of the underdog, representing a rebellious, antiauthoritarian spirit. It is perhaps in this context that they became famous for knowing secret martial arts techniques. Most famously, it is said that tengu trained Minamoto no Yoshitsune, one of the great warriors of Japanese history. Yoshitsune was the younger brother of Minamoto no Yoritomo, the leader of the victorious Genji forces during the Genpei War (1180–1185), the great civil conflict that led to the founding of the Kamakura government. As a Genji general, Yoshitsune was famous for his military skills, which, according to legend, he learned from tengu when he lived as a child at Kurama Temple in (current-day) Kyoto. This explanation for his military prowess seems to have become part of popular cultural imagination quite early. The Kamakura-period *Heiji monogatari* (The tale of Heiji), for example, notes simply that "it is told that Yoshitsune night after night was taught the manual of arms by a Tengu . . . in Kurama-yama. That was the reason why he could run and jump beyond the limits of human power."[37]

The relationship between the tengu and Yoshitsune, or Ushiwaka as he was called as a child, has been elaborated in a Noh play, *Kurama tengu,* and in a lesser known dramatic-literary form called *kōwakamai,* from the

Muromachi period. This latter work, titled *Miraiki* (Chronicle of the future), opens with Ushiwaka training by himself every evening in a wooded area behind Kurama Temple. Some tengu spot him there and at first resent his intrusion into their territory. But when they recognize that he is training to avenge the death of his father, one tengu says to the others: "We are known by the name of *tengu*—there is a reason for this. We were humans long ago, but studying well the dharma we felt there was nobody more knowledgeable, and because we swelled with pride, we could not become Buddhas and fell into the Way of Tengu [Tengu-dō]. But even though this pride caused us to fall into this path, there is no reason we should not know pity. So let us help Ushiwaka, teach him the method of the tengu so he can attack his father's enemy."

And so, appearing to him as yamabushi, the tengu invite Ushiwaka back to their dwelling place. Ushiwaka is suspicious of these monklike figures but, feeling adventurous, agrees to accompany them. He is soon spirited away to a mountain he has never before seen: a beautiful place, thickly wooded, with rocks towering majestically, the fragrance of flowers, and the sound of a waterfall. They enter a magnificent temple, where a hundred tengu are playing musical instruments. Ushiwaka joins them for a wonderful meal with foods from the mountains and the rivers, flavored with all kinds of spices.

The tengu (who presumably still appear as monks or yamabushi) then proceed to enact a kind of play, in which one by one they assume roles of key players in the Genpei conflict, for which Ushiwaka is training. Essentially they perform the future for him, explaining his own role in the conflict and even informing him that, after the last battle, he will fall out of favor with his older brother. All their predictions, of course, are accurate: indeed, the reader or viewer of *Chronicle of the Future* would already know that Yoshitsune would end up being killed, infamously, by his older brother. Interestingly, however, there is no explicit military training involved in the tale—perhaps simply receiving this vision of the future is enough to make Ushiwaka a superior warrior. When the tengu have finished their tale, they give the boy a small iron ball as a token of his visit, and then they disappear. Suddenly Ushiwaka finds himself on a branch of a pine tree behind the temple. He thinks, "Well, I was tricked by tengu."[38]

The tengu here, and in the Noh play as well, are portrayed as generally benevolent creatures eager to assist Ushiwaka in his fight for justice; here we see the more helpful side of their character. Whether this reflects a general change in attitude toward tengu or not is difficult to ascertain, but it clearly demonstrates the tengu's deep involvement with the human world.

Spiriting Away

During the Edo period, tengu developed into the long-nosed, winged, monklike form for which they are most famous today, a shift in appearance that scholars cannot clearly explain.[39] Perhaps one reason for this change, however, was their increasing identification with humans and the workings of humanity, as if the tengu realm were a strange mirror of the human world. Indeed, reflecting the highly structured society of Tokugawa-period Japan, tengu were portrayed hierarchically, with the human-shaped, long-nosed tengu, called *daitengu* (big tengu), flanked by a posse of birdlike karasu tengu called *kotengu* (small tengu).

It was also during this period that tengu became increasingly associated with mountain worship and deeply embedded in all manner of local folk belief. They were often invoked as an explanation for mysterious happenings. The sound of a tree falling in the forest, for example, might be attributed to the machinations of a tengu and called *tengu-daoshi* (tengu knocking-down). A loud guffaw echoing through the forest was called *tengu-warai* (tengu laugh).[40]

Other times, tengu might cause real mischief. In a certain location in Gifu City, for example, it was said that a tengu made his home in a large pine tree. If a fisherman wanted to go fishing nearby, the tengu would throw rocks at him in order to get him to reconsider. And if that did not stop him, the tengu would proceed to overturn his boat.[41]

Most famously and frighteningly, tengu were often the perpetrators of something called *kamikakushi:* kidnapping by a god, translatable as "spiriting away," or more literally, "hiding by a deity." The details of such occurrences vary, but usually the story goes like this: A young boy or adolescent suddenly disappears. His family and the villagers search frantically but to no avail. Then, some time later, he shows up in a strange place—in a tree, or in the eaves of a house—dazed but otherwise unharmed.

Figure 7. Daitengu and kotengu (also known as karasu tengu).
Original illustration by Shinonome Kijin.

Sometimes he is able to recount a story of being abducted by a stranger,
usually an older man, who took him off to distant places.

A story from Takayama in Gifu Prefecture, for example, tells of a boy
employed by a merchant family. The boy receives a new pair of geta
(wooden sandals) from his master and plans to wear them that evening.
However, his master warns him that if he wears his new geta in the
evening, "a tengu will take him away." But the boy is so thrilled to have the
new footwear that he surreptitiously puts them on anyway and strolls out
into the street—and is not seen again. When his master realizes he has
disappeared, a big commotion ensues and a troop of people is enlisted to

search. Finally, about a week later, they find the boy standing on a bridge, looking exhausted. He explains that as he was walking along that evening in his new geta, a large man with a long nose and wings on his back came up to him and said, "Get on my back and I will take you to a good place." The boy did as he was told, but after that, he remembers nothing. "The next thing I realized I was standing here on this bridge." The tale ends with the comment "They say that it was a tengu."[42]

Similarly, Yanagita Kunio records an episode from 1877 that took place in Kanazawa City in Ishikawa Prefecture, and which was related to him as a childhood memory by the novelist Tokuda Shūsei (1871–1943). In the house next to Tokuda's, a young man of about twenty disappeared from under a large persimmon tree, leaving only his geta. After searching for a long time, everybody suddenly heard a loud sound in the attic, like something falling. When Tokuda's older brother went up to investigate, he discovered the young man lying there. After he carried him downstairs, they saw that his mouth was green, as if he had been chewing tree leaves. When he recovered sufficiently, he explained that a large man had come and taken him away; they had traveled here and there, eating wherever they went. After a while, he told the man he had to go and he made his escape—and that's when they found him in the attic.[43]

There is, in fact, no specific mention of a tengu in this story, and certainly throughout history there must have been instances in which children accidentally got lost or killed, or abducted by other humans. Although different yōkai (including kitsune and oni) may be implicated in such kidnappings, at least as far back as the Kamakura period the tengu has been the most commonly blamed perpetrator of this kind of crime. The Ushiwaka legend mentioned earlier, for example, fits the pattern.

Even in the modern period, the correlation of such abductions with supernatural powers is clear. Yanagita relates another story, from 1907, of a boy who disappears during a festival in which villagers are making offerings of rice to the deities. When the boy is found in the attic of a house, he explains that an older man took him from house to house to feast on the food provided there, and indeed his mouth is covered with rice.[44] Again, there is no explicit mention of tengu, but it is clear that the boy was in the company of a supernatural being; we can also see obvious similarities to Tokuda Shūsei's legend.

Perhaps the most famous example of a supernatural abduction during the Edo period is the story of the boy Torakichi, who claimed to have been taken on a series of mystical journeys around the world, and even to the moon, by an accomplished tengu. His adventures came to the attention of nativist scholar Hirata Atsutane, who interviewed him extensively and recorded his findings in a text called *Senkyō ibun* (Strange tidings from the realm of immortals). Although the text was inflected with Atsutane's particular religious and political perspectives, it reveals details, both fantastic and mundane, about the residents of the otherworld, including animals (real and legendary) and all sorts of demons.[45]

In contemporary Japan, the idea of kamikakushi is still well known, primarily because of Miyazaki Hayao's blockbuster anime *Sen to Chihiro no kamikakushi* (2001), which was appropriately translated into English as *Spirited Away*. Although no tengu appear in the film, and the way in which the characters are "spirited away" is quite different from the legends noted here, the movie's success at the box office brought the word and concept of kamikakushi back into the popular imagination. Recently the concept has featured in literature and visual media and even as the theme for several websites.[46]

Meanwhile, in contemporary Japan, tengu are often invoked as symbols of local identity, although they still retain their mystical, historical associations. In Hachiōji City, to the west of central Tokyo, for example, Mount Takao features several tengu statues, tributes to the legends associated with them in the area. And at the Takao-san Yakuō-in Temple on the mountain, there are statues of a long-nosed daitengu and beak-nosed kotengu. Appropriately, too, the tengu's association with shugendō is still very much alive: the temple is a center of worship by mountain ascetics, where practitioners still undergo austerities such as waterfall training and fire walking.[47]

The tengu image and name are also commonly used for merchandise. There is a popular chain of inexpensive *izakaya* (restaurant-bars) called Tengu, for example, which uses a stylized image of the long-nosed being as its icon. There is also a famous sake made in Ishikawa Prefecture called Tengumai (Dance of the tengu). In short, tengu have a long history, and although they have undergone many changes, they remain one of the most distinctive and vital yōkai in Japan today, with roles in local community life, religion, tourism, and commerce.

MUKADE

Centipede

The mukade is a species of centipede: a real animal that is also considered a yōkai.

Mukade beliefs and legends are found throughout Japan. The most famous comes from the Ōmi region, present-day Shiga Prefecture. There are of course different versions, but the story takes place during the Heian period. The Dragon King living in Lake Biwa disguises himself as a gigantic snake and lies down across a bridge, preventing anybody from crossing. But when a warrior named Fujiwara no Hidesato (nicknamed Tawara Tōta or Tawara no Tōta) steps over the snake without showing the slightest fear, the Dragon King knows he has found his man. He promptly recruits Hidesato for the job of subduing a giant mukade on Mount Mikami. (In some versions, it is the beautiful daughter of the Dragon King who recruits Hidesato.)

Hidesato finds the giant mukade coiled seven and a half times around Mount Mikami. After shooting several arrows into the creature to no effect, he finally moistens the tip of an arrow with his own spit and this time kills the mukade. Legend has it that among the rewards he receives from the Dragon King is a large bell, which he donated to Miidera Temple, where it is still on display today.[48] Bad relations between snakes and mukade persist in beliefs throughout Japan.[49]

It is not difficult to imagine why the mukade might be considered a yōkai. Examined closely, a real centipede is completely alien to the human world. With its "hundred" legs it seems to possess supernatural—or at least unfamiliar—powers of propulsion. Its pincerlike mouth looks vicious, and indeed, a real mukade's bite is extremely painful and can be poisonous. Moreover, mukade in Japan can be six or seven inches long and are notoriously difficult to kill. As with Hidesato's experience, they rarely die on the first attempt. Contemporary mukade lore suggests that the best way to subdue them is to cut them into pieces with a sharp pair of scissors.

Figure 8. Mukade in Shiga Prefecture, near Lake Biwa. Photograph by author.

NURIKABE

Plaster Wall

The nurikabe is probably most famous as one of the standard characters in Mizuki Shigeru's *Gegege no Kitarō* series, where it appears as an animated rectangular wall with eyes, arms, and legs. The most famous early folkloric reference to the nurikabe is in Yanagita Kunio's "Yōkai Glossary," which collected yōkai names and descriptions from many parts of Japan. Yanagita describes the nurikabe as a mysterious phenomenon: "Found on the coast of Onga County in Chikuzen [present-day Fukuoka Prefecture]. When [you are] walking along a road at night, suddenly a wall appears in front of you, and you cannot go anywhere. This is called *nurikabe* and it is feared. It is said that if you take a stick and strike at the bottom of it, it will disappear; but if you hit at the top part, nothing will happen."[50] Similar examples of nuri-kabe phenomena have been documented elsewhere in Kyushu, such as *tanuki no nurikabe* (nurikabe caused by tanuki) found in Ōita Prefecture. In this case, the walker suddenly is unable to see in front of himself or herself.[51]

For his part, Mizuki describes a personal experience with a nurikabe-like encounter that occurred when he was in New Guinea during World War II. Exhausted and alone, he is walking through the "dark jungle" at night eager to rejoin his companions and wary of enemies, when suddenly he feels as if he is stuck in "coal tar," unable to move forward or to either side. Completely at a loss for what to do, he sits down to rest for a few minutes, and when he tries to walk again it is as if nothing at all had happened.[52]

Many years later, Mizuki gave visual form to Yanagita's description as well as his own experience; the resulting yōkai exemplifies the way a phenomenon can be fleshed out and made real through visual imagery and the addition of eyes and limbs to endow it with agency. Whereas Yanagita states that a wall "appears," Mizuki creates the wall's appearance. Moreover, through the popularity of Mizuki's work, and the fact that the nurikabe is one of the standard characters in his *Gegege no Kitarō* series, the nurikabe of Japanese folklore has been transformed from an obscure, local experience with no visualizable form to a nationally recognized character.

Although this trajectory, from Yanagita's description to Mizuki's character, accurately depicts the development of the nurikabe in the twentieth century, it turns out that Mizuki's image is not the first visualization of the phenomenon. In 2007, scholars discovered an image labeled "nurikabe" in an 1802 picture scroll archived at Brigham Young University in the United States. This Edo-period nurikabe illustration looks very different from Mizuki's—more like a flat-faced, three-eyed elephant. The discovery suggests that oral and visual traditions do not always materialize in tandem with each other, and that the "same" yōkai may be reimagined, reenvisioned, and reinvented multiple times. Mizuki reportedly was happy about the discovery and called it "significant."[53]

MIKOSHI-NYŪDŌ

The mikoshi-nyūdō is usually described as an exceedingly tall monklike figure you might encounter while walking through the mountains.

Sometimes he starts off small, but as you look up at him, he keeps growing and growing. Although the word *nyūdō* refers to a Buddhist monk, literally somebody who has "entered the way," the mikoshi-nyūdō is not necessarily an actual monk. However, he often *looks* like one, with a shaved head and severe features. Folkloric records of mikoshi-nyūdō are found throughout Japan, where he is also known by alternative names, such as *miage-nyūdō* and sometimes just *mikoshi*. In some cases, it is said that he is a shape-shifting animal such as a tanuki or kitsune in disguise.

Meeting a mikoshi-nyūdō can pose a serious problem, but there is often a way to escape. In one region of Okayama Prefecture, for example, it is said that if you move your line of vision from the feet of the mikoshi-nyūdō up to his head, he will devour you. But if you start with his head and move down to his feet, you can escape unharmed.[54] Yanagita Kunio records a yōkai called a *nyūdōbōzu*, which he explains is the same as a mikoshi-nyū-dō: "At first it looks like a small monk less than three shaku [*shaku* = approx. a third of a meter], but as [you] get closer it becomes [more than] seven or eight shaku tall. It is believed that if you are first to say, 'I saw you,' everything will be all right, but if it says this [first], you will die."[55]

Since at least the Edo period, images of the mikoshi-nyūdō have appeared in a wide variety of texts. The early encyclopedia *Three Realms*, for example, explains that this yōkai is "tall and has no hair. The folk [*zoku*] call it mikoshi-nyūdō. It is said that it leans over a person's shoulders from behind and stares him in the face."[56] In his first catalog, Toriyama Sekien also includes a mikoshi-nyūdō (labeled only *mikoshi*), which he draws as a long-necked, balding figure peering out from behind a tree.[57]

Later in the Edo period, the mikoshi-nyūdō became a standard yōkai character in popular literature, especially the illustrated kibyōshi genre, where he emerged as a leader of yōkai. In these images and narratives, his neck became longer and more flexible, giving him the ability to peer over all sorts of folding screens and other barriers and making him an ideal partner for the extendable-necked female, rokurokubi.[58] The imagery of the long neck is both phallic and snakelike, managing to be simultaneously comical, suggestive, and creepy.

The word *mikoshi* can mean to "look through" a barrier of some sort, but it can also mean to "foretell" or *look through* the present into the

見越の道

Figure 9. Mikoshi-nyūdō. Original illustration by Shinonome Kijin.

future. Although this meaning does not seem to be explicitly discussed in the folkloric record, perhaps it hints implicitly at the mikoshi-nyūdō's supernatural powers. Written with different kanji, *mikoshi* also refers to the vehicle or portable shrine in which a deity is carried during festivals or other events. In the Amakusa region of Kumamoto Prefecture, a legend tells of a man encountering a tall mikoshi-nyūdō who sticks out his tongue and threatens to lick him. The man prays desperately: eventually a sword-wielding deity appears and glares angrily at the creature, who proceeds to fly away in a mikoshi-like vehicle. The name and narrative development here seem to be based on a play on words or confusion of language.[59]

The mikoshi-nyūdō is ambiguously positioned between deity and demon. Not only does this particular version refer to a sacred vehicle reserved for transporting gods, but also the very name—*nyūdō*—has Buddhist overtones. Powers of vision, too, are important for this yōkai; even in this legend from Kumamoto, it is not the sword but the deity's mighty glare that banishes the monster.

YAMAMBA OR YAMAUBA

Mountain Crone, Mountain Hag, or Mountain Witch

The yamamba, or yamauba, is an old woman who lives in the mountains. The word *yamamba* literally means "mountain old woman" but might be more loosely rendered as "mountain crone," "mountain hag," "mountain witch," or even, as one translation puts it, "malevolent ogress."[60]

The yamamba is one of the best-known yōkai in Japan. In legends, folktales, and local beliefs, she is often portrayed as a hideous witchlike being who kidnaps women from local villages, eats livestock and small children, and torments anybody who wanders into her territory. At the same time, there are also positive portrayals of the yamamba in which she is a deific and beneficial presence.

Most commonly the yamamba is described as tall, with a large mouth (sometimes slit from ear to ear), long hair, and piercing eyes.[61] In addition to appearing in local folklore, she is the protagonist of a famous Noh play (*Yamamba,* attributed to Zeami) and stars in several literary texts from the Muromachi period to the present.[62] In his first codex, Toriyama Sekien drew a bony Yamamba with long hair, seated in front of a mountain peak and holding a tree branch in her hand. She seems to be emerging from the mountainside, like an anthropomorphic version of the old, wizened landscape itself.

In many characterizations, the yamamba is a demonic woman who harms or kills anybody unfortunate enough to cross her path in the mountains; she may also descend from her mountain habitat to terrorize people in the lowlands. A folktale collected in the early twentieth century in Tokushima Prefecture, for example, tells of a mother who leaves her three children at home while she goes to visit the grave of her dead husband. She warns the children that there is a yamamba in the mountains, and that they should not open the door for anybody. Sure enough, after a short while, the yamamba appears at the door of the house, claiming to be the mother. The appropriately suspicious children inspect her hand and see that it is covered with hair, so they refuse to let her in. She goes away and shaves her hand, but next the children suspect her because of her rough voice. Eventually, the yamamba does manage to get into the household, where she proceeds to devour the youngest child. After a long series of events, and the help of the "deity of the sky," the two older boys eventually escape and the yamamba is killed.[63]

While this is just one of many narratives featuring a yamamba, it reflects the danger and fear associated with her. At other times, however, she is drawn sympathetically, as a woman of great strength and resources who has managed to survive hardship. Numerous legends attest to her benevolence. In some regions, for example, she readily assists with household work, such as spinning thread. Or she may suddenly appear at a marketplace to purchase something; the money received from her is said to bring good fortune.

In one part of Kōchi Prefecture, the yamamba's ambiguity is clearly reflected in local belief. If you meet a yamamba in the mountains, it is said, you will incur the "yamamba's curse," suffer from illness of an unknown origin, and require the services of an exorcist to free yourself. On the other hand, in the same region, it is told that a household visited by a yamamba will prosper.[64] Within this particular set of beliefs, then, transgressing the yamamba's home (that is, the mountains) can cause misfortune; but inversely, allowing her to enter your own home brings about wealth.

Clearly then, the yamamba has mysterious powers but cannot be succinctly labeled as either good or evil. With so many variations, it is difficult to find absolute commonalities, except to characterize her as a woman who lives in the mountains or, more accurately, as a woman who does not—or *cannot*—live in a village with other people.[65] Because of her ambiguity, scholars have suggested there is a link between the yamamba and mountain deities; in a complex argument, for example, folklorist Orikuchi Shinobu (1887–1953) speculates that she can be considered the wife of the mountain god (*yama no kami*).[66] Whatever her origins, however, clearly the yamamba is closely associated with the furtive powers and dangers of the mountains. And mountains, of course, not only are a source of wealth for a community, providing wood and food and water, but also represent uncharted territory, a space of undomesticated nature into which humans must venture only with care and respect.

The yamamba is also associated with motherhood and birthing and might be considered, in modern terms, a fierce and exemplary single mother. Most famously, in some narratives a yamamba is said to be the mother of the legendary boy hero Kintarō, who would grow up to be Sakata no Kintoki, faithful retainer of the great warrior Raikō and one of his lieutenants in the conquest of the oni Shuten dōji. Legends connecting these various characters, and describing Kintoki as the son of a yamamba, developed through popular-culture narratives, dramas, and illustrations during the Edo period and became particularly widespread with the production of Chikamatsu Monzaemon's *Komochi yamamba* as a bunraku puppet drama in 1712.[67]

A set of beliefs collected in Gifu Prefecture during the mid-twentieth century neatly encapsulates a number of the ideas associated with the yamamba. In a certain community, there was a rock, some four meters high, known as Yamamba-iwa (Yamamba rock). On the rock could be seen the image of a yamamba's face, "with one closed eye, no nose, and a large mouth with missing teeth." It was said that "long ago, wandering through the mountains, there was a frightening yamamba who lived by sucking the blood and eating the meat of birds and beasts." She could be terrifying to behold, but when she was in good spirits she would come down to the village and help farmers with their work, "easily doing the same amount of labor as four or five men."

Once she complained that her scalp was itchy, and somebody took a look and discovered that it was crawling with centipedes and caterpillars. They gave her an old comb, and she "happily scratched herself as she went back home into the mountains." Every December, she would buy some sake at the market, take it up into the mountains and not return for the entire winter. When she died, the people of the village buried her at the base of a large rock, which gradually eroded over the years into the image of a yamamba's face. It was said that if the face appeared to be crying, it would soon rain; if it seemed happy, the sun would shine. It was also said that if a woman prayed at the rock, she would produce abundant milk for her child.[68]

The yamamba here is hideous and frightening but simultaneously well respected, benevolent, and associated with motherhood. Her legend is, literally, engraved in the landscape. This one specific example reflects the complex of ideas associated with her figure, as well as the interplay and mutual influences of popular culture and folklore.

The word *yamamba* (or *yamauba*) does not seem to appear in Japanese texts until the Muromachi period; before that, such witchlike women were generally portrayed as female oni.[69] Whether classified as yamamba or not, demonic women can be found as far back as the *Kojiki* and the *Nihonshoki* episode in which the Yomotsu-shikome, the "hags of Yomi," chase Izanagi from the underworld. They also appear in numerous medieval setsuwa and Noh plays.[70]

That said, it is important not to conflate all female demon figures. The female oni is often characterized by her jealous rage—in fact, this rage is sometimes the very thing that turns a regular woman into a demon in the first place. This is, for example, one characteristic of the demonic female *hannya* mask used in many a Noh play. Akin to male oni, the female oni is distinguished by horns sprouting from her head. In contrast, most descriptions of yamamba do not include horns; nor generally is her monstrousness attributed to jealousy or sexual passion.

The yamamba is clearly a multifaceted and often contradictory being. In contemporary feminist analysis, she is a figure of great interpretive value. Living on the edge of society, in the mountains, she becomes a symbol of the marginalized Other, the outcast, or perhaps someone who has purposefully chosen to live off the grid. As a woman in particular, she comes to represent resistance to patriarchy and hegemonic gender relations. It is no coincidence that at the turn of the current century, *yamamba* became the name of a Japanese fashion-related subculture featuring

山姥

Figure 10. Yamamba. Original illustration by Shinonome Kijin.

young women who bleach their hair white and artificially darken the color of their skin. As an extreme cultural statement, the yamamba fashion threatens normative standards, drawing on the dangerous and rebellious spirit of this yōkai of folklore.

KIJIMUNĀ

Probably the most widely known yōkai of the Okinawa and Ryukyu Island region in the south of Japan, the *kijimunā* is a trickster figure akin to a kappa. It is also considered a tree spirit like a kodama. There is no simple English translation for *kijimunā*.

Within Okinawa, there are numerous local names for the creature, including *kijimuna, kijimun, kimuyā, bunagai, bunagayā, michibata, handanmii,* and *akagandā,* among others. As suggested by the variety of names, there are also many regional versions; but kijimunā are often described as having both hair down to their shoulders and hairy bodies. In some locales, they are the size of an infant or small child and covered in red hair; elsewhere they are large and completely black; and in some places they are said to possess gigantic testicles. They tend to reside in trees, such as fig trees and other types native to the region.[71]

Kijimunā like to play tricks on people by, for example, giving them dirt and making them believe it is rice. They can be violent and troublesome, robbing people walking alone at night. But they can also befriend humans, helping them catch fish or do work in the mountains. A fish provided by a kijimunā is always missing one eye because, it is said, the kijimunā has eaten the other. You can break off a friendship with a kijimunā or cause it to leave the area by giving it something it hates, such as an octopus or a chicken, or by burning down or hammering nails into the tree in which it lives.[72]

A legend collected in the Shimajiri district in Okinawa clearly exemplifies the double-edged, ambivalent character of the kijimunā. There was a man called Kujira-dono, who spent his days working hard and his evenings fishing in the ocean. Once, while fishing, he noticed a man he had never seen before; he greeted him and eventually the two became friends, meeting every night at the same place and occasionally even sharing their catch. Kujira-dono noticed some strange things about the man—an accent he could not place, for example, and the fact that his clothing always seemed wet. When he asked him where he lived, the strange man only gestured vaguely to a mountain in the distance. Kujira-dono eventually became more and more suspicious and one day ventured to ask him again where he came from and what his village was called. Suddenly the man's eyes flashed, and he said, "Today is no fun, so I am going home." Kujira-dono followed him through the woods and into the mountains, where he eventually came to a gigantic old mulberry (*kuwa*) tree. And then the man just disappeared, as if swallowed up by the tree.

That night, when Kujira-dono told his wife about the experience, she immediately realized that her husband's friend must be a kijimunā. The next day, Kujira-dono went to their fishing spot and greeted the man as usual. But while they were fishing, Kujira-dono's wife found the old mulberry tree and set it on fire. When the kijimunā returned to find his home destroyed, he was distressed and angry and eventually just disappeared. Kujira-dono and his wife were afraid and moved to another village far away.

Several years later, Kujira-dono had to travel to town. Late at night, as he walked alone on the road, he saw a light coming toward him. When it got closer, he recognized the kijimunā. He was frightened, of course, but screwed up his courage and greeted his old companion. The two old friends went out for a drink and had a lively time telling stories. At one point, Kujira-dono forgot himself and told about the time, five years earlier, that he banished a spirit from an old mulberry tree.

The kijimunā listened carefully and then stood up, whipped out a small knife, held down Kujira-dono's hand, and cut off his five fingers. He then just disappeared. In extreme pain, Kujira-dono managed to make it home, where he eventually died in agony. In her sadness, his wife carried his body back to his hometown. When she stripped off his clothing to dress him in his funeral garb, she discovered that his entire body was the color of rust.[73]

On a lighter note, the kijimunā name is also currently associated with Kijimunā Festa, an international performing arts festival for young people held every summer in Okinawa City. The festival symbol is an image of a crazy-haired, cute, red kijimunā.[74]

NINMENJU OR JINMENJU

Human-Faced Tree

In one of his many encyclopedic compendia of yōkai, Mizuki Shigeru describes a tree in Aomori Prefecture that, according to legend, would bleed when cut. He suggests that this strange plant might be a version of the ninmenju (alternatively *jinmenju*), a tree with human heads instead of flowers.[75] Such a yōkai tree was pictured two centuries earlier by Toriyama Sekien, who explains that it is found "in the mountains and valleys. Its flowers are like human heads. They do not speak, but merely laugh constantly. If they laugh too much, it is said, they will fall off."[76]

In Sekien's illustration, the tree skirts the left side and top of the page, with a spiky-leafed branch bearing small bald heads. Sekien apparently developed this image from one in the *Three Realms;* interestingly, however, in the *Three Realms* there is a man standing to the right of the tree. More intriguing still is that this entry is not in the section on plants but in the section on "peoples from foreign lands."[77] In fact, the focus is not the tree itself but the land with which it is associated: a place called Daishi. The *Three Realms* passage refers to an earlier Chinese text, the *Sancaituhui* (c. 1609), where the land is called Da-shi, possibly from *tazi*, a Persian word meaning "Arab." If we continue back in time and along the Silk Road, we find different versions of the great Persian epic poem *Shahnama* (Book of Kings) by Firdawsi (d. 1020), with illustrations of a man conversing with a tree bearing humans heads. The man, it turns out, is Alexander the Great (Sikandar or Iskandar), and the illustrations portray his legendary encounter with a talking tree, sometimes called the Wakwak Tree, that prophesied his death.[78]

By tracing this complex lineage, we can see images and ideas moving across space, time, and cultures. Here a picture of Alexander the Great becomes associated with "foreign lands" and enters Japan (through China) during the Edo period (a time, ironically, known for its relative isolation). Eventually man and place disappear, leaving only a mysterious tree located somewhere in "the mountains and valleys"—a plant monster that joins the world of Japanese yōkai. This tree yōkai, in turn, not only becomes part of the cultural imagination of Japan but also comes to be associated with a local legend in one corner of the country.

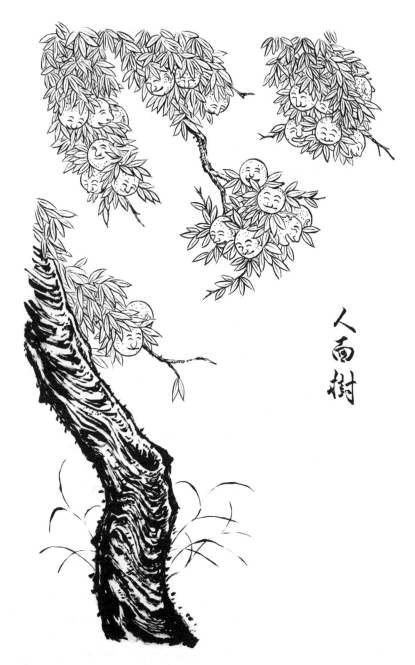

人面樹

Figure 11. Ninmenju. Original illustration by Shinonome Kijin.

The process demonstrates one of many ways in which "Japanese" yōkai come into being. It turns out that a seemingly indigenous monster may have originated with a Persian illustration of Alexander the Great! Interestingly, many scholars have focused on how Alexander's travels introduced monsters and "marvels of the East" into the Hellenistic world and the Western imagination.[79] The talking or laughing heads of the nin-menju tell us that such monstrous influences went both ways. Even in so-called premodern times, there were global connections through which legends and imagery were transmitted and transformed across time, language, continents, and cultures.

6 Water

Japan is made up of numerous islands and surrounded by ocean. It is also full of rivers, creeks, marshes, and ponds. Historically much of the arable land has been farmed through wet-rice cultivation, in which paddy fields are flooded during the growing season. Water control and irrigation are critical to Japanese economic life, and water plays a large part in the cultural imagination. All the yōkai in this chapter are connected in some way with water.

NINGYO

Mermaid or Merman

Legends of human-fish hybrids, often called mermaids or mermen, are found throughout the world. In Japan, the earliest documented account of a ningyo (literally, "human-fish") appears in the *Nihonshoki,* where it is recorded that near (present-day) Osaka in the year 619, a fisherman caught something "shaped like a child. It was neither a fish nor a person, and its name was unknown."[1] Historically, the implications of a ningyo sighting varied; it might be considered a sign of prosperity to come or, alternatively, interpreted as an omen of impending catastrophe, such as a typhoon, earthquake, or tsunami.[2]

Either way, however, ningyo were thought to possess great powers. One famous belief was that eating ningyo meat would bring you long life. Sometimes just looking at a ningyo was considered good fortune. A woodblock print from 1805, for example, shows a female ningyo from Ecchū-no-kuni (current-day Toyama area), with the comment that "a person who looks even once at this fish" will have a long and happy life, free of natural disasters and bad things.[3]

The story of Happyaku bikuni (also called Yao bikuni), the "eight-hundred-year nun," is one of the best-known legends (or complexes of legends) associated with the ningyo; the tale reveals the mixed blessings that long life can bring. A version recounted in the Wakasa-Obama area (present-day Fukui Prefecture) tells of a man who invites a guest to his house to eat a rare fish, a ningyo that he has caught in his nets. Put off by the idea of eating the flesh of a human-faced creature, the guest carefully manages to avoid the meat—but his host insists that he take some home, where, inadvertently, his sixteen-year-old daughter eats it. In the years to come, it is discovered that the daughter, miraculously, does not seem to age; as time progresses, her parents and friends all die and she is left lonely. Eventually she becomes a nun and travels throughout the country doing good things for everyone she meets. At the age of eight hundred, she returns to Wakasa-Obama to enshrine herself in a cave by the sea. Just before entering the cave, however, she plants a single camellia tree near the entrance, saying, "When this tree withers, please think that I have died." According to legend, the tree has not yet withered.[4]

The size, shape, and countenance of ningyo vary. Generally the upper body of the creature—sometimes just the head, sometimes the arms as well—is humanlike, while the lower body is fishlike. The inverse has also been found on occasion. In many Edo-period illustrations, ningyo also have horns protruding from their otherwise humanlike heads.

A number of mummified mermaids can still be found today. These mummies seem to have been artfully constructed during the Edo period by Japanese (and possibly other Asian) fishermen, who would stitch together the upper body of a monkey and the lower body of a fish. Mermaid-making like this, which required a sophisticated knowledge of taxidermy, may have been a way for seafaring people to pass the time and perhaps make a little extra money.[5] Several of the existing examples of these creatures are found in Holland and were most likely sold or traded to Dutch sailors by Japanese fishermen.

The most notorious desiccated mermaid was the one displayed in 1842 by the great American showman P. T. Barnum. Called the "Feejee Mermaid," this ugly, shriveled, two-foot-ten-inch-long mummy was a cause célèbre when Barnum showed it with great fanfare in New York. It not only made viewers rethink their common conception of the mermaid as an attractive woman who just happens to have the tail of a fish, but it also set off a debate among naturalists and the general public about the possibility of mermaids in the first place.

Some twenty years earlier this same ningyo had made a stir on the other side of the Atlantic, where "throughout the autumn of 1822, the mermaid was London's greatest scientific sensation: people thronged to see it, and most newspapers had articles about 'the remarkable Stuffed Mermaid.'"[6] The ningyo was first brought to London by Samuel Barrett Eades, an American sea captain, who had purchased it from Dutch merchants in Holland. The Dutchmen claimed that they had bought it from a Japanese fisherman who had caught it in his net. The ultimate fate of the Feejee Mermaid is unknown—though it was probably destroyed in a Boston fire in the 1880s. But in its sensational global sojourn, from Japan to Holland to Britain to the United States, this one small yōkai seems to have made a remarkable impression on a great number of people, inspired debates among scientists and the general public, and played a small but meaningful role in Western cultural history.[7]

Over a hundred years later, in 1990, a yōkai called a *jinmengyo*, or "human faced-fish," became an instant media sensation in Japan when a weekly magazine published a photo of a carp that had what looked like a human face, found in a temple pond in Yamagata Prefecture. This occurred almost directly on the heels of rumors about a human-faced dog (*jinmenken*), so it was likely a sort of copycat yōkai phenomenon. As recently as 2008, jinmengyo sightings have been reported, and these may be the result of a trick of light created by the pattern of reflective scales on the heads of certain kinds of fish; when seen through the water from above, the fish appears to have the features of a human face.[8] Although the jinmengyo may not be historically related to the ningyo, the hybrid of human and fish is still part of the cultural imagination and still causing viewers to question, or play with, the limits of possibility.

KAPPA (ALSO KAWATARŌ)

The kappa is associated with water, usually rivers, ponds, or swamps. It is one of the most famous of all yōkai in Japan. Different legends and beliefs about it are distributed throughout the country, but generally speaking, the kappa is thought of as scaly or slimy, greenish in color, with webbed feet and hands, and a carapace on its back. Sometimes it resembles a monkey, sometimes a giant frog or turtle. It is the size of a young child but disproportionately strong. A concave indentation or saucer on top of the kappa's head contains water; if this water is spilled, the creature loses its super strength. Kappa are mischievous and sometimes deadly, notorious for pulling horses and cattle into the water; they have also been known to drown young children and extract their internal organs through their anuses.

Despite these murderous proclivities, kappa can be both playful and exceedingly honest. They especially enjoy sumō wrestling and like to challenge passersby to a match. One tactic for defeating a kappa in sumō is simply to bow beforehand; when the kappa bows in response, it spills its strength-giving liquid from the saucer on its head. The kappa is at once a dangerous, demonic monster—a reason to warn children about swimming in a river or pond—and an amusing, if disgusting, water sprite. While Chinese lore has certainly influenced its development, and comparable water creatures exist elsewhere in world folklore, the kappa as described here is considered a distinctly Japanese creation.

Kappa are fond of certain foods, including melons, eggplants, and especially, cucumbers. In many places, children were warned not to go swimming after eating cucumbers, because they might be attacked by a kappa; in some communities, there is a tradition of leaving cucumbers at shrines or in the water as offerings to appease the resident kappa. In fact, in Japan and much of the rest of the world, sushi rolls made with cucumbers are called *kappa maki,* named for the kappa's love of this summer vegetable.

Numerous local rituals and festivals, particularly in agricultural communities that depend on water for irrigation, celebrate kappa as water deities (*suijin*). When treated appropriately, the local kappa will ensure ample water for irrigation; if neglected or treated with disdain, it will cause drought or flooding. The kappa, therefore, can be considered simultaneously a deity and a demon, depending on the perspective of the human beings with whom it is in contact.

The Word

Literally meaning "river" (*kawa*) "child" (*warabe*), the name *kappa* seems to perfectly describe the little beast itself—a child of the river. But *kappa* is actually only one of many variant words for the creature, whose wide distribution throughout Japan is reflected in its many local types—there are more than a hundred regional variations. Scholars have tried to classify the various names or types of kappa found throughout Japan, organizing them into "lineages." Ishikawa Jun'ichirō, for example, has mapped out names in accordance with their possible derivations; some reflect the creature's physical resemblance to a child (e.g., *kawappa, kawako, kawatarō*), others its resemblance to a monkey (e.g., *enkō, enko*), a turtle (e.g., *dangame*), or an otter (e.g., *kawaso*); still other names indicate the kappa's behavior (e.g., *komahiki*, or "horse puller").[9]

The word *kappa* itself was originally a regional term used in the east of Japan, from the Kanto area to Tohoku, but has now become the generic label for the creature, commonly used in academic works and in popular culture.[10] The ubiquity of the label raises the question of how much the *name* of the thing determines the *nature* of the thing. In my own fieldwork, for example, I interviewed a number of older residents of the small community of Teuchi in Kagoshima Prefecture. They told me how, as children, they were warned about a terrifying water creature called a gamishiro. When I asked them to describe it, one of them told me it was "just like a kappa." Most likely, however, when they were children they never actually heard the word *kappa;* only after they were older, and had heard descriptions of the kappa from elsewhere, did they attach this label to their own local water creature—and with the label, they also imported some of the kappa's particular characteristics.

Similarly, folklorist Itō Ryōhei notes that several years ago, when he taught a class on Japanese culture at a university in Taiwan, he asked his students to draw pictures of oni, tengu, and kappa. Of these three, it was the kappa images that were most similar to each other: "a small cute creature, a head with hair surrounding a saucer, a beak and webbed hands and feet, and a shell on its back." As Itō points out, this is how a Japanese person would probably illustrate a kappa.[11] In other words, not only has the kappa—both name and image—become unified or generic within Japan, but also, through mass media and other means, it has been transmitted overseas.

If we take *kappa* as a generic label for a whole range of water creatures, then we can trace its earliest documented appearance to the *Nihonshoki*, in which it is explained that in the year 379 a snakelike water creature called a *midzuchi* had been killing travelers near a particular river. The district warden, "a man of fierce temper and of great bodily strength, stood over the pool of the river-fork and flung into the water three whole calabashes, saying:—'Thou art continually belching up poison and therewithal plaguing travellers. I will kill thee, thou water-snake. If thou canst sink these calabashes, then will I take myself away, but if thou canst not sink them, then will I cut up thy body.'" In the end, the midzuchi fails in his efforts to sink the gourds and is duly dispatched by the warden.[12]

Whether or not the water-snake or spirit portrayed in this early period can be considered a kappa or perhaps a "pre-kappa," it was not until the Edo period that the creature became a major yōkai presence.[13] That was when the kappa started to appear in many a local legend, as the protagonist in numerous lighthearted popular illustrated texts and as the focus of academic and protozoological studies. The earliest known mass-produced image appears in the *Three Realms*, under the label *kawatarō*, accompanied by the following description:

> About the size of a ten-year-old child, the kawatarō stands and walks naked and speaks in a human voice. Its hair is short and sparse. The top of its head is concave and can hold a scoop of water. Kawatarō usually live in the water, but in the light of the late afternoon, many emerge into the area near the river and steal melons, eggplants, and things from the fields. By nature the kawatarō likes sumō; when it sees a person, it will invite him [to wrestle]. . . . If there is water on its head, the kawatarō has several times the

strength of a warrior. . . . The kawatarō has a tendency to pull cattle and horses into the water and suck blood out of their rumps. People crossing rivers must be very careful.[14]

Kappa were also among the first yōkai illustrated in Toriyama Sekien's *Gazu hyakkiyagyō*, where the label reads simply, "Kappa, also called kawatarō." Along with such encyclopedic treatments, kappa appeared as protagonists in kibyōshi and other graphic literary works. Through these inexpensive and widely circulated formats, the kappa image became relatively standardized, and this mass-produced urban version in turn influenced localized rural versions.

Kappa versus Kawatarō

Scholars have traced images of the kappa to different regions, broadly dividing the country between east and west. The shell-bearing, amphibious yōkai was generally found in eastern Japan, from the Kanto (Edo) region to Tohoku. In western Japan, from Kansai to parts of Shikoku and Kyushu, the creature was called a kawatarō (or some variation of this name) and was hairy and walked upright and monkeylike. It is no coincidence, for example, that the "kawatarō" in the *Three Realms* quoted earlier looks much like a monkey; the author, Terajima Ryōan, was from Osaka, in the west of the country. Similarly, a 1754 text called the *Nihon sankai meibutsu zue* shows a group of kawatarō from Bungo (modern-day Ōita Prefecture) in Kyushu walking upright and playing near a river; the text describes them as "the size of five-year-old children and having hair all over their bodies."[15] In 1776, when Toriyama Sekien created an image labeled "Kappa, also called kawatarō," he neatly, and perhaps consciously, subsumed the name and image of the western kawatarō under the name and image of the eastern kappa. In the ensuing years, and certainly by the late nineteenth and early twentieth centuries, this generally amphibious, slimy version of the creature, called by the name *kappa*, would become the yōkai we know today.[16]

Kappa Characteristics

Keeping in mind this complex history of regional variants and creative interaction, we can identify a number of widely noted kappa traits. As mentioned earlier, kappa are, for example, exceedingly fond of cucumbers. On the other hand, they are repelled by certain materials, such as iron—an aversion common to many water spirits around the world.[17] Their inability to cope with calabashes, or gourds, as demonstrated in the *Nihonshoki* passage quoted earlier, persists even in a much later folk narrative known as the "Kappa muko-iri" (Kappa bridegroom) tale. A farmer offers to give his daughter to anybody who can successfully irrigate his fields. He had assumed this would be a human being, of course, but it is the local kappa who eventually performs the task and receives the daughter's hand. The prospective bride, understandably, is not keen on the relationship and challenges the kappa to sink some gourds in the river. Unable to complete this impossible assignment, the kappa exhausts himself, forsaking the marriage.[18]

Particularly in the northern part of Japan, kappa were known for pulling horses into the water: in some regions they are called komahiki, or "horse-puller." This nasty penchant for drowning horses (and sometimes cattle) is balanced by the fact that, in most of these narratives, the kappa fails. Its attempt backfires and the kappa, or just its arm, is pulled by the startled horse all the way back to the stable. In this emasculated condition, the kappa is receptive to human negotiation, and often, in order to regain its freedom or get its arm back (the arm can be reattached within a certain number of days), it will pledge, for example, to stop harassing passersby, to help with work in the fields, or perhaps to teach its captors secret medicines and techniques for setting bones.

This last trait, the kappa's knowledge of medicine, is a motif found throughout Japan. In some cases, an ancestor's negotiation with a captive kappa is touted as the origin of a family's lineage as medical doctors. A legend from Ehime Prefecture reflects not only this secret medical knowledge but also another nasty habit of the kappa (in this case, called an *enko*):

> Long ago, the maid [of a doctor's household] went to the outhouse at night, and out of the toilet reached a hairy hand—perhaps a human, perhaps a monkey; she didn't know what—and made to stroke her buttocks. She was frightened and told her experience to the doctor.
>   On hearing this, the doctor grabbed a sword, exclaimed, "I'll go conquer this thing," and entered the outhouse. And sure enough, when a hand

reached out of the toilet the doctor grabbed it and chopped it off with his sword. He brought the hand inside and put it in his examination room.

The next evening, there was a knock at the front door; assuming it was a patient, the doctor went out and discovered that it was the enko whose arm he had chopped off the day before. "Doctor," the enko said, "please return my arm. If I don't apply medicine and reattach it quickly, I won't be able to re-attach it at all. I won't do anything bad anymore," it apologized, "so please return my arm."

When the doctor at first refused, the enko signed a pledge promising to teach him secret knowledge and how to make a medicine for mending bones, and so it seems the doctor then returned his arm. After this, it is said, the doctor prospered as a specialist in the setting of bones.[19]

The kappa's interest in stroking human buttocks is connected with another, more devious trait—namely, its desire for an organ called the *shirikodama*. The shirikodama is characterized as a ball positioned at the opening of the anus; if your shirikodama is snatched away by a kappa, you will die. Of course, biologically speaking, there is no such organ, but one explanation for the belief is that the bodies of drowning victims have an "open anus," as if something had been removed.[20] In some cases, it is said, the kappa's objective is not the shirikodama itself but the internal organs beyond it.

Modern Kappa

Despite their potentially devious and disgusting behavior, kappa flourish in modern Japan. They have gradually been cleaned up—domesticated and made safe—and are often used for nationwide advertising campaigns and the promotion of local tourism. This process of domestication certainly started with the kappa's comic appearance in kibyōshi and other Edo-period formats. In the twentieth century, the creature made a particularly famous literary appearance, as the protagonist of Akutagawa Ryūnosuke's short novel *Kappa* (1927), a social satire narrated by a human who journeys to a land of kappa. In his depiction of kappa characters, with their similarities to and differences from humans, the author poignantly critiques certain aspects of modern Japanese society. Akutagawa was already well known when he wrote *Kappa;* his suicide soon after its appearance brought atten-tion to the satirical contents and kappa characters of his final novel.[21]

The kappa's appearance also developed throughout the twentieth century. The artist Ogawa Usen (1868–1938), for example, was famous for his depictions of kappa frolicking joyfully. As in Akutagawa's novel, the kappa became stand-ins for humans. This is also clear in the popular manga of Shimizu Kon (1912–1974), whose *Kappa tengoku* (Kappa heaven), complete with female kappa (rare in folklore) and "salaryman" kappa (nonexistent in folklore), began nationwide circulation in the *Asahi Weekly* in 1953. Kojima Kō (b. 1928) also illustrated naked female kappa, with pink nipples and thick eyelashes, similar to humans but for their patterned shells and the delicate blue saucers perched on their heads. Images by both these artists were used in advertising campaigns, most famously by Kizakura sake. In the 1960s, Mizuki Shigeru published a serialized manga titled *Sanpei the Kappa*. The kappa's role as a national icon, and as a metaphor for the Japanese consumer, can also be seen in its use as a mascot for the DC Card (a credit card). In this case, the kappa is paired with another popular yōkai—the tanuki.[22]

The kappa's commercial power is also recognized on the local level. In the 1970s and 1980s, when many people were moving to the cities, rural communities throughout Japan began to develop local kappa-lore for "village revitalization" projects. By celebrating the kappa's association with agriculture and a rapidly disappearing rural lifestyle, communities branded themselves nostalgically as traditional hometowns, attracting tourists and selling products based on these images.

Similarly, this slimy creature that once terrorized people and animals venturing near the water has now become a symbol of unspoiled nature. You can find cutesified kappa images posted near rivers, imploring people not to litter or spoil the environment. In other words, a yōkai that used to represent the violence and unpredictability of the natural world, and especially water, has now literally become a poster child for the effort to stop the sacrifice of nature.

Even while kappa serve different purposes on the local level, they continue to appear nationally (and internationally) in popular media, especially film. Mizuki Shigeru's 1960s manga *Sanpei the Kappa* returned as an animated series in the 1990s, and a kappa character played a starring role in the *E.T.*-like feature film *Kappa* (1994). The early twenty-first century has already witnessed several kappa-related films, such as director Miike

Figure 12. Kappa and kawauso. Original illustrations by Shinonome Kijin.

Takashi's *Yōkai daisensō* (*The Great Yōkai War*, 2005); *Desu kappa* (*Death Kappa*, dir. Haraguchi Tomo'o, 2010), starring a mammoth mutant kappa stomping through Tokyo; and Imaoka Shinji's *Onna no Kappa* (2011, English title: *Underwater Love*), a fantasy soft-porn musical. The kappa remains a vibrant and versatile character, more often than not providing satirical, if not frightening, commentary on contemporary human society.

Finally, as one of Japan's best-recognized yōkai, the kappa has also appeared internationally, famously in *Harry Potter and the Prisoner of Azkaban* (1999) and Rowling's bestiary *Fantastic Beasts & Where to Find Them* (2001).[23] Although the kappa is not celebrated specifically as a shape-shifter, it turns out to be very capable of adapting to all sorts of different environments. After its humble beginnings as a repulsive water creature in a Japanese river, it has now traveled the world.

KAWAUSO

River Otter

Kawauso are found in various regions throughout the country, where they are known for deception and mischief similar to that of kitsune and tanuki. And like kitsune and tanuki, kawauso are also related to a real mammal, in this case the river otter.

Since at least the Edo period, the kawauso has been famous for assuming the guise of an attractive human in order to deceive other humans. In some literary accounts, it is portrayed as a particularly cruel yōkai, transforming itself into a beautiful woman in order to kill a man. Tales of otters taking the guise of beautiful women are also found in early Chinese texts.[24]

In some local folklore, kawauso are conflated with kappa, performing the same types of mischief and similarly challenging humans to sumō. In fact, the names *kawauso* and *kawaso* are sometimes used as variant labels for kappa. At the very least, kawauso and kappa are close relatives: Toriyama Sekien's kawauso, walking upright and wearing a sedge hat, appears in his earliest text—on the page facing the kappa.

Both the image of the kawauso and the word itself are deeply linked with the Japanese river otter (*Lutra lutra whiteleyi* or *Lutra lutra nippon*), which once swam in abundance throughout the Japanese archipelago. Eating shrimp and fish, these sleek carnivorous creatures grew to be about a meter long. Given their quick, flashing movements and expressive faces, it is easy to imagine them possessing shape-shifting and deceptive capabilities.

Unfortunately, they also possessed highly desirable fur, which was primarily sold to foreign traders. And more recently, during Japan's postwar period of rapid industrialization, many rivers were dammed and polluted, gradually destroying the kawauso's natural habitat. A wild otter was spotted in Kōchi Prefecture in 1979, but none have been seen since. In September 2012, the Japanese Ministry of the Environment officially declared them extinct.[25]

HYŌSUBE

The *hyōsube*, also called *hyōsuhe*, *hyōzunbo*, and *hyōsubo*, is a water yōkai, perhaps a species of kappa, found especially in Saga and Miyazaki Prefectures in Kyushu.[26] In his first catalog, Toriyama Sekien draws the hyōsube as a goofy-looking creature with an extremely hairy body (but bald head); he does not provide any written description or other information.

ひやうすべ

Figure 13. Hyōsube. Original illustration by Shinonome Kijin.

Even though the creature is thought to be related to the kappa, Sekien's hyōsube seems to be on the veranda of a house, and there is no water in sight. Sekien's image also resembles a hyōsube found in an earlier yōkai picture scroll, the *Hyakkai-zukan* by Sawaki Sūshi, where it is also illustrated in a comic fashion but with no explanation.[27]

GAMISHIRO, GAMISHIRŌ, OR GAMESHIRŌ

The gamishiro lives in the ocean near the village of Teuchi on the island of Shimo-Koshikijima off the west coast of Kagoshima Prefecture. While the creature seems to be localized to this small area, it shares many characteristics with the kappa. Like the kappa, for example, it is particularly fond of cucumbers. But whereas most yōkai of the kappa family tend to haunt rivers and small pools of water, the gamishiro lives in the ocean.

There are no extant illustrations of the gamishiro, and it has been all but forgotten by younger islanders. However, it seems to have been well known in the past. In 2012, for example, one fifty-eight-year-old island native told me that when he was a child he was warned not to go swimming in the ocean after eating cucumbers, because he would be attacked by a gamishiro. Looking back, he suggests this may have been a way for adults to prevent children from stealing cucumbers, a summer crop on the island. His parents, both in their eighties, confirmed that they too were told the same thing as children, so the belief has been consistent for at least eighty years or so. Another islander in her fifties recalled being told that she should not go swimming alone in the ocean because a gamishiro would grab her leg and pull her under. In retrospect, she interprets this as a way for her elders to remind her of the dangers of swimming alone in the ocean. She has no recollection of an association with cucumbers.

Generally there is no specific physical description associated with the gamishiro: it is just a frightening and dangerous "thing" lurking in the waters. However, another Teuchi resident, in his late eighties, described the creature as being similar to a kappa, with a cavity on its head and clawlike limbs. As a child he was warned that the gamishiro lurked particularly in two deep pools of water in the bay, and that it would pull you down by grabbing your Achilles tendon. He recalled that when he was a child a young relative of his was almost drowned in one of these pools; when he was rescued, everybody checked his ankles for marks of the gami-shiro's claws, but there were none.[28]

It is possible that the "gami" in "gamishiro" is related to the word *kami*, the general Japanese word for deity. The alternate name *gameshirō* has also been recorded for this same oceangoing yōkai.[29] The *game* part of the word is a name for kappa-like creatures found in various different regions and may imply an association with the turtle, or *kame*.[30] The variety of names and the possible associations with deities, other yōkai, and turtles demonstrate the flexibility of such vernacular designations. The fact that there are no known illustrations or other visible images of this particular yōkai also allows it to remain vague and changeable but still dangerous and potentially frightening.

MŌRYŌ

The *mōryō* has a complex and somewhat vague history, but the name derives from Chinese sources and indicates a deity or demon associated with water. *Mōryō* is one part of the longer word *chimi-mōryō*, an inclusive term for all sorts of yōkai, which has been used in Japan since at least the Edo period. *Chimi* refers to spirits associated with the mountains, while *mōryō* is linked with water.[31]

In the *Kinmōzui* (1666), an early Japanese illustrated encyclopedia, there is a brief entry for oni that explains, "*Oni* is *chimi*, which is the spirit of an old thing; *mōryō* or *mizuchi*, which is a water deity [*suijin*]; and also the tree spirit [*kinomi*] or *kodama;* mountain demon [*sanki*] or *yama-zumi.*"[32] About fifty years later, in the *Three Realms*, the mōryō is given its own entry, in which it is described as a creature the size of a "three-year-old child, black and red in color, with red eyes, long ears, and beautiful hair." Judging from the illustration, the mōryō looks harmless, much like a human child but for the elongated upright ears. The author goes on to note, however, that this creature "likes to eat livers from dead bodies."[33]

In *Konjaku gazu zoku hyakki* (1779), Toriyama Sekien develops this image with a description very similar to the one found in the *Three*

Realms: "Its figure is like that of a three-year-old child. It is red and black in color. It has red eyes, long ears and beautiful hair. It is said that it likes to eat the livers of dead bodies." In contrast to the innocent-looking creature illustrated in the *Three Realms,* however, Sekien's mōryō has sharp nails and hairy ears and is pulling a body from the ground; a broken Buddhist stupa indicates the site of the disrupted grave. There is no mention of any relationship with water.[34]

More recently, the mōryō has been pictured in manga and anime by Mizuki Shigeru.[35] It was also the title character of Kyogoku Natsuhiko's second novel, *Mōryō no hako* (The box of the mōryō; 1995), which won the Mystery Writers of Japan Award for Best Novel (1996) and was later made into a live action film (2007), a manga (2007–2010), and a television anime (2008).[36]

AZUKI-ARAI

Bean-Washer

The *azuki-arai* is a yōkai that creates the sound of azuki (or adzuki) beans being washed in a river, pond, or well. The phenomenon is found throughout most of Japan, though the name may differ from region to region; for example, it is called *azuki-suri* and *azuki-sarasara* in parts of Okayama Prefecture, *azuki-sogi* in one village in Yamanashi Prefecture, and *azuki-goshagosha* in part of Nagano City. Along with making the sound of washing, sometimes it is heard singing. Similar sounds of washing have also been attributed to tanuki, kitsune, kawauso, and mujina.[37]

While the origin of the azuki-arai is most likely the sound of water running across pebbles or through leaves, the connection with azuki is also important. In Japan, azuki (*Phaseolus angularis*) and other beans are symbolically powerful. During the Setsubun celebration in early February, for example, family members in many parts of Japan throw soybeans while shouting, "Out with oni, in with good fortune!" and then each eats as many beans as his or her age. The magical properties of the beans ward off evil and usher in good fortune for the year to come. Similarly, special events such as weddings, graduations, and other achievements are often celebrated by eating *seki-han,* rice cooked with red azuki beans.

小豆洗い

Figure 14. Azuki-arai. Original illustration by Shinonome Kijin.

Although the folk phenomenon of the azuki-arai described earlier is auditory, at least as far back as the Edo period a visual image was also associated with it. In an 1841 illustrated book of spooky tales by Takehara Shunsen, for example, there is a story of a disabled Buddhist acolyte who enjoys, and is exceedingly skilled at, counting beans. One day, an evil monk throws him down a well, and afterward his spirit appears at twilight and is heard washing and counting beans. The narrative is illustrated with an image of an awkwardly bent man with a crazy smile and a demonic glint in his eye, his hands thrust into a bucket of beans. Mizuki Shigeru's azuki-arai image is clearly based on this one, and an even more developed character appears in the film *The Great Yōkai War* (2005).[38]

Azuki-arai is also an alternative name for the *chatate-mushi* (literally, "tea-brewing insect," *Psocoptera*), a family of insects known for making noise at night in the paper shoji dividers of households. The noise they make is said to be similar to the sound of the brewing of tea (*cha o tateru*) or, as it were, the washing of beans.[39]

7 Countryside

The yōkai in this chapter live and appear in the countryside, by which I mean any sort of rural setting—from a wooded mountain to a farming village. This designation is necessarily broad and somewhat vague, occupying the expansive space between the Wilds of nature and the busy streets of Village and City. The yōkai here might appear by a shrine or small shelter in a lonely forest, but they also might come right down to a farmhouse or field or a bridge in town. Some of the yōkai in this group, particularly tanuki and kitsune, seem to be at home in almost any setting. Many of these yōkai assume animal form, and all of them are forces of nature— metaphors for the mysteries of the natural world that make their presence known to the humans who would try to control it.

SUNAKAKE-BABĀ

Sand-Throwing Granny

In "Yōkai Glossary," Yanagita Kunio writes that this yōkai is "found in various locations in Nara Prefecture. [She] threatens people by sprinkling sand on them when they pass through places such as the shadows of a lonely forest of a shrine. Although nobody has ever seen her, it is said that she is an old woman."[1] Sunakake-babā (alternatively *sunakake-baba*) has also been recorded in Hyōgo Prefecture and elsewhere in the Kansai area. In some regions of the country, similar mischief is attributed to monkeys or tanuki (*sunakake-tanuki*).[2]

Despite the fact that "nobody has ever seen her," Mizuki Shigeru illustrates sunakake-babā in his catalogs and has also transformed her into one of the standard yōkai characters in his *Gegege no Kitarō* series.[3] If not for Mizuki's influence it is likely this yōkai would have remained relatively obscure, collected in Yanagita's work and perhaps remembered in a few communities around Nara. But because of Mizuki, she is now one of the most well recognized of all yōkai.

YUKI-ONNA

Snow Woman

The yuki-onna is a female yōkai who appears on snowy nights or in the midst of a snowstorm.

Specific names, beliefs, and narratives vary from region to region. In Miyagi Prefecture, for example, she is called *yuki-banba;* in parts of Nagano Prefecture she is known as *shikkenken;* in Yamagata Prefecture, *yuki-jorō;* and in Miyazaki Prefecture and the Satsuma region of Kagoshima Prefecture, she is known as *yuki-bajo* (*bajo* being a local term for "old woman").

In Iwate and Miyagi Prefectures in northeast Japan, it was said that if you saw yuki-onna, your spirit would be drawn from your body. In parts of Aomori Prefecture, her behavior is similar to that of the ubume: she will ask you to hold her baby. In some parts of the country, such as Tōno, in Iwate Prefecture, she appears on a set date; elsewhere her appearance is random and witnessed only by particularly lucky (or unlucky) individuals. She is variously explained as the spirit of the snow, as the ghost of a woman who died in the snow, or even—in Yamagata Prefecture—as a moon princess who was kicked out of the sky-world, and who descends, dancing, along with the snow.[4] In one form or another, the yuki-onna seems to have been commonly known throughout the country; Toriyama Sekien puts her in his earliest catalog, along with other yōkai for whom no explanation was needed.[5]

Even with this widespread distribution throughout Japan, the yuki-onna is probably best known today because of a tale written in English by Lafcadio Hearn in his *Kwaidan* of 1904; translated into Japanese, it has been widely read over the last century. Hearn explains in the preface that the yuki-onna narrative he recounts was related to him "by a farmer of Chōfu, Nishitama-gōri, in Musashi province, as a legend of his native village."[6] One night, two woodcutters are caught in a terrible snowstorm and take shelter in a hut. The younger of the two, Minokichi, witnesses a beautiful woman in white blow white smoke in the face of his older companion, a cold breath that, he later discovers, takes the older man's life. The mysterious white woman then stoops down to breathe on Minokichi's face, but pulls back at the last second—leaving him alive but with a warning that she will kill him if he ever reveals what he saw that night.

The next year, Minokichi meets a beautiful young woman named (somewhat suspiciously!) O-Yuki. They are soon married and lead a happy and fruitful life together, replete with ten children. One night, however, Minokichi gazes at his wife and, lost in reverie, tells her of his encounter with yuki-onna so many years earlier. In that instant, his wife flies into a rage and cries, "But for those children asleep there, I would kill you this moment!" And with that, she melts "into a bright white mist that spired to the roof-beams, and shuddered away through the smoke-hole."[7]

Although Hearn attributes the narrative to a local farmer, scholars have doubted the veracity of this claim because his fully developed love story is significantly more complex than any known local legends concerning yuki-onna. Indeed, Hearn himself had much earlier mentioned the simplicity of such legends in an 1893 letter to Basil Hall Chamberlain: "The Japanese fancy," he wrote, "has its 'Snow-women' too—its white spectres and goblins, which do no harm and say nothing, only frighten and make one feel cold."[8] It is possible then that Hearn combined a simple Japanese legend with more complex and stylish European literary images of a "femme fatale." One scholar suggests he was specifically influenced by Charles Baudelaire's poem "Les Bienfaits de la Lune" (The moon's blessings).[9]

Hearn's yuki-onna tale also incorporates a variety of folk motifs—particularly the notion of marriage between human and nonhuman. Common to such tales is the end of the marriage when the husband, often by accident, breaches a promise and the wife returns to her true form. In Japan, this motif occurs as far back as the *Kojiki* and *Nihonshoki;* it is found in the widely distributed legends "Hagoromo" (Feather mantle) and "Tsuru-nyōbo" (Crane wife), and there are numerous examples of men who have married kitsune. The motif is also common in folklore of other cultures, such as Gaelic legends of the *selkie.* Such diverse sources were likely an influence on Hearn as he successfully developed an evocative literary narrative and created an image that survives to this day, in Japan and abroad, as the most resonant image of the snow woman.

KAMAITACHI

Sickle Weasel

You are walking outside and suddenly discover that your leg has been cut as if with a sharp blade. This is said to be the work of a kamaitachi— literally a "sickle weasel." The kamaitachi is an extremely widespread yōkai phenomenon found throughout Japan, but probably most common in the so-called snow country of northern Honshu. In most cases, the creature inflicts its wound on the lower part of the body, on the shin or the calf, and often there is no pain or blood associated with the cut.[10] Beliefs and narratives about kamaitachi vary from place to place, but the creature is often said to ride in with a powerful gust of wind or on a whirlwind; in some places the phenomenon is known as *kamakaze,* or "sickle wind."

The origins of the word *kamaitachi* are unclear but may stem from a play on *kamae-tachi,* which could be translated as "poised sword."[11] Regardless of whether this play on words led to the name or not, it is easy to imagine a weasel as a stealthy culprit sneaking in like the wind, inflicting a wound, and disappearing. In fact, zoologically speaking, weasels are famous for their speed, moving "quickly and tirelessly, investigating every hole and crevice."[12] Extremely skilled hunters with razor sharp teeth, they can kill animals much larger than themselves, leaving only a small wound and taking just enough meat or blood for their immediate energy requirements. The fact that a weasel can slip into small places and leave almost no trace of its passage on the body of its victim may be one reason they are associated with mysterious phenomena.

Although the word and phenomenon precede it, one of the earliest and most influential images of a kamaitachi is a sharp-clawed weasel in a spiraling whirlwind found in Toriyama Sekien's first catalog. But there are also very different ways of characterizing the phenomenon; in Gifu Prefecture, for example, the kamaitachi is reported to consist of a trio of three gods: the first one pushes over the victim, the second inflicts the injury with a blade, and the third administers a healing salve. The wound does not bleed and is not painful.[13]

Attempts have been made to explain the kamaitachi phenomenon scientifically. It has been attributed to changes in air pressure caused by whirlwinds or to pieces of debris picked up by a strong gust of wind. Such explanations, as Murakami Kenji points out, are themselves a form of folk belief, and nothing has been proven scientifically.[14] With this in mind, it is worth mentioning that as early as 1911 the phenomenon was taken seriously as a medical condition worth international attention. Under the heading of "Spontaneous Wounds," the *British Medical Journal* introduced a report by a Japanese doctor about

> a form of wound which occurs spontaneously and is frequently seen in Japan, the so-called Kamaitachi disease. The wound is suddenly formed. . . . Usually it occurs on one of the lower limbs, sometimes the face. . . . It is known by meteorologists that during thunderstorms a temporary vacuum may occur in places as a result of stray air currents, and if a part of the body comes into such a space a tear may result from the internal pressure unmodified by the action of external pressure. The cases usually occur in outlying mountain districts, rich in trees and streams, and it is in just such districts that in a thunderstorm atmospheric conditions can most readily produce a vacuum of the kind described.[15]

It is no coincidence that such a scientific analysis comes at the end of the Meiji period, exactly when Inoue Enryō's rationalist explanations of yōkai had become common in intellectual circles.

In contemporary Japan, the kamaitachi lends its name and mystery to one of the first "sound novels," or interactive fiction games. Originally made by Chunsoft in 1994, versions (and sequels) of the game have been available for play on PlayStation, Game Boy, Android, and other platforms.

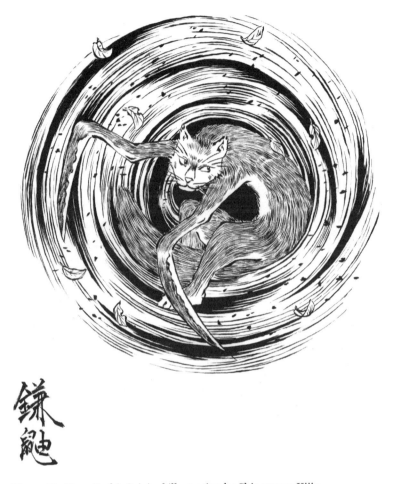

Figure 15. Kamaitachi. Original illustration by Shinonome Kijin.

KITSUNE

Fox

The kitsune, or fox, is one of the most famous yōkai in Japan; and perhaps more than any other, it has also fascinated people outside the country. Although *kitsune* is the most common generic term for this yōkai, foxlike creatures are also known by different regional names, including *ninko, osaki-gitsune, kuda-gitsune,* and *nogitsune.*

The kitsune is multitalented, appearing in local folklore, historical records, literary texts, theatrical performances, and contemporary popular culture. It can be a dangerous shape-shifter and it can possess people; but it is also a standard feature of Inari worship, and stone statues of kitsune are stationed at shrines throughout the country. With so many different incarnations and meanings, it is fair to say that in Japan today the kitsune—a charming and cunning deceiver that emanates an aura of danger and malevolence—is admired, worshipped, and feared.

Many early Japanese tales of kitsune can be traced back to China, where the creature was also known for its shape-shifting talents, most notoriously taking on the guise of beautiful, seductive women. Some of these tales were told in highly literary forms and came to Japan in written texts.[16] In China, the word *huli,* a combination of the kanji for *kitsune* and *tanuki,* generally indicates a fox; in Japan the same kanji compound, pronounced *kori,* refers to all sorts of supernatural and troublesome occurrences (and includes tanuki as one of the culprits).[17]

In Japan, kitsune and tanuki are both famous for their ability to shape-shift and deceive others. Tanuki tend to be comical and less adept at their deceptions; kitsune appear to be more serious about their performances, and their abilities are better honed. Both creatures are members of the Canidae family. The folkloric characteristics of the kitsune, like those of the tanuki, reflect its zoological traits as a creature that can live on the edges of human society—visible one moment and gone the next. The most common fox in Japan is the red fox (*Vulpes vulpes*), which is also "the most widely distributed carnivore in the world."[18]

Kitsune are mentioned in the earliest Japanese texts, such as the *Nihonshoki,* where they seem to appear as omens, either good or bad.[19] But they have also been turning into beautiful women and attracting men since at least the ninth century, when one such affair was recorded in a setsuwa collected in *Miraculous Stories.* A man met "a pretty and responsive girl," married her, and the two had a son. At around the same time, their dog gave birth to a puppy, which insisted on barking at the wife. One day it startled her: "Terrified, she suddenly changed into a wild fox and jumped up on top of the hedge." In the end, the couple is forced to separate, but their love remains strong and the wife comes every night to sleep with the man, and from this, the text explains, we get the word *kitsune:* to come (*kitsu*) and sleep (*ne*).[20]

The etymology offered here is not generally taken seriously today, but such narratives of faithful and caring fox-wives are found throughout Japanese history, some more embellished than others. One from the *Tales of Times Now Past* is particularly elaborate. The year is 896, and a man named Kaya no Yoshifuji, who lives in the village of Ashimori in Bitchū Province, is left to his own devices when his "wife went up to the Capital, leaving him all alone. He was far too randy a fellow to stand this for long. One evening at twilight, he was out for a stroll when he spotted a lovely young girl he had not seen before, and wanted her right away. She tried to run when he grabbed at her, but he caught her and asked who she was. Very sweetly, she answered, 'Nobody.'"

Eventually Yoshifuji goes back with the girl to her house, an attractive home filled with servants. That evening, they sleep together: "He was so taken with her that he forgot all about his wife. As for his house and children, he never gave them a thought. He and the girl pledged each other eternal love." His new wife is soon pregnant, and when she gives birth, "Yoshifuji had not a care in the world."

Meanwhile, back at his human household, Yoshifuji's disappearance causes a great commotion and a thorough search is undertaken, but to no avail. His family prays, reads Buddhist sutras, and carves an image of an Eleven-Headed Kannon.

The narrative then cuts back to Yoshifuji's new home, where a man with a stick suddenly appears. Yoshifuji's new family runs away in terror, and the man pokes at Yoshifuji, forcing him out of a narrow passageway: "This was the thirteenth evening after Yoshifuji's disappearance. The people at his old home were still shaking their heads over what had happened when a strangely dark, monkeylike creature crawled out from under the storehouse nearby. What could it be? Through the jabber of the excited onlookers came a voice saying, 'It's me!' It was Yoshifuji." Yoshifuji explains about his wonderful new life and his new child. A servant is sent to investigate the storehouse, and foxes run off in every direction. Although there was little space under the storehouse, "that was where Yoshifuji had been. Obviously a fox had tricked him. He had married the fox and was no longer in his right mind." His thirteen days in the vulpine otherworld had seemed like thirteen years to him. A monk and an onmyōji are summoned to pray for him and exorcize him, and he is bathed over and over. When he "finally came back to himself he was horribly embarrassed," but he "lived on in good health another decade and died in his sixty-first year."[21]

The narrative is wonderfully complex, presenting different perspectives—a man's journey into the otherworld of the kitsune realm and, simultaneously, his family's search for him. The fox herself does not appear as a demonic and deceptive monster, but is more like an innocent victim of a man's libidinous desires. Yoshifuji's casual abandonment of his first wife, followed by the abandonment of his second (fox) wife, suggests that in the gender dynamics of the time, the status of women and foxes may not have been all that far apart. As with many setsuwa, the "moral" is not necessarily clear, but at least on one level we can interpret the tale as a warning not to take one's family for granted.

Another famous example, in which the narrative of love between fox and human inspires pathos, is the story of Abe no Yasuna, father of the great onmyōji Abe no Seimei. Yasuna was said to have married a white fox called Kuzunoha. The legend appeared at least as early as 1662 in a written work called *Abe no Seimei monogatari* (The tale of Abe no Seimei), but it garnered greater popularity through its later dramatization in both puppet theater and Kabuki. The most famous scene in the Kabuki version is the *henshin* (transformation) in which an actor performs a quick change from human to fox, a stunt that not only flaunted an actor's skill and the special effects of Kabuki but also played off the kitsune's notorious shapeshifting powers.[22]

Tales of *kitsune-nyōbo*, or fox-wives, were collected as late as the twentieth century. Yanagita Kunio, for example, records one from a rural part of Ishikawa Prefecture. A man went outside one night to use the outhouse, and when he came back he discovered that his wife had doubled—there were two of her in the room. They looked indistinguishable, and he could not decide which one was the real one and which one was a bakemono. He asked them all sorts of difficult questions, which they both answered with ease. Finally, he made the decision that one of them was just not quite right, so he chased her away and kept the other woman as his wife. In the years that followed, the household prospered and she gave birth to two boys.

One day, the boys were playing hide-and-seek, and they noticed that their mother had a tail! Now that her true nature had been discovered, the fox-wife could no longer stay with the family, and she departed in tears. But during planting season she appeared again, this time in her fox form, and circled the family's rice paddies. That year, and in succeeding years, the rice stalks appeared to be empty, and the tax collector determined that the family owed nothing. But when they cut the stalks, brought them into the house and peeled back the husks, they found that they were full of rice . . . and since they didn't have to pay taxes on their income, the family became wealthy.[23]

Inari Worship

The connection with rice cultivation in this narrative is no coincidence. In fact, kitsune are connected with the worship of Inari, the kami of the rice fields. Depending on the time and place, Inari has also been associated with farming, fishing, fertility, prostitution, and even warfare. Inari worship in some form has presumably existed since at least the Nara period, but it was not until the eleventh century or later that foxes became linked with it, and not until the Edo period that Inari shrines proliferated throughout the country—according to some statistics there may be almost forty thousand of them today.

The kitsune is not the Inari deity itself, but rather the messenger or attendant of Inari. And in this capacity, a pair of stone foxes typically stands guard in front of Inari shrines throughout Japan. The connection between Inari worship and the complex of beliefs associated with the kitsune of folklore is not straightforward, but it is clear that the two overlap and mutually influence each other, if not in religious doctrine than certainly in the popular imagination.[24]

Fox Possession

The kitsune's dangerous ability to possess or bewitch humans is generally known as *kitsune-tsuki* (fox possession). Instances of possession have been recorded from the time of *Miraculous Stories* well into the modern period. Historically, kitsune-tsuki took many forms and occurred for a variety of reasons. Although the term *kitsune-tsuki* is not actually used in the setsuwa about Yoshifuji mentioned earlier, certainly such a tale of obsessive and deluded love can be thought of as a possession story. More commonly, however, during kitsune-tsuki events a fox would take control of a person's body in order to communicate a message from the other-world or sometimes simply to torment him or her.[25]

There were various ways of dealing with a possession, but in many cases an exorcist would be called in and he would transfer the possession to a medium—as in this setsuwa:

> Once, someone in a certain house was possessed by a spirit, and when it had been transferred to a medium, it spoke through her, as follows: "I am no evil spirit, only a fox who happened to come wandering by. I have a young family at home in my den who were hungry, so I came in here because it seemed to me that in a place like this there would be some food lying about. Please give me a feed of rice-cakes and I'll go." The people of the house had some rice-cakes made and offered a trayful to the girl, who ate a few and said how delicious they were. "She only pretended it was a fox possessing her because she wanted some rice-cakes," grumbled the onlookers.
>
> The spirit then spoke again. "Will you please let me have some paper, so that I can wrap this up and take it home for the old lady and my children to eat." A large parcel of rice-cakes was wrapped up in two pieces of paper, and the girl stuffed it down inside her dress, with the end sticking out by her chest. She now said to the exorcist, "Drive me out and I'll go away." "Out, out!" he cried, and the girl stood up, after which she fell flat on her face. Presently she got up again and the parcel in her dress was missing.
>
> What a strange thing that it should have vanished![26]

Although the narrative presents a relatively frivolous—though still creepy—instance of possession, in other situations the life of the victim might be in danger or the fox might be acting out of revenge. *Miraculous Stories*, for example, tells about a monk who is called in to cure a sick man:

> As long as he chanted a formula, the patient was cured. If he stopped, however, the disease would return at once. . . . Making a vow to cure the patient at any cost, the monk continued chanting the formula. Then, possessed by a spirit, the patient said, "I am a fox. I won't surrender easily, so don't try to force me!" The monk asked, "Why?" The patient replied, "This man killed me in his previous life, and I am taking revenge on him."

Eventually, the patient dies, and a year later, one of the monk's own disciples is lying sick in the same room. A visitor comes to see the monk, and happens to tie his dog to a post. The monk sees the dog struggling hard against its chain and tells his visitor to set it free:

> As soon as the dog was released, it ran into the room of the sick disciple and came out with a fox in its mouth. Although the visitor tried to restrain the dog, it would not release the fox but bit it to death.
>
> It was evident that the dead person had been reborn as a dog to take revenge on the fox. Ah! Revenge knows no limits.[27]

Centuries later, the theme of possession, revenge, and dogs is still relevant. An Edo-period text, for example, reports that a man named Kakubē was taking a nap when a family of playful foxes disturbed him. He chased most of them away, but he caught and tormented one of the cubs, half killing it. Soon after this incident, Kakubē was possessed by the parent fox and fell into a state of madness and frenzy. A shugendō practitioner was called in, and he caused the fox "to borrow Kakubē's mouth." The fox explained that it was tormenting Kakubē because he had hurt its child. However, the fox continued, once in the past a dog was pursuing it and this same Kakubē chased the dog away. "It is because he tormented my child that I have possessed Kakubē in order to punish him," the fox said, "but since I owe him for helping me in the past, I will leave it at this." And with that, Kakubē seemed to wake up and return to himself.[28]

Symptoms of kitsune-tsuki varied. There are descriptions of "afflicted persons who ate gravel, ashes, hair, or combs, wandered the mountains and fields making piles of stones, jumped into rivers or ran into the mountains, etc."[29] In 1894, Lafcadio Hearn wrote, "Strange is the madness of those into whom demon foxes enter. Sometimes they run naked shouting through the streets. Sometimes they lie down and froth at the mouth, and yelp as a fox yelps."[30] Kitsune-tsuki (and other forms of possession) persisted throughout Hearn's time, and similar phenomena are still occasionally identified today. But during the Meiji period, modern Western medicine was called on to redefine fox possession as a form of mental illness treatable by psychiatrists. A German doctor named Erwin von Bälz (1849–1913) wrote the first Western scientific treatise on the subject, in 1885, giving it the medical label *alopecanthropy*—akin to lycanthropy, the belief that a person can become a wolf or werewolf.[31]

All these examples of fox possession entail a fox who chooses to enter the body or psyche of a person. But sometimes, it was thought, possession was caused by people who could send out spirit foxes at will to do their bidding. Known as *kitsune-tsukai* (fox-employers) or *kitsune-mochi* (fox-owners), such people were said to be members of hereditary lineages, families that passed the ability to control a fox from one generation to the next. In regions where this belief persisted, the position of fox-owners was troublesome: people identified as such were often individuals who came from wealthy families whose fortune was attributed by others to their devious manipulation of foxes against their enemies. These families were viewed negatively, their relationship with foxes considered a contagion that others wanted to avoid. In some places, instead of kitsune, other animal familiars could be employed in the same fashion; these included kitsune-like creatures called *osaki* and *kuda*, as well as snakes and dogs (known as *inugami*). While such beliefs are certainly not common anymore, cases of discrimination because of presumed fox-ownership were, as recently as the 1950s, noted in the news.[32]

Foxfire and Fox Weddings

The kitsune is a real animal that treads the borders between this world and that. This ambiguous character, and some of the traits that we have already seen, are clear in the *Three Realms* encyclopedia:

> For the most part, kitsune have a long life, and many have lived for several hundred years. . . . When a kitsune is suffering, its call is very much like the crying of an infant; when it is happy, it sounds like [somebody] beating on a hollow container. By nature, kitsune are afraid of dogs; if chased by a dog, the kitsune will most certainly emit a fart in its urgency. The odor is so bad that the dog cannot come closer. When a kitsune is going to transform itself, it will always place a skull [on its head], pray to the Big Dipper, and transform into a person. . . . It deceives people, attacking them and also exacting retribution. Kitsune like rice cooked with deep fried foods and azuki beans.[33]

One of the kitsune's favorite foods is *abura-age*, thin sheets of deep-fried tofu. Noodle shops throughout Japan today serve kitsune udon: udon noodles topped with abura-age. Additionally, abura-age can be formed into small pouches and filled with sushi rice to make a delicacy called *inari-zushi*, likewise named for its association with foxes.

The entry in the *Three Realms* also mentions another kitsune talent: "By striking its tail [against the ground], it causes fire to appear."[34] In fact, the kitsune's ability to make fire, known as *kitsune-bi*, or "foxfire," is an old explanation for mysterious fire balls that were occasionally seen. In some locations the fire was attributed to the kitsune's tail, and in other regions to its breath. The Ōji Inari Shrine in Tokyo was particularly famous for foxfire; it was said that kitsune from all over the area would congregate at the shrine every New Year's Eve. The foxfire they created could be seen for miles around, and based on its brightness the local humans would predict whether that year's harvest would be good or bad.[35]

Because of their relationship with fire, kitsune were sometimes blamed for actually starting fires. One setsuwa, for example, tells of a retainer for the governor of Kai who spots a fox one evening while he is heading home. He shoots the fox in the hindquarters with an arrow, and the fox, clearly in pain, manages to disappear. The man continues on his journey, but "a quarter of a mile from home he saw the fox running ahead of him carrying a flaming brand in its mouth. What could it be up to? He spurred his horse on. On reaching the house, the fox changed into a human being and set the house on fire. The retainer was ready to shoot as soon as he got within range, but the human changed right back into a fox and got away. The house burned down."[36]

Another phenomenon associated with kitsune is *kitsune-no-yomeiri*, a "fox's wedding." The expression is used to signify the seemingly contradictory weather phenomenon that occurs when the sun is shining while it is raining. It was at mysterious, paradoxical times like this that foxes got married, or alternatively, it was the mysterious powers of foxes that caused such paradoxical meteorological phenomena. In several records from the Edo period, people claim to have witnessed kitsune wedding processions. In one case, boat captains were employed to ferry what looked like a noble entourage, lit with lanterns, across the river. But in the morning, the captains discovered that the money they had received for their labor had transformed into nothing but leaves. This is a vivid example, but in most cases the phenomenon was noted simply as a procession of lights seen in the distance.[37] Parades of light may be rare these days, especially in

Figure 16. Kitsune and tanuki. Original illustrations by Shinonome Kijin.

well-lit urban areas, but even today whenever it is raining and the sun is shining, somebody is sure to mention that a fox is getting married.

TANUKI

Raccoon Dog

Tanuki are among the most common yōkai. Folktales and legends about them are found throughout Japan, and tanuki have long been a presence in literature and art, in children's books, and more recently in films, anime, manga, video games, and advertising. Generally they are characterized as supernatural trickster figures, often comical and mischievous but not necessarily murderous, though in some narratives they come across as vicious.

Tanuki are real animals: in English they are sometimes called badgers or, more accurately, "raccoon dogs." They are small, primarily nocturnal, omnivorous mammals that look like a cross between raccoon and possum. Native throughout East Asia, tanuki have spread to Scandinavia and much of northern Europe. They have a high rate of reproduction, as well as the ability to eat human-made foods and live close to human settlement. The tanuki is a beast of the borders, ecologically skirting the line between culture and nature.[38]

The traits of the animal tanuki are reflected in its yōkai image: tanuki seem to exist simultaneously in this world and the otherworld. In folklore they are tricksters, often portrayed as somewhat bumbling and potbellied, with a penchant for drinking sake, changing shape, and impersonating Buddhist monks. One of the tanuki's most famous characteristics is its gargantuan scrotum, which it employs for all sorts of creative shape-shift-ing—numerous woodblock prints and other images illustrate the powers of this magnificent paraphernalia. Accordingly, in contemporary Japan tanuki are fertility symbols, signs of prosperity and good fortune: in front of restaurants, bars, and sake shops, you can find a ceramic statuette of a plump, wide-eyed, cheerful tanuki standing upright and adorned with a straw hat, a jug of sake in one hand. On the streets of a modern city, the creature radiates a sense of joviality and traditional welcome.[39]

The first documented appearance of a tanuki-like creature is in the *Nihonshoki*, where it is called a mujina.[40] During the Heian and Kamakura periods, tanuki started appearing in setsuwa. *Tales from Uji*, for example, includes a story in which a mountain hermit, after years of deep devotion, begins to receive nightly visits from the Bodhisattva Fugen on his white elephant. One evening a hunter who brings food to the hermit is invited to witness the holy vision. But when Fugen appears, radiating a beautiful light, the hunter is suspicious. Why would he, a killer of animals, be per-mitted this glimpse of the divine? And so he fits an arrow to his bow and shoots at the image. The light goes out and a crashing sound is heard. In the morning, hunter and hermit follow a trail of blood to the bottom of a ravine where they find a dead tanuki with an arrow in its chest.[41]

Historically, tanuki are often associated with foxes or kitsune, and in some cases the two creatures are interchangeable; the term *kori*, which combines the kanji for kitsune and tanuki, was used to refer to all manner of supernatural occurrences.[42] Although generalizations are always diffi-cult, for the most part kitsune seem to be sly and dangerous creatures that assume the shape of a seductive woman; in contrast, tanuki are more comical, often taking on the shape of a pudgy monk or other not-so-seductive figure. As in the setsuwa related earlier, despite the temporary success of their transformations, tanuki often end up dead.

During the Edo period, the image of the tanuki as a ribald trickster and somewhat inept shape-shifter continued to develop. For example, the famous folktale "Bunbuku-chagama" (The lucky teakettle) concerns a tanuki's distinct inability to sustain its transformation. In one simple version of the tale, for example, a junk dealer asks a friendly tanuki to transform into a teakettle, which he does with no problem. The junk dealer then sells the kettle to a Buddhist priest, who puts the kettle on the fire. First the kettle complains about the heat, and then out pops the tanuki's face, feet, and "big fat tail," and the creature escapes into the mountains.[43] In more elaborate versions of the tale, an entrepreneurial priest ends up marketing the walking, talking teakettle as a moneymaking attraction. During the Edo period, this comical image of half transformation made for all sorts of wonderful imagery in wood-block prints and other visual forms.[44] As an animated household object, the teakettle is also reminiscent of tsukumogami.

Although the tanuki image from the Edo period onward was generally a lighthearted and even friendly one, occasionally the tanuki of lore could be quite nasty. The famous folktale "Kachi-kachi yama" (Crackling-fire mountain), for example, tells of a tanuki that not only kills and cooks an old woman in soup, but then transforms itself into the woman's shape to serve the soup to her husband. This tale, too, comes in hundreds of versions, some more graphic than others, but in most cases the murderous tanuki ends up experiencing a gruesome set of tortures: being set on fire, given a hot pepper salve to rub on its burns, and eventually drowning.[45]

The tanuki's shape-shifting talents are used not just to transform itself; it can also reshape the landscape. Many local legends, for example, concern somebody walking home after a night of sake drinking and getting hopelessly lost in familiar terrain that has been magically transformed by a playful tanuki. In some cases, this is because the tanuki uses its powers to create an elaborate optical illusion. In other cases, the mischief is of a more mundane nature: an early-twentieth-century legend, for example, tells of "a tanuki who is in the habit of throwing sand. When a person is passing through at night, the tanuki will rain down so much sand that the person will lose his way, and then the tanuki will guide him to a river or waterside and cause him to fall in."[46] Tanuki are also adept at leading people astray by imitating sounds, creating what we might call sonic mirages.

They are particularly notorious for making uncanny drumming noises by thumping their ample bellies (*hara-tsutsumi*).[47]

The tanuki can also be found in the Edo-period encyclopedic *Three Realms*, which describes its appearance and habitat and then casually mentions that "just like kitsune, old tanuki will often change shape [henshin] and become yōkai. They always hide in a hole in the ground and emerge to steal and eat grains, fruits, chickens, and ducks. . . . And also, they enjoy themselves by thumping on their bellies." The entry goes on to describe ways to cook tanuki and various uses for tanuki skin (particularly good for making bellows, apparently).[48]

But even as tanuki were being recorded with this sort of zoological detail, they continued to appear as characters in the spooky narratives of hyaku-monogatari, such as in this one:

> In Bishū, a samurai with a salary of two thousand *koku* had lost his wife. Every night, she was all he could think about. Then one night, when he set down his light and nodded off, his dead wife, beautifully made up and appearing exactly as she had in life, came to his bedroom. She looked [at him] longingly and made to get under the covers. Surprised, the samurai said, "Is it possible for a dead person to come back?" He grabbed her, pulled her toward him, and he stabbed her three times with his sword: she disappeared into thin air. His retainers rushed in, lit torches, and searched everywhere, but there was nothing. When morning broke, they discovered a trace of blood on the hole of the door latch. Thinking this was very strange indeed, they searched and found a hole in a grove located at the northwest corner of the property. They dug this up and found an aged tanuki, stabbed three times and lying dead.[49]

Tales of tanuki are too varied and numerous to generalize beyond noting that in the popular imagination of Edo-period Japan, the creature was at once a common everyday animal and a dangerous, vexing, and often comical shape-shifting yōkai. While sometimes tanuki appear as fleshed-out characters in a story, often they simply serve as default explanations for the otherwise unexplainable—odd sounds in the forest, a sense of being watched, and strange occurrences of all sorts.

During the Meiji period, tanuki continued to appear in oral tales and even, on occasion, made it into the newspapers. One widely distributed story was the legend of the phantom, or counterfeit, train (*nise-kisha*), in which tanuki articulate (futile) resistance to the steam train, perhaps the most pervasive symbol of modernizing Japan. Here is a version of the legend reported in the *Tōō Nippō* newspaper on May 3, 1889:

> Just before arriving in Okegawa [station, opened in 1885] one evening, a steam train that had left Ueno [in Tokyo] encountered another train, with its steam whistle blowing, advancing along the same tracks from the opposite direction. The train driver was surprised; he hastily reduced his speed and blew his whistle wildly. The oncoming train did the same, blowing its whistle insistently. However, the train that had appeared close [at first] did not seem to come any closer. When he fixed his eyes on it, the train seemed to be there but it also seemed not to be there; it was very unclear, so he increased his speed so much that he was going to crash into the other train. But the other train just disappeared like smoke, leaving not a trace. However, where it had been, two old tanuki the size of dogs were found lying dead on the tracks, having been hit by the train. Thinking they were terrible nuisances and now they would get their comeuppances, the driver skinned them and used the meat for tanuki soup. What a surprise that such a thing could occur these days, during the Meiji period.[50]

In this kind of legend, tanuki continue their role as shape-shifting yōkai living on the edge of human society. Well into the twentieth century, tanuki were the go-to explanation for anything strange—and in some areas of Japan, they still are. In my own research, I interviewed a man, then in his seventies, on an island in Kagoshima Prefecture. He told me a story he had heard as a "true story" when he was a child—the events would have taken place in the 1930s. Here is an abbreviated translation:

> Of course, there's absolutely no way there can be a train on this island. But in spite of that, this guy's asleep and, you know, in those days bathrooms were outside, so you had to put on geta and go outside or you couldn't use the toilet. . . . So this guy wakes up in the middle of the night and goes out to the toilet, . . . and he hears the *chiin, chiin,* sound of a train. He's never seen a train before, never even heard the *chiin, chiin,* sound of a train before. Only maybe he's heard about it in rumor—that the train goes *chiin, chiin,* . . . you know, he's just heard people talking about it. So he hears *chiin, chiin,* and believe it or not a train comes along. And he thinks, "Wow, that's a train," and he runs and leaps aboard. . . . And then the train gradually goes along the coast, and [he hears], "This is Jugoya-baba; are

there any departing passengers?" The guy thinks, I'm already on board so I may as well ride on to the last station. . . . The next stop is Kunboigawa, so [he hears], "This is Kunboigawa," and . . . then there's that shrine, Suwa-jinja, and they arrive there and it says, "Last stop, Suwa-jinja." In the old days there was a rocky shore there, so they get to the shore, and then the guy gets off and arranges the area, making a nice spot for himself.

Meanwhile, his wife [back home] is thinking, he went out for a piss and he hasn't come home yet. And they were just newlyweds, so she's wondering what could have happened, where could he have gone? So she calls the fire department and the search begins. The firemen search throughout the area, and when they find the guy, he tells them proudly, "Hey, I came out here by train."

That's the story. Nobody's sure what it was, but it was probably a tanuki. There are a lot of people tricked by tanuki, so it was most likely a tanuki for sure.[51]

Even though the story could be thought of as frightening—a man getting lost in the middle of the night and having to be rescued by the fire department—it was apparently related as a comical but true story. Interestingly, in some ways it is akin to the kamikakushi, or spiriting away, narratives more often associated with tengu. In this case, however, the tanuki appears once more as a shape-shifter who is more playful than harmful. This may be one reason that, as the twentieth century progressed, tanuki also became common commercial characters, appearing as ceramic figurines in front of shops and as mascot characters.

The tanuki continues to be visually represented today, in manga and anime, including Studio Ghibli's 1994 animated feature film, *Heisei tanuki gassen ponpoko* (*Pom Poko*, dir. Takahata Isao). The film takes place in the late 1960s, during a period of economic growth and urbanization, and tells of a community of tanuki living on the outskirts of Tokyo. Humans are planning to build a new suburb there, which will destroy the tanuki's native home. In a desperate attempt to stymie the human plan, the older tanuki teach the younger tanuki how to shape-shift, and together they create illusions and roadblocks to stop the construction of the suburb.[52]

The tanuki has also made a name for itself internationally. In Nintendo's Mario Bros. video game franchise, for example, there is a raccoonlike figure with various magical abilities called "Tanooki." A tanuki also appears

Figure 17. Tanuki demonstrating their shape-shifting talents and paraphernalia. Ichiyūsai Kuniyoshi (1797–1861). Courtesy of International Research Center for Japanese Studies.

as a big-balled protagonist in *Villa Incognito* (2003) by American novelist Tom Robbins.

Throughout its long history in Japan, the tanuki has constantly plied its trade as a shape-shifter. It has also shifted its shape with each historical moment to conform to diverse media and different social contexts. In today's Japan, it is simultaneously a real animal, a fun-loving supernatural trickster, and a mutable character for commercial and creative experimentation.

MUJINA

Similar to tanuki and kitsune, mujina are found throughout Japan and are known for causing mischief and for shape-shifting. In contemporary Japanese, *mujina* generally refers to a mammal called *anaguma,* or Japanese badger (*Meles anakuma*), which is found throughout much of the country, excluding Hokkaido. In some regions, however, *mujina* is also a local name for tanuki. Whether referring to a badger or a tanuki, legends about mujina tend to resemble legends about tanuki; in some cases the two creatures are interchangeable.[53]

The earliest reference to a mujina is found in an entry for spring of the year 627 in the *Nihonshoki:* a mujina appeared in Michinoku Province (in northern Honshu), where it transformed itself into a person and sang.[54] Numerous legends throughout Japan tell of mujina that turn into monks; various temples possess calligraphy and other art said to be the handiwork of a mujina.[55] Toriyama Sekien's mujina sits at an *irori* (sunken hearth), looking distinctly half human and half animal. The brief text compares the creature's shape-shifting talents to those of tanuki and kitsune, mentioning that the old mujina in the picture managed to sustain its monk disguise and carry out its duties all day until it nodded off after eating and "let its tail come out."[56]

Perhaps not coincidentally then, the *Three Realms* (citing the Chinese *Bencao gangmu*) explains that mujina "like to sleep. Even when people come close, they will not awaken; if a person sees this and bangs on a piece of bamboo, the mujina will wake up, but it will soon go back to sleep again."[57]

BĀBŪ

This is a general name for yōkai found on Kami-Koshikijima, a small island off the west coast of Kagoshima Prefecture. According to a book of local history and folklore, *bābū* refers to "a yōkai or frightening imaginary thing." In order to quiet crying children, people would say "the bābū is coming" or "the bābū is here."[58] I have not been able to find reference to bābū elsewhere, and this is just one example of an extremely localized yōkai. Examples of similarly rare or obscure creatures can be found throughout Japan, often recorded only by local scholars and providing evidence of the richness of regional variation and imagination.

KUBI-KIRE-UMA

Headless Horse

Kubi-kire-uma (also *kubi-nashi-uma*) is, as the name implies, a yōkai horse with no head. Folklore concerning the kubi-kire-uma is found in various places throughout Japan, but especially in Fukui Prefecture and the four prefectures of Shikoku. While legends of the kubi-kire-uma vary, these creatures are sometimes characterized as steeds on which deities ride when they come visiting on New Year's Eve or the Setsubun holiday. That is, like many yōkai and mysterious phenomena, kubi-kire-uma appear at moments of transition—in this case during the liminal time between the end of the old year and the start of the new.[59]

NUE

This hybrid creature appears in medieval texts, most famously *The Tale of the Heike* (Kakuichi text, composed 1371), where it is subdued by Minamoto no Yorimasa (1106–1180).

Most likely the *nue* originated in China and was considered a bird of some sort. Its earliest appearance in Japan is in the *Kojiki* and, soon after, in the *Manyōshū* poetry collection (eighth century). In the latter it is called *nue-dori* (nue-bird) and said to make a sad call in the forest at night; after the call of this strange bird was heard, purification ceremonies were performed in the palace.[60] The bird in question here is probably what is now called a *toratsugumi* (White's thrush, *Zoothera dauma*). The kanji for *nue* consists appropriately of two components: "night" and "bird."

The *Wamyō ruijū shō* (Japanese names for things classified and annotated; 931–938) describes the call of this bird as being a portent or omen. By the time of *The Tale of the Heike,* however, the nue had become a chimera-like hybrid made from the head of a monkey, the legs of a tiger, and a snake's tail, all linked by the inherently shape-shifting body of a tanuki.[61]

The episode in *The Tale of the Heike* describes two events in which Minamoto no Yorimasa, a warrior and poet, is called on to shoot a nue out of the sky. In the first instance, a black cloud was seen over the emperor's residence every night at the hour of the ox, and the emperor felt a sense of dread. When Yorimasa looks up into the cloud, he sees "in it a strange shape." He fits an arrow into his bow, and praying, lets it fly. He hits his mark:

> Everyone there brought up light
> for a good look at whatever it was:
> a monkey's head, a badger's body,
> a snake's tail, the limbs of a tiger,
> and a cry like that of a thrush.
> "Frightening" is hardly the word.[62]

Because of his success, Yorimasa gains a reputation as a subduer of strange monsters and goes on to kill another nue during the reign of a subsequent emperor.

In the fifteenth century, Zeami (1363–1443) composed a Noh drama in which the tale is expressed from the deeply sad perspective of the slain nue:

> Such aimless misery, my body a caged bird,
> My mind a blinded tortoise clinging to a floating log;
> Bogwood buried in the sightless back
> And yet not fully buried,
> Why should my spirit linger on?[63]

The forlorn nature of the nue's lament perhaps ties the nue to its earliest association, in the *Manyōshū,* as a bird with a sad call.

Figure 18. Nue, in the style of Toriyama Sekien. From *Kaibutsu ehon* (Edo period; artist unknown). Courtesy of International Research Center for Japanese Studies.

The nue does not seem to have been a common yōkai in local lore, but it was certainly well known. Sekien includes it in one of his catalogs, with the tip of its tail a vicious-looking snake's head. He mentions its association with the Yorimasa legend and also says simply that it lives deep in the mountains.[64]

RAIJŪ

Thunder Beast

The *raijū*, or thunder beast, is said to come down to earth with a lightning bolt during a thunderstorm; lightning scars on a tree were sometimes attributed to raijū. Although not the best-known yōkai today, raijū were exceedingly common during the Edo period: numerous documents, illustrations, and even mummified bodies record their appearance in regions throughout Japan. In these materials raijū come in a wide variety of sizes and shapes, ranging from squirrel- or weasel-like creatures to beasts more akin to dogs or large cats.[65]

Clearly, lightning and thunder were mysterious, frightening, transcendent phenomena for people in the past (and present), and it is not surprising that they were associated with deities and mysterious creatures. The exact relationship between raijū and thunder gods varies from region to region, but the direct inspiration for the raijū itself most likely came to Japan through China; scholars believe the Chinese materia medica text *Bencao gangmu,* imported to Japan in the early seventeenth century, was a primary cause of the plethora of raijū sightings and documentation later in the Edo period.[66]

To people during this time, Yumoto Kōichi suggests, the sky was completely unexplored territory. Whereas the depths of the ocean may have been hard to penetrate, human beings had a direct relationship with the sea and could make a living through fishing and diving. The sky on the other hand, though always present and visible, was simply not accessible. It was a place of the imagination, where otherworlds and mysterious phenomena were always possible.[67]

In the twentieth century, attempts were made to scientifically explain raijū as animals startled or knocked out of a tree by thunder and lightning.

Figure 19. Raijū and tsuchinoko. Original illustrations by Shinonome Kijin.

That is, the theory is that raijū may be a "misinterpretation" of a real animal, and various creatures have been nominated as the most likely model. One fairly recent theory posits that the creature is derived from a small, tree-dwelling animal called a *hakubishin*, a masked palm-civet (*Paguma larvata*), found in parts of China, Taiwan, and Southeast Asia. It is commonly believed that the hakubishin appeared in Japan only after World War II, when soldiers brought them back from Southeast Asia as pets and they escaped into the wild. Because Edo-period images of raijū bear a striking resemblance to these creatures, however, some scholars are now convinced that hakubishin have been in Japan since much earlier.[68] Whatever the case, the discussion inspires productive interaction between folkloric knowledge and scientific inquiry.

TSUCHINOKO

The *tsuchinoko* is a short, thick, snakelike creature. In some places, it is said to be poisonous or to continue living even after its head has been cut off. Perhaps its most distinguishing characteristic today, however, is simply its elusiveness, along with the quest this has inspired to prove whether it actually exists. In the language of cryptozoology (the study of "hidden animals"), tsuchinoko is a cryptid; or to use a Japanese categorization, it is a *UMA*—an unidentified mysterious animal.[69]

The word *tsuchinoko* can be interpreted variously, depending on the kanji, as "child of the earth" or, more commonly, "small mallet" or "mallet child," a reference to the creature's short, stocky shape, similar to that of a Japanese tool known as a *tsuchi*, which can be used as a hammer, mallet, or pestle. In fact, one kind of small pestle is actually called a tsuchinoko, and it is certainly likely that the name or shape of the yōkai and the name or shape of the tool are linked.[70] In addition to *tsuchinoko*, there are numerous regional names for the creature, including *gigi-hebi* and *bachi-hebi* (Akita Prefecture), *koro* and *koro-hebi* (Fukui Prefecture) and *tsuchi-korobi* (Tottori Prefecture), to mention just a few.[71] Another common variant is *nozuchi* (field mallet).

Since at least the Edo period, people have reported seeing or hearing about tsuchinoko. For example, an urban legend from the city of Kanazawa recorded in 1807 explains that there is a particular slope in the city where strange things have occurred. It is overgrown and somewhat spooky even in the daytime. One evening during a light rain, a man saw something moving along the slope in a rolling, tumbling fashion. On looking more carefully, he discovered that it was a kind of pestle, but as thick as a mortar and completely black. It was moving here and there. Then suddenly it let out a burst of laughter, made a sound like thunder, erupted in light—and disappeared. Several people had seen similar things in the past, and in each case the witness was ill for a few days afterward.[72]

The various different images and beliefs about tsuchinoko-type creatures came together in the 1970s during a so-called tsuchinoko boom. The boom was set off with the publication of a book called *Nigero tsuchinoko* (Tsuchinoko, escape; 1973) by Yamamoto Soseki (1919–1988), an angler and author who wrote about his own sighting of a tsuchinoko and collected eyewitness accounts from others. Yamamoto memorably described the creature he saw as looking like a beer bottle. Images in the book were picked up in manga and other mass media venues, and excitement about the tsuchinoko spread. The book was a key factor in making the name *tsuchinoko* into a generic label for all such snakelike creatures; it was also instrumental in transforming the tsuchinoko from yōkai (mysterious, supernatural) to UMA (real animal but hard to catch).[73]

In the opening years of the twenty-first century, there was another tsuchinoko boom, this one occurring when a farmer in a small town in Okayama Prefecture happened upon the remains of a mysterious creature. The discovery set off a frenzy in the mass media, with tabloid newspapers, magazines, and television shows stirring up excitement.[74] Eventually the body was examined by a biologist, who pronounced it "probably a *yamakagashi* [tiger keelback snake, *Rhabdophis tigrinus*] but not a normal one." The town itself had quickly become identified with the tsuchinoko (there had been earlier sightings as well), and today tsuchinoko is a local brand—you can, for example, buy tsuchinoko wine.[75]

8 Village and City

This chapter introduces yōkai associated with human settlements, such as cities, towns, villages, and suburbs—essentially any place people gather in large numbers. Again, such designations are necessarily vague: some of the yōkai listed in this chapter, such as hitotsume-kozō, are not associated with a particular kind of place and might just as easily be found in the rural setting of the countryside. On the other hand, tōfu-kozō and kamikiri seem to be cosmopolitan in their hauntings. Not surprisingly many yōkai here originally emerged during the Edo period, a time characterized by the intensive development of urban centers. Some, such as kuchi-sake-onna and jinmenken, haunt the modern cities and suburbs that developed during the rapid-growth period of the late twentieth century.

HITOTSUME-KOZŌ
One-Eyed Rascal

Hitotsume-kozō is a widely distributed yōkai distinguished, as its name implies, by having a single eye. This yōkai often assumes the size and shape of a young boy about ten years of age, and sometimes he has only one leg and a very long tongue. Translating the word *kozō* is difficult: although strictly speaking it refers to a Buddhist acolyte, it is also commonly used to signify a boy and sometimes has a slightly derogative or casual tone, as in "kid," "urchin," or "rascal." In the Edo-period merchant world, it also indicated a menial employee, such as an errand boy.

Narratives about hitotsume-kozō vary; in general he is not portrayed as particularly evil or deadly but is more like a troublesome mischief-maker. In some legends, he scares people by showing a face lacking a mouth and nose but having one large eye in the middle. Occasionally he uses his long tongue to lick people. There are, however, traditions that portray hitotsume-kozō in a more sinister light, as a bringer of disease and misfortune, a creature to be avoided at all costs. Particularly in the Kanto region, there was a belief that on certain days households were subject to visitation by hitotsume-kozō. In order to ward off this threat, residents put certain objects, such as bamboo baskets, outside their homes.[1] The word for bamboo basket, *mekago*, is constructed of the characters for *eye* and *basket*; one interpretation of its effectiveness against hitotsume-kozō is that because it has so many eyes (holes), it frightens off yōkai who have only one.[2]

In 1917, in one of his earliest essays on yōkai, folklorist Yanagita Kunio examined the widespread traditions concerning hitotsume-kozō in an attempt to trace an earlier, "authentic" set of Japanese beliefs. He claims in the essay, titled simply "Hitotsume-kozō," that "with only a little variation, this yōkai has crossed most of the islands of Japan." He goes on to present the "bold hypothesis" that the tradition of hitotsume-kozō represents a remnant of earlier customs involving human sacrifice.

Long ago, Yanagita contends, there were rituals in which a human was sacrificed. The victim would be selected through divination the year before the ritual was scheduled to take place, and "in order to distinguish him from the others, one of his eyes might be poked out. This person, who was to work in a sacred capacity, would be treated with a certain amount of hospitality and respect." Although "human knowledge advanced and such bloody rituals came to an end," Yanagita explains, the notion that a one-eyed person could receive sacred intelligence from the deities persisted. Many generations later, this connection between one-eyedness, the sacred, and the status of being doomed or outcast, would survive in the form of hitotsume-kozō:

一津目小僧

Figure 20. Hitotsume-kozō. Original illustration by Shinonome Kijin.

Like most obake, hitotsume-kozō is a minor deity that has become divorced from its foundations and lost its lineage. . . . At some point in the long distant past, in order to turn somebody into a relative of a deity, there was a custom of killing a person on the festival day for that deity. Probably, in the beginning, so that he could be quickly captured in the event of an escape, they would poke out one eye and break one leg of the chosen person. And then that person would be treated very favorably and afforded great respect. . . . After a while, [this sort of sacrificial rite] came to an end, and all that remained was the ritual in which the eye was poked out. . . . And in due course, the time came when putting out the eye became a superfluous procedure. . . . Meanwhile, it was long remembered that the sacred spirits [*goryō*] of the past had one eye; it is only natural that when this deity became separated from the control of the higher gods and started to wander the mountains, fields and roads, it came to be seen as exceedingly frightening.[3]

Although there is no actual evidence for Yanagita's assertion about the connection between human sacrifice and hitotsume-kozō, his comments are significant because they associate the sacred and godlike with the outcast, doomed, or deformed. Like so many yōkai, hitotsume-kozō is ambiguous: both worshipped and feared, held in reverence but also excluded, a deific liminal being doomed to wander on the edge of human society. Moreover, hitotsume-kozō also exhibits an imbalance—one eye and one leg—that sets it apart from "normal" human society; his visible physical disability hints at special invisible abilities. One-eyed monsters, such as the Cyclops of the Greek pantheon, and one-legged or lame beings with supernatural powers, are found in folklore from different cultures around the world.

ISOGASHI

Busy-Body

This is a gangly, sinewy yōkai, running with his head in the air and a huge tongue dangling out of his mouth. The name *isogashi* is evidently a play on the word *isogashii*, meaning busy or hectic, and this yōkai seems to be the incarnation of that particular state of being.

The isogashi makes only rare appearances. It is featured, complete with label, in the *Hyakkiyagyō emaki* (1832) by Oda Yoshi, owned by the

Figure 21. Isogashi. From an Edo-period picture scroll called *Hyakkiyagyō emaki* (artist unknown). Courtesy of International Research Center for Japanese Studies.

Matsui family in Kumamoto.[4] It appears alongside other yōkai in the scroll, but there is no explanation—just the name written in hiragana. A very similar creature, but with no name attached, can be found in another hyakkiyagyō emaki that is probably also from the late Edo period.[5] Again there is no explanation, but perhaps in the case of the isogashi no caption is needed: with its flailing arms and lolling tongue, this creature is clearly busy.

UBUME

Birthing Woman

The ubume is found in various forms throughout the country and in collections of ghost stories, religious texts, and other documents. Although details vary, she is most commonly thought of as an incarnation of a woman who has died during childbirth. She appears at a crossroads or on a bridge as evening falls, her lower body covered with blood, crying and cradling her infant in her arms. She asks a male passerby to hold the baby, and then she leaves. In his arms, the baby gradually gets heavier and heavier until the man cannot move at all for fear of dropping it. (In some versions, the baby turns into a stone.) Ubume narratives have many different outcomes, and it is not always clear what becomes of the baby or the woman; but at least in a number of legends, the man is rewarded for his efforts with great physical strength, a trait he passes down to his descendants.[6]

Ubume-related narratives and beliefs vary significantly from region to region, as does the specific name associated with her. In Shiga Prefecture, for example, there is an *ubume-tori*, and on Sado Island in Niigata Prefecture there is an *ubu*.[7] Textual portrayals of the ubume can be found as far back as the Heian-period *Tales of Times Now Past*.[8] During the Edo period, she is described in the 1687 *Kokon hyaku-monogatari hyōban*, and her image as a yōkai became solidified through illustrations in picture scrolls such as the *Hyakkai-zukan* and the *Bakemono zukushi* and in Toriyama Sekien's catalog. She also became a standard character in fiction and a popular trope in Kabuki drama, where she was one model for the ghost of Oiwa-san, the vengeful spirit who returns from the dead to haunt her cruel and cheating husband, in a famous play by Tsuruya Nanboku IV (1755–1829), *Tōkaidō Yotsuya Kaidan* (1825).[9]

Today the standard kanji characters associated with the ubume define the situation in which she died: 産女, literally "birthing woman."[10] Sekien, however, chooses characters with readings not readily associated with the pronunciation *ubume*, or with the image of a ghostly woman holding a baby, but rather with a legendary Chinese bird: *kokakuchō* (姑獲鳥). The kanji combination here is somewhat confusing, but the name seems to suggest, very loosely, something like: "bird on the hunt to become a surrogate mother." These same characters are found in the *Tales of Times Now Past*, and they are also used in an entry in the *Three Realms*, which pictures a small bird, called *taufūnyau* or, colloquially, *ubume-dori* (ubume bird), perched in a tree. With reference to earlier Chinese texts, the *Three Realms* explains that this bird becomes a woman when its feathers are removed: "Because this is the incarnation of a woman who has died in childbirth, she has breasts and likes to steal other people's children, raising them as her own."[11] When Sekien draws the ubume, he shows the woman from legend, standing in a river and clutching a baby to her breast, but he labels his picture with the "bird" characters, simultaneously referencing both Chinese precedents and Japanese legends.[12]

Figure 22. Ubume and nuppeppō. Original illustrations by Shinonome Kijin.

Death during childbirth was not uncommon before the modern period, and the ubume may be related to similar yōkai, most famously the *koso-date-yūrei*, or "child-rearing ghost." Found in many parts of Japan, legends tell of a mysterious woman who comes night after night to buy candy from a particular shop. Finally, one night the suspicious shopkeeper follows her. She disappears into a graveyard, and then he hears a baby crying. A grave is dug up and they find the corpse of a recently buried woman who had died during pregnancy. By her side in the grave is a live, healthy baby. In many of the legends, the baby grows up to be a prominent monk.[13]

As a yōkai, then, the ubume embodies grave and real concerns about pregnancy and safe delivery. She also represents the self-sacrificing spirit of motherhood. Various Buddhist temples in Japan today are associated with the ubume, safe childbirth, and motherhood; similarly, place-names throughout the country include the word *ubume*.[14]

Award-winning mystery writer and yōkai researcher Kyōgoku Natsuhiko draws on the image of the ubume and the theme of childbirth in his debut novel, *The Summer of the Ubume,* which was also made into a film of the same title in 2005 (dir. Jissōji Akio).[15]

NUPPEPPŌ

This yōkai looks like a somewhat amorphous fleshy blob, with fatty folds vaguely taking on the shape of eyes, nose, and mouth. It also has saggy, semiformed arms and legs, so it appears to be a kind of walking—or rather, staggering—lump of flesh. Despite this disgusting description, however, the *nuppeppō* is generally illustrated as somewhat cute and humorous.

The nuppeppō image can be found in Edo-period texts, including Sekien's *Gazu hyakkiyagyō* and emaki such as *Bakemono zukushi*, *Hyakkai-zukan*, *Bakemono emaki*, and *Hyakkiyagyō emaki*. However, none of these works explain the characteristics or behavior of the creature, and it does not appear in any known legends or beliefs during this time.

By the late twentieth century, presumably through the creative energies of Mizuki Shigeru, the character of the nuppeppō had become more fleshed out (pun intended). Mizuki explains, for example, that this yōkai (he writes "nuppefuhofu") is the "spirit of flesh" that haunts deserted temples; if a monk chooses to sleep in such a temple, he might be awakened by the creature walking through the hallways. The objective of its nocturnal wanderings is unknown, but since this yōkai may be "the flesh of a dead body walking by itself, it is not a particularly pleasant thing."[16]

The word *nupperi* (also *nopperi*) means "flat-faced," and it is likely that the nuppeppō derives its name or countenance, or both, from this connection. The idea of a flat or expressionless face also coincides with that of a related yōkai, the nopperabō, which may be a later, more developed version of the nuppeppō.[17]

NOPPERABŌ OR NUPPERABŌ

This yōkai looks like a human until you see its face, which is completely featureless, lacking eyes, nose, mouth, and any kind of expression—a face as smooth as an egg.

The iconic nopperabō legend is recounted by Lafcadio Hearn in *Kwaidan*. Late at night, a man was walking along the edge of a moat when he came upon a young woman crouching at the edge of the water, crying with her face in her sleeve. He asked what was wrong and if he could help, but she did not respond. Finally she turned around, "dropped the sleeve, and stroked her face with her hand;—and the man saw that she had no eyes or nose or mouth,—and he screamed and ran away." He saw a light up ahead, which turned out to be the lantern of a traveling soba-noodle stand, and "he flung himself down at the feet of the *soba*-seller" and tried to explain what he had seen. "'Was it anything like THIS that she showed you?' cried the soba-man, stroking his own face—which therewith became like unto an Egg. . . . And, simultaneously, the light went out."[18]

This type of tale is common. In Aomori Prefecture, for example, where the nopperabō is called a *zunberabō*, there is a story about a man walking through the mountains singing, who hears a voice singing the exact same song only more skillfully. He asks who it is, and a blank-faced zunberabō appears and says, "Me!" The man escapes to a nearby village and recounts his experience to an acquaintance there. The acquaintance asks, "Did that zunberabō look like this?" and turns to him with the same blank face. The man faints and, it is said, dies soon afterward.[19]

Similarly, in Higo Province (present-day Kumamoto Prefecture), this yōkai is called *nopperabon*. A man is traveling through the mountains, when night falls. He is relieved to see a lantern up ahead and calls at the house to see if he can stay for the night. An old woman comes to the door—with no nose, eyes, or mouth. The traveler runs in fright, coming eventually to a village. When he describes his encounter to a young woman there, she asks whether that "bakemono looked like this"—and shows him her blank face.[20]

In the Hearn story quoted earlier, Hearn never mentions the name *nopperabō*. In fact, he calls the short narrative "Mujina," a reference to a tanuki-like creature with a reputation for shape-shifting mischief. While Hearn's use of *mujina* here may be misleading, in many regions nopperabō is indeed attributed to the machinations of shape-shifting animals, such as mujina, kitsune, and tanuki. In the 1994 anime *Pom Poko*, tanuki enact a scene reminiscent of the one portrayed by Hearn; the victim in this case is a policeman, who runs for help to a convenience store—an updated version, perhaps, of Hearn's soba stand.

The nopperabō is most likely related to the nuppeppō, though the key difference here is that the nopperabō has a head and face (but no features on it), in contrast to the nuppeppō, who has no body but *just* a face. Both *nupperi* and *nopperi* mean "flat-faced." The suffix *bō* literally refers to a monk but can also indicate a young boy; here (and in other examples) it seems to anthropomorphize (or yōkai-ify) the thing being described—that is, the nopperabō is the personification of facelessness.[21]

In Miyazaki Hayao's film *Spirited Away*, there is a being called a "kaonashi," literally "no-face." There are no folkloric records of a yōkai with this name and exact description, but it may be at least in part inspired by the nopperabō.

KAMIKIRI OR KAMIKIRI-MA

Hair Cutter or Hair-Cutting Demon

Kamikiri (also *kamikiri-ma*) refers to a strange phenomenon in which a person's hair is suddenly cut. It was documented especially during the Edo period in collections of urban legends and other contemporary observations, such as *Shokoku rijindan* (1743) and *Mimi bukuro* (1814).

In *Shokoku rijindan*, for example, poet Kikuoka Senryō (1680–1747) reports that during the early Genroku period (1688–1704) men and women walking home at night might suddenly have their hair cut off right at the point where it was tied. This occurred all over Japan but was particularly common in Matsuzaka City (in current-day Mie Prefecture). Some people would not even realize their hair had been cut off, and it would remain lying in the street. In one case, it was not until a woman arrived home that people told her her hair was gone—at which point she fainted in terror. The phenomenon was also reported in several places in the city of Edo, where the victims were female shop employees.[22]

Miyata Noboru notes other instances of kamikiri attacks throughout the Edo period, labeling it a "serial crime" and pointing out that most victims of kamikiri were young women, and that the incident usually occurred at twilight. One explanation at the time was that it was caused by "a demonic wind blowing in from a foreign place [*ikoku*]," and that to counter it you had to call on the winds of the deity of Ise to protect you. Apparently, spells were intoned to this effect, and some women would write out the words of the prayer on a piece of paper they inserted into their hairpins.[23]

Various other explanations were offered. It was suggested, for example, that this might be caused by kitsune. In *Mimi bukuro*, Negishi Yasumori (1737–1815) explains that in one particular neighborhood three women had their hair cut off. Finally a wild fox was caught and its belly sliced open. They found female hair inside.[24]

Another common explanation takes the strange *phenomenon* of having one's hair cut and transforms it into a strange *creature* that does the cutting. Specifically it was said that the culprit was a *kamikiri-mushi*, a "hair-cutting insect."[25] Although there are no eyewitness accounts of this insect-yōkai, it was visualized in Edo-period picture scrolls such as *Bakemono zukushi* and *Hyakkai-zukan*, where it was shown in action with a devilish birdlike face, a pincer hand, and a lock of freshly cut hair falling to the ground. Toriyama Sekien does not include a kamikiri in his catalogs, but does draw a scorpion-like yōkai labeled *amikiri*, or "net cutter." Significantly, the amikiri comes right after his image of a kamaitachi, a yōkai similarly known for its ability to cut.[26] One possible reason for the association of kamikiri with the insect world stems from its similarity in sound to *kamakiri*, the Japanese word for a praying mantis—a large insect that seems ready to attack with scythelike (*kama*) front limbs, and which is in fact carnivorous.

It is worth noting also that hair has long been symbolically significant in Japanese culture. In Heian-period texts such as *The Tale of Genji*, long luxurious female hair projected beauty, sexuality, and wealth. In *Genji*, as well as later military tales such as *The Tale of the Heike*, both women and men cut off their hair on becoming Buddhist nuns or monks. The phrase "cut off one's hair" became a kind of shorthand for taking religious vows and renouncing the material world. At other times, too, such as the *genpuku* coming-of-age ceremony held to celebrate a boy's initiation into manhood, cutting off hair represented a symbolic change in status. Throughout the Edo period, hair also revealed a great deal about people: women's hairstyles could vary with age, marital status, social position, and employment. For men, the topknot (*chonmage*) transmitted information on status, profession, and lineage. All this is to say that the kamikiri resonated meaningfully in Edo society: having your hair cut suddenly and without your knowledge would have been a violent physical and symbolic experience.

Figure 23. Kamikiri and tōfu-kozō. Original illustrations by Shinonome Kijin.

TŌFU-KOZŌ

Tofu Boy

This yōkai seems to have appeared suddenly during the An'ei period (1772–1781), particularly in the popular literary form of kusazōshi, especially the illustrated books known as kibyōshi, or "yellow covers." Tōfu-kozō flourished during this time, lingered into the Meiji period, and then was forgotten, reemerging only recently as scholars began to explore kibyōshi and similar texts.[27] There is no known folkloric evidence of the tōfu-kozō; he appears to be a character born within the popular literature and mass media of the Edo period.

Even within this context, however, tōfu-kozō assumed a variety of appearances. Most typically he was pictured as a small boy, often with an oversized head, wearing a bamboo rain hat and holding a block of tofu, as if delivering it or offering it to somebody. There are variations on this: in some cases he has a single eye (like hitotsume-kozō), or is sticking out his tongue, and sometimes he has claws instead of feet. One of the most common, if not defining, features is a Japanese-maple-leaf (*momiji*) shape imprinted on the side of the tofu he is offering. In general, he is comical and cute, and as literature scholar Adam Kabat points out, no matter what story you read, tōfu-kozō is never portrayed as being explicitly bad. Rather there is something a little lonely about him; he is often shown walking behind people who don't seem to want to talk with him.[28]

Because of his sudden appearance in the second half of the eighteenth century, the origins of this little creature remain an intriguing mystery; he may have been born of a play on words of some sort, or he may have first been promoted as an advertising mascot. He also may be a topical reference to a now forgotten popular sensation or news event.[29] One unusual recent theory suggests a connection between tōfu-kozō and an Edo-period smallpox epidemic that claimed the lives of numerous children and often left survivors pockmarked and occasionally blinded. Because the cause of the illness was not readily understood, a variety of folk remedies were employed, including the use of particular colors and designs that were believed to ward off the smallpox god (hōsō-gami). Similar design patterns can be found on the tōfu-kozō's clothing as it is illustrated in kibyō-shi texts, suggesting that he may have developed as a popular-culture parody of the smallpox god, or perhaps he was a charm to protect against the illness.[30] Whatever his origins, the tōfu-kozō took on a life of his own as an odd little character who seemed to take pleasure in surprising people with his offer of tofu.

NEKOMATA
Split-Tailed Cat or Forked Cat

BAKENEKO
Monster Cat or Goblin Cat

There are numerous examples of yōkai cats in Japanese folklore, where they are portrayed as everything from lighthearted tricksters to vicious monsters. Presumably the quiet, intelligent mien of the cat, along with its stealthy prowling behavior and powerful vocal abilities, contributes to a sense of mystery and otherworldliness. In Japan, like many places in the world, cats seem to occupy an ambiguous position in human lives; they sit calmly, purring, on our laps one minute and go off chasing rats the next. They are both domestic and wild, comfortable in either urban or rural environments, simultaneously an intimate part of the human world and part of the natural world. Perhaps it is not surprising that cats, both feral and domestic, play an important role in yōkai folklore.

One common cat yōkai, the *nekomata,* is characterized by a forked tail. It was said that when a cat reached a certain age, its tail would bifurcate and it would begin acting in a dangerous and suspicious manner. One early nekomata story, from the year 1233, tells of a creature with eyes like a cat and a body like a large dog. It devoured seven or eight people in a single night.[31] In many cases nekomata are described as exceedingly large cats living in the mountains and forests, but they are also found in populated cities and towns.[32]

Toriyama Sekien illustrates a nekomata in his first catalog; it stands on two legs on the outer veranda of a house, with a small towel (*tenugui*) on its head. Another cat—presumably not a yōkai—sits on the ground below it, while a third seems to be looking out from inside the house. Although Sekien does not explain anything here, the nekomata is portrayed as betwixt and between the human and natural worlds. It is wild but wears a towel on its head, stands on two legs like a person, and is perched literally on the outer edge of a human habitation, with one cat outside (feral?) behind it and another inside (domestic?) in front of it. The fact that there is no commentary suggests that the nekomata was such a commonly recognized yōkai that explanation was not necessary.[33]

Another yōkai cat is called *bakeneko,* which might be loosely translated as "monster cat." While bakeneko generally look no different from regular cats—no split tail like a nekomata—their monstrousness is similarly attributed to age. In some parts of Japan it was said that a pet cat kept longer than a certain number of years (the exact number varied by location) would kill its master or, more commonly, turn into a bakeneko and perform all sorts of mischievous acts. Such misbehavior might be comical—speaking in a human voice, for example, or dancing around with a towel on its head—or it might be terrifying, such as turning into a human, molesting travelers, possessing people, or manipulating the bodies of the dead.[34]

The most famous bakeneko narrative is "Nabeshima no bakeneko sōdō" (The disturbance of the bakeneko of Nabeshima), a legend that developed

Figure 24. Nekomata, in the style of Toriyama Sekien. From *Kaibutsu ehon* (Edo period; artist unknown). Courtesy of International Research Center for Japanese Studies.

from a succession dispute, known as the Nabeshima Disturbance, that occurred in Hizen (present-day Saga Prefecture) in the late 1500s. Some versions of the Nabeshima legend are simple tales of revenge, while others recount a complex plot featuring a demon cat in the guise of a woman who is foiled only by the intense loyalty of one of the Nabeshima clan retainers. The narratives themselves probably did not originate until the late Edo period, long after the original disturbance, but they became popular through sensationalist Kabuki and *kyōgen* plays, as well as through woodblock-print illustrations. In the twentieth century, versions of the tale were made into movies, such as *Hiroku kaibyō-den* (*The Haunted Castle*, 1969, dir. Tanaka Tokuzō).[35]

KUDAN
Human-Faced Bovine

The *kudan* is a cow or bull with the face of a human. Upon being born it will utter a prophecy and then die. It is said to appear at times of social upheaval or rapid change, and its prophecy often concerns a natural disaster or an epidemic of some sort. The prophecy is guaranteed to come true. Kudan are quintessential examples of what Yumoto Kōichi calls "prophesy beasts" (*yogenjū*).[36]

Evidence of the kudan is first found during the Edo period, when it is mentioned primarily in *kawaraban* newssheets. The earliest known reference is to a prediction made in 1705 about the harvest for the following year. A famous 1836 kawaraban, complete with line drawing of a bull with a human face, explains that the newssheet itself can be posted in the house, where it will ward off evil and bring good fortune.[37] In other words, the kudan itself may be an omen of bad things to come, but the *representation* of the kudan on paper is, in the parlance of religious studies, apotropaic—it can protect against these very things.

Along with images of kudan, physical representations (made through skillful manipulation of the carcasses and skins of cows or pigs) and mummified bodies were displayed at misemono spectacle shows. Kudan appeared throughout the Meiji period, during times of epidemic and hardship, and even during World War II, when a rumor circulated that one had predicted Japan would lose the war.[38]

The kanji that signifies *kudan* (件) is constructed of two parts perfectly indicating its hybrid nature: 人 meaning *person* and 牛 meaning *cow* or *bull*. This character is commonly found in Edo-period deeds and legal agreements, where the phrase *kudan no gotoshi* was used as a pledge meaning roughly: "It is guaranteed to be as stated here." Literally

Figure 25. Kudan and nurarihyon. Original illustrations by Shinonome Kijin.

translated, however, the phrase reads, "Like the kudan," presumably a reference to the fact that what the kudan says is guaranteed to come true. Scholars suspect that the phrase, and the kanji character itself, may have preceded the yōkai. In other words, the character, made from the elements for *human* and *bovine*, inspired wordplay in which the yōkai—constructed from human and bovine elements—was imagined.[39] Given this use of the phrase in legal contracts, the kudan's prophecies would be, as it were, legally binding.

NURARIHYON OR NŪRIHYON

There is some confusion about the exact identity of the nurarihyon. An image of a big-headed, bald, monklike figure appears under this name in Sawaki Sūshi's *Hyakkai-zukan* of 1737; Sekien also draws a similar image in his first catalog almost forty years later. It is possible that Sekien's original name for this yōkai was *nūrihyon,* with *nurarihyon* being a later misreading.[40]

Neither of the images mentioned here has a description, so the nature of the creature is uncertain. In recent years, however, the nurarihyon seems to have acquired various characteristics: particularly his role as a leader of yōkai, and his tendency to sneak into your house and drink your tea. This is, for example, how Mizuki Shigeru describes the nurarihyon in one of his many compendia.[41] These traits, however, are not found in known folklore or documentary materials, and their origins are difficult to trace. Tada Katsumi points out that in 1929, folklorist Fujisawa Morihiko (1885–1967) labeled an image of nurarihyon with the caption "leader of yōkai" (*yōkai no oyadama*). Fujisawa provides no explanation or rationale for this designation, but ever since that time nurarihyon has occupied this leadership role.[42]

A somewhat different yōkai, too, goes by the name of *nurarihyon*. This one is an ocean yōkai reported in the Okayama area. The name presumably comes from onomatopoetic interpretations of its actions: a spherical object like a human head is seen bobbing in the water; when sailors reach out to seize it, the object slips away (*nurari-to*) and disappears under the waves, only to bob up (*hyon*) a few seconds later. This happens over and over again.[43]

Similarly, in a standard Japanese dictionary, the word *nurarihyon* is described as being synonymous with *nurarikurari*, which refers to something (or somebody) with no place to grab onto. In this case, *nurarihyon* is written with the characters for "slippery" and "gourd," and an analogy is made to a famous Japanese proverb about the futility of attempting to catch a catfish with a gourd.[44] It is possible that this word for a hard-to-grasp slippery thing is entirely unrelated to the monk figure illustrated by Sawaki and Sekien; however, one might easily imagine a connection between the elusive bobbing object in the ocean and a slick, bulbous-headed (catfishlike) yōkai who slips in and out of your house. Certainly the idea of something that is definitely there but ultimately ungraspable is a tempting metaphor for yōkai in general—perhaps one of the reasons nurarihyon has come to be a leader in the pantheon.

Indeed, despite or perhaps because of its elusiveness, the nurarihyon is a darling of modern mass media. Mizuki features one as a recurring character in his manga and anime, and more recently he has become the title character for a manga series by Shiibashi Hiroshi called *Nurarihyon no mago* (Grandchild of nurarihyon). The series commenced publication in 2008 in the manga magazine *Shūkan shōnen janpu* (*Weekly Shōnen*

Jump) and has since been made into a television anime series; it is also popular in its English-language translation as *Nura: Rise of the Yōkai Clan.*

TOIRE NO HANAKO-SAN
Hanako of the Toilet

Toire no Hanako-san is a ghostly girl who haunts school bathrooms. She is the protagonist of a popular contemporary legend that has circulated widely throughout Japan since at least the 1980s, though there are also older variants. Details differ from school to school, but typically it is said that if you go to the girls' bathroom on the third floor and knock three times on the door of the third toilet stall, a girl's voice will answer. In some versions, the door swings open but nobody is there. Sometimes it is explained that Hanako will answer if you call her name or say, "Hanako-san, let's play!" And in some versions, Hanako does appear: a little girl with a bob haircut, dressed in a white blouse and red skirt.[45]

Common to many versions of the legend is the emphasis on the number three, and one alternate name for the girl yōkai is "Hanako-san of the third [toilet]" (*Sanbanme no Hanako-san*). An old variant of the legend from 1948 (collected in Iwate Prefecture), for example, explains that among the students of a particular elementary school there was a taboo about using the third toilet in the bathroom behind the gymnasium: "If you went in there and called, 'Hanako-san of the third,' a large white hand would suddenly reach out of the toilet."[46]

The other critical element of the legend, of course, is the bathroom. In fact, bathrooms are surprisingly common sites for yōkai encounters. Legends of kappa reaching their hands out of outhouse toilets, for example, are found throughout Japan. In many ways the bathroom is a dangerous liminal space, exactly the sort of no-man's-land that yōkai like to frequent. In particular a school bathroom is *shared*, and in this sense it is very public; at the same time, however, it is also the most private of spaces, in which a person literally exposes herself. Moreover, a toilet—with its hole leading to somewhere else—can be thought of as a kind of portal to another world. The bathroom, then, is a distinct space in the school, with its own special function (and its own special odors); it is a space of vulnerability and transition and potential danger.

Schools, too, are particularly vital spawning grounds for spooky lore and yōkai legends, so much so that in the last thirty years an entire genre of eerie story has grown up around them. In the 1980s and 1990s, folklorist Tsunemitsu Tōru (b. 1948) collected and analyzed many of these so-called *gakkō no kaidan*, or "eerie tales of the schoolhouse," leading eventually to a number of books, television series, and several films. The legend of Toire no Hanako-san was also made into a manga and two hit films in the 1990s; a new film was released in June 2013.[47] As with most contemporary legends, there is a feedback loop between popular-culture depictions of the legend (and character) and the oral narratives related in local schools, with students incorporating details from manga and movies into the word-of-mouth versions and vice versa.

The school environment functions as a small community, with each set of students representing a different generation; legends are passed from one generation to the next, reinterpreted and re-created in accordance with the needs and anxieties of the current group of students occupying the school. In some variants of the Hanako legend, Hanako is described as the ghost of a student who died. In this context, she becomes a kind of ancestral spirit, the belief in her existence transmitted through time and across generations.

The legend might also be analyzed in terms of the anxieties of the young girls who commonly tell it. In middle school and the upper grades of elementary school, presumably many girls are concerned about puberty and menstruation—physical experiences that can be frightening and mysterious, and that they may confront in the school bathroom. Perhaps it is no coincidence that when Hanako-san does appear, her skirt is bright red, the color of blood.[48]

ROKUROKUBI

Pulley Neck

NUKEKUBI

Removable Head

The rokurokubi appears as a normal woman whose head can become completely detached from her body or, alternatively, remain attached by a long threadlike neck. In either case, the head has the ability to fly around and act of its own accord. During the Edo period, narratives about rokurokubi appeared in several hyaku-monogatari collections and other texts, and Toriyama Sekien includes an image in his *Gazu hyakkiyagyō*. Although rokurokubi are usually portrayed as female, there are also male rokurokubi and occasionally even an entire family of them.

The idea of a rokurokubi with a fully detachable head most likely came from Chinese folk and literary sources. The *Three Realms*, for example, references several Chinese texts that describe a "flying-head tribe," glossed as *rokurokubi*, living in parts of China and Southeast Asia. At night, their heads separate from their bodies and, with ears flapping like wings, fly around chomping on insects; in the morning the heads reattach themselves.[49]

The word *rokuro* refers to a pulley, a device that facilitates the extending or retracting of a rope or cable. In Japan, visual images of the rokurokubi generally show the neck stretching and swirling in a snakelike fashion, while the head is never completely separated. During the Edo period, lighthearted narratives of rokurokubi appeared in numerous illustrated kusazōshi texts; sometimes she is paired with mikoshi-nyūdō, a male yōkai endowed with an elongated, elastic neck.[50] The rokurokubi has long provided a fascinating subject for visual artists, including Kawanabe Kyōsai and Mizuki Shigeru. More recently, she has appeared in films, where computer graphics extend the imagistic possibilities of her stretchable neck.

In *Kwaidan*, Lafcadio Hearn records a compelling story of a rokurokubi or nukekubi encounter, the first extended discussion of this yōkai in English. A samurai-turned-wandering-priest finds himself staying the night with a woodcutter and his family. After reciting prayers until late into the night, the priest gets up to get some water to drink and discovers the woodcutter and his family lying in their sleeping room, with no heads! He realizes that he has "been lured into the dwelling of a Rokuro-Kubi." Sneaking outside, he sees the heads flitting around and eating worms and insects. He also overhears them discussing how delightful it will be to devour the "traveling priest." Fortunately, however, he recalls an old text in which it is written that if you "remove the body to another place, the head will never be able to join itself again to the neck. . . . When the head comes back and finds that its body has been moved, it will strike itself upon the floor three times,—bounding like a ball,—and will pant as in great fear, and presently die."[51] Using his cunning, as well as his great strength, the priest escapes with his life and a souvenir head.

The notion of a detachable head that flies around at night while the body sleeps or is otherwise unaware of what is going on may be related to a belief that the spirit can become separated from the body. As early as the Heian period, narratives tell of *ikiryō*, spirits of living people who detach from their bodies to possess others or wreak havoc, all without the knowledge of their owners. This is most famously portrayed in Murasaki Shikibu's *The Tale of Genji;* in a series of disquieting episodes, the spirit of the jealous but still-very-much-alive Lady Rokujō slips from her body to haunt and torment her rivals—all without her own knowledge. The case of the rokurokubi also raises profound philosophical questions about the seat of the spirit and the intellect—whether a "person" is defined as head or body or as a perfect linking of both.

KUCHI-SAKE-ONNA

Slit-Mouthed Woman

Kuchi-sake-onna, literally "slit-mouthed woman," is the name of a modern female yōkai. She is the protagonist of a contemporary legend that first appeared at the end of 1978 and spread throughout Japan within a few months. As with all such legends, there are many variations, but the basic narrative describes her as an attractive young woman, perhaps in her twenties or early thirties, who wears a white mask over her mouth, a common practice in Japan for somebody with a cold. In the case of the kuchi-sake-onna, however, the mask covers up a mouth hideously slit from ear to ear. She stands on an urban or suburban street, often at dusk, and approaches children on their way home from school:

> This woman with a white mask and long hair would come from behind and tap you on the shoulder. When you turned to look, she would ask, "Am I pretty?" [*Watashi kirei?*] If you said, "Yes, you're pretty," she would ask, "Even like this?" [*Kore demo?*], and remove the mask and threaten you. Or if you said, "You're not pretty," she would come chasing after you. When I parted with my friends on the way home from school, and it was getting dark, I would be frightened if I thought about it.[52]

Figure 26. Rokurokubi and kuchi-sake-onna. Original illustrations by Shinonome Kijin.

For six months, the legend traveled throughout Japan, assuming local characteristics wherever it went, scaring children walking home from school alone, and reportedly inspiring extra police patrols in some locations.[53] The basic story became so well known that even today the phrases *Watashi kirei?* and *Kore demo?* can have an eerie ring to them.

Many attempts have been made to link kuchi-sake-onna to earlier demonic female yōkai in Japan, and certainly one can find connections with ubume, yuki-onna, yamamba, and others. The sudden reveal of her hideous mouth may even be related to the *gabu*, a type of mechanical head used in Bunraku puppet theater since the Edo period: with a pull of a string, an attractive female face turns demonic, complete with a slit mouth, sharp teeth, and sometimes horns. Additionally, the ear-to-ear slit-mouth motif is sometimes found in descriptions of both oni and yamamba. Whatever her precedents, however, the kuchi-sake-onna was first documented in Gifu Prefecture in December 1978; by June 1979 there were reports in every prefecture.[54] According to one set of statistics, some 99 percent of children in Japan were aware of the legend in one form or another.[55]

As the kuchi-sake-onna narrative traveled through the country, it took on local characteristics and was often set in streets and neighborhoods familiar to the tellers. The story itself also became more and more elaborate. Sometimes the kuchi-sake-onna carried a scythe or a knife and threatened to slit her victim's mouth to make it like hers. Her behavior might depend on the way you answered the question *Am I pretty?* Often the only way to escape was to respond with an ambiguous "So-so."

She also acquired various personality traits and backstories. It was said that she was fond of a hard candy known as *bekkō-ame*. She had once been an Olympic athlete and could run extremely fast. But you could escape her if you ran into a record shop or repeated the word *pomade* (*pomādo*) three times. The number three appears again and again in the legend cycle— there are sometimes three kuchi-sake-onna sisters, for example, and the kuchi-sake-onna is often associated with place-names containing the character for "three" (e.g., Sangenjaya, Mitaka).[56]

Versions of the legend include explanations for her slit mouth, often attributing it to a horrible mistake incurred during cosmetic surgery:

> The kuchi-sake-onna came into being because there was this very beautiful woman, but she was concerned that her mouth was too small so she went to a certain cosmetic surgery clinic and had an operation. But there was a mistake with the operation to make her mouth larger, and the instant she saw her face after the operation, she went insane and became the kuchi-sake-onna. Usually she wears a large mask and asks people "Am I pretty?" If they say "Yes," she will remove the mask, say, "Even like this?" and show her mouth. If you see that and try to escape, she will come after you, and kill you with a scythe. She is exceedingly fast and can soon catch anybody, but she has the weakness of not liking the odor of pomade, so if you say "pomade," it is said that you can escape her.[57]

And from Kanagawa Prefecture:

> There are three sisters. The oldest had cosmetic surgery, and mistakenly her mouth was slit open. The second sister was in a traffic accident and her mouth was slit open. Because of that, the youngest sister went insane, slit open her own mouth, and was put into a mental hospital. She escaped and

has appeared in town. Her hair is long, she always wears a mask, and [she] holds a scythe in one hand. If you give her candy [bekkō-ame], she won't chase after you. Or if you say "pomade" you can run away.[58]

There are many descriptions of the kuchi-sake-onna's image and behavior, but several motifs are common: (1) she is a young woman, (2) her mouth is slit from ear to ear, (3) she asks, "Am I pretty?" and (4) her mouth is covered by a mask, the removal of which is frightening. Although methods of escape, types of weapon, clothing, and so on all vary, these four elements seem key to her identity and to the storyline of the legend.

One reason the legend spread so rapidly is that the kuchi-sake-onna became a media darling: in addition to being spread by word of mouth, her story was broadcast nationwide on television and late-night radio and discussed in weekly magazines and sports tabloids. The legend seems to have reflected real social concerns, such as the alienation children might feel while growing up in a world of concrete apartment complexes. It has also been suggested that she represented a monstrous version of an "education mama," a term for an overly enthusiastic mother who pressures her children to do well in school.[59] I argue that the mask also symbolizes awareness of environmental illnesses, since at the time such masks were occasionally worn to protect against air pollution. This practice is even more prevalent today in Japan and other (especially Asian) countries, where masks are used to filter out polluted air and allergens.[60] Moreover, during the 1970s the women's liberation movement became more and more active in Japan, so the legend's appearance at this time might reflect social anxieties over changing roles for women.[61]

The commotion over the kuchi-sake-onna died down after about six months, but by that time she had already become a permanent member of the yōkai pantheon, an example of a modern urban-suburban monster. She has been famously illustrated by Mizuki Shigeru, of course, and has appeared in numerous other manga and anime. She has also surfaced in Korea (wearing a red mask) and, more recently, become a film star, mentioned in the blockbuster horror movie *Ringu* (*Ring*, 1998, dir. Nakata Hideo) and featured as the protagonist of a series of Japanese horror movies (*Kuchi-Sake-Onna* [*Carved: The Slit-Mouthed Woman*], dir. Shiraishi Kōji, 2007; *Kuchi-Sake-Onna 2* [*The Scissors Massacre*], dir. Terauchi

Kōtarō, 2008). The example of the kuchi-sake-onna demonstrates the way in which "folk" knowledge is profoundly intertwined with popular media and commercial culture, as well as with broader social anxieties. It also reminds us that yōkai are not merely a thing of the past but are constantly being created and re-created.

JINMENKEN

Human-Faced Dog

In the second half of 1989, an urban legend featuring a dog with a human face, called a jinmenken, caused excitement across Japan, primarily among elementary school children. The rapid transmission of the rumor was propelled by mass media, especially weekly magazines and sports tabloids. The modern precedent for a yōkai becoming a media sensation had been established by the kuchi-sake-onna almost exactly ten years earlier, but the jinmenken may have been even more prominent in this context than its predecessor.[62] Perhaps because of their propulsion through mass media rather than by word of mouth, stories about jinmenken never became complex and seem to have been told more for comic effect than out of belief or fear—at least among adults.

In most cases, an encounter with a jinmenken was brief, startling, and comic: you see a dog rummaging through garbage, it looks up at you with a human face and says, "Just leave me alone [*hottoite kure*]!"[63] A variety of similar utterances were attributed to the dog, but in most cases the implication was something akin to "What do you think you're looking at?" Sometimes the encounter would occur while people were driving: running at a tremendous speed, a dog would overtake the car and then look back with its human face. The jinmenken was variously explained as the result of a DNA experiment or as the ghost of a person hit by a car while walking a dog.[64]

There have been occasional accounts of dogs with human faces in Japan since at least 1810, when it was reported that a human-faced puppy was put on display in a spectacle show (misemono), where it proved exceedingly popular.[65] A jinmenken rumor may also have circulated among surfers in the 1950s.[66] Famously, a dog with the face of a man appears in the 1978 American film *Invasion of the Body Snatchers* (dir. Philip Kaufman). It is unclear whether the appearance of the jinmenken in Japan in the late 1980s and early 1990s was related to any of these previous versions.

More to the point is that the jinmenken fits into a fairly common yōkai pattern of nonhumans with human faces; these include the jinmenju (human-faced tree), ningyo (mermaid), jinmengyo (human-faced fish), and kudan (human-faced bovine). Such creatures literally embody the betwixt and between of yōkai—they are neither human nor animal but a hybrid of both. As such, they are the site of contact between different worlds and may possess distinct powers of communication. Indeed, the utterances of such creatures are often seen as especially meaningful, and some—like the kudan—are famous as "prophesy beasts" for their ability to see into the future.[67]

With this in mind, we may see the jinmenken in a slightly different light. With the anticlimactic punch line—"Just leave me alone!"—the narrative is superficially lighthearted and humorous. But it is also funny distinctly because we are expecting a more profound and meaningful utterance—an omen of future fortune or catastrophe. The humor pivots on this unfulfilled expectation and the shock when we realize that this unique creature not only speaks like a human but also utters something as mundane and everyday as the average human.

Taking the analysis one step further, however, perhaps there is a more profound meaning to the utterance. There is an undertone of sadness and social commentary embedded in the joke: "Leave me alone" implies a weariness with always being stared at or pointed to. At a time when Japan was struggling with issues of otherness and changing attitudes toward foreignness, the jinmenken, as an unusual and anomalous (monstrous?) being, may have offered a subtle critique of social conformity and mainstream attitudes toward disability, hybridity, and difference.

9 Home

Yōkai may reside in the wilds, in the water, in the country, and in cities and villages, but we don't necessarily have to travel far to find them: they also live in the *home*. In fact, these domestic (but undomesticated) creatures may be some of the most frightening of all yōkai because they share with us, whether we know it or not, the places we think of as our own, the places where we feel most secure. These are intimate yōkai. When we see the signs they leave—marks on the ceiling, a pillow in the wrong place—they remind us that we are never actually alone and never completely in control. The otherworld of yōkai overlays our own world and can even seep into our dreams—yōkai are always with us.

YANARI

Sounding House, House Sounds, or Poltergeist

Yanari refers to unexplainable sounds within a house, the kind of phenomenon often called a poltergeist today. In an old Japanese house, yanari would be heard through the rattling of fusuma and shoji screens and other mysterious noises at night.

Figure 27. Yanari and kasa-bake. Original illustrations by Shinonome Kijin.

The first known reference to yanari appears in *Gazu hyakkiyagyō*, where Sekien illustrates them as little anthropomorphic oni-like figures, scratching and hammering at the outside beams and foundations of a wooden house. He provides no explanation or description with the image, other than the word *yanari* (literally, "sounding house").[1] Since the yanari appear in his first codex, containing mostly well-known traditional yōkai for which no explanations were necessary, it is possible that Sekien was simply illustrating a commonly known poltergeist phenomenon. However, he may have been the first person to actually affix a concrete visual image— little demon figures—to this phenomenal yōkai, effectively transforming an intangible aural occurrence into an embodied living being.

KASA-BAKE, KASA-OBAKE, OR KARAKASA-BAKE
Umbrella Monster

Although there are no known narratives or folk beliefs associated specifi-cally with the kasa-bake (also called *kasa-obake* or *karakasa-obake*), this umbrella monster has become a staple of yōkai iconography, appearing in everything from Edo-period games to contemporary live-action films and anime. The kasa-bake is generally portrayed as an old-style Japanese umbrella (made of oil paper on a bamboo frame) with two arms, one eye, a long tongue and—in place of a handle—a single leg with a wooden geta sandal. The kasa-bake is a decidedly lighthearted and loveable image, particularly in film versions, in which it hops around on its single leg.

A yōkai in the shape of an umbrella appears in an early Edo-period picture scroll, *Hyakkiyagyō-zu*, attributed to Kanō Tōun (1625–1694).[2] In his *Hyakki tsurezure bukuro* of 1784, Toriyama Sekien also includes a yōkai he calls *hone-karakasa* (bone umbrella). Both these images, however, are quite different from the image that would become popular in later years. A particularly representative version of the one-eyed, one-legged, long-tongued kasa-bake is found on an illustrated sugoroku board game (a popular form of play throughout much of the Edo period) made by Utagawa Yoshikazu.[3] This is the image that, much later, Mizuki Shigeru developed in his manga, and it is also the character used, for example, in the 2005 film *The Great Yōkai War*.[4]

Whatever its origins, the kasa-bake is clearly associated with the concept of tsukumogami, household tools and objects that become yōkai after a hundred years. Additionally, the one-eyed, one-legged nature of the kasa-bake suggest that it is cognitively related to many other yōkai—such as hitotsume-kozō—that have one eye or one leg, attributes common to deities and monsters of other cultures as well.

It is also worth noting that, since the Edo period, some umbrellas were known as *ja-no-me-gasa*, "snake-eye umbrellas," but it is unclear whether there is a direct relationship between these and the kasa-bake yōkai. Presumably ja-no-me-gasa were so named because of a circle of color placed around the circumference of the canopy near the peak. When the umbrella was opened, the top appeared like a single eye of a snake.

MOKUMOKUREN

Eyes Everywhere

Late afternoon and you are traveling through the forest. You come to an old abandoned house, potential shelter for the evening. You are alone but have an unshakable sense that somebody, or something, is watching you. Such an eerie phenomenon, the feeling of being watched, was translated into an image by Toriyama Sekien in his *Konjaku hyakki shūi* of 1781. The yōkai he portrayed is called the *mokumokuren*, which might be translated as "eyes-eyes continuously" or "eyes everywhere." Sekien's picture shows the corner of a seemingly abandoned house, overgrown with weeds. The shoji screen is ragged and ripped, but in each section of paper there is a set of eyes.

On closer inspection, the eyes seem to have a quizzical, almost comical expression. Sekien's description, too, is playful: "a house, in which long ago somebody lived, has many eyes. It must be the house of somebody who played *go*."[5] The joke here is that in the game of go, squares on the board are referred to as "eyes," and the designated counter for the playing pieces is also "eyes."[6] So Sekien is simultaneously creating a potentially frightening image and making a (somewhat goofy) pun. The mokumokuren, therefore, is a good example of the way a strange phenomenon (the sense of being watched) is transformed into a living creature (a house with eyes), and it is also a good example of the playfulness of Sekien's catalogs.

There is no known documentation predating Sekien's mokumokuren image, so scholars suspect that he may have simply created this yōkai.[7] As with so many of his creations, however, this one was later redrawn by Mizuki Shigeru, who adds a terrified man leaping out of the house. He also provides a folkloric backstory about a lumber merchant from Edo who travels up to the Tsugaru region of northeast Japan to purchase some wood; with nowhere else to sleep, he spends the night in an abandoned house. When eyes appear all around him, he is not the least bit frightened: "on the contrary, he plucked the eyes out one at a time, put them in a bag, and took them back to Edo, where he sold them to an eye doctor."[8] Although Mizuki himself does not mention it, this story had been recorded earlier by folklorist Yamada Norio, who does not use the term *mokumokuren* but titles the brief narrative "Eyes of the Shoji" (Shōji no me).[9]

The mokumokuren seems, oddly, to be a particularly relevant image for today's global surveillance society. The notion of eyes embedded within the shoji of a house can also be thought of as a visualization of the eyes of society—the eyes of all those people around you, watching and evaluating your behavior. Indeed, there is a Japanese proverb—*Kabe wa mimi ari, shōji wa me ari*—that means: "The walls have ears and the shoji have eyes." In a sense, then, the community itself is a kind of yōkai, always keeping an eye on you—even when you think you are alone.

AKANAME

Scum-Licker

This yōkai appears for the first time in Sekien's *Gazu hyakkiyagyō*, where it is pictured as a small, anthropomorphic creature, scratching its head and sticking out its tongue as it creeps suspiciously around the corner of a bathhouse. Like most of the other entries in this particular codex, there is absolutely no explanation. We can infer from its inclusion in a catalog with common yōkai such as tanuki and tengu that the akaname, too, may have been well known at the time, although specific legends and folk beliefs are lost to us now.

The word *aka* refers to dirt, grime, or sweat and also describes the coating of scum that accrues to the sides of a bathtub. Some scholars believe that Sekien's akaname is similar to, or based on, the *akaneburi* discussed in *Kokon hyaku-monogatari hyōban* of 1686, in which yōkai and other mysterious phenomena are explained. There the akaneburi is described as a creature formed from an accumulation of dust and grime and living in a bathhouse or dilapidated house.[10]

Mizuki Shigeru bases his own illustration on Sekien's but shows it actually licking an old wooden bathtub. He also notes that this yōkai is not known particularly for anything other than licking the aka off the tub, but that having a creature like this come into your house at night is certainly creepy—and a good reason to make sure your bathtub is clean. In this way, Mizuki suggests, the akaname can be thought of as a yōkai who provides a lesson about cleanliness.[11]

Interestingly, another word pronounced *aka,* but written with different kanji, is derived from Sanskrit (*arghya*) to indicate sacred water used as an offering to Buddha. It is tempting to imagine that the akaname might also be a yōkai who would stealthily lap up water offered during religious rites. Unfortunately, there is no evidence of a connection here, but this sort of homonymic wordplay is just the sort of thing Sekien was famous for.

Figure 28. Akaname and tenjōname. Original illustrations by Shinonome Kijin.

TENJŌNAME

Ceiling Licker

The *tenjōname*, literally "ceiling licker," is a tall, bony creature with frilly hair and an extraordinarily long tongue. The first documented reference to this yōkai is Toriyama Sekien's *Hyakki tsurezure bukuro* of 1784, where it is pictured seemingly suspended in midair, licking a wooden ceiling.

The title of the catalog itself contains the phrase *tsurezure*, and the tenjōname entry appropriately references the famous essay collection containing this same phrase, *Tsurezure-gusa* (*Essays in Idleness*, 1333), by the monk Yoshida Kenkō (c. 1283–c. 1350). In entry number 55 of this text, Kenkō writes that "a room with a high ceiling is cold in winter and dark by lamplight."[12] The description Sekien includes with his tenjōname plays off this assertion: "It is said that if the ceiling is high, [the room] will be dark and in winter it will be cold; but this is not because of the way the house is made. Rather, it is entirely due to the machinations of this yōkai

[*kai*]. Just thinking about it will give you the creeps."[13] In other words, it is not the architecture that makes it cold and dark but the tenjōname.

It is possible that this yōkai existed in folklore before being illustrated by Sekien, but there is no evidence of this, and many scholars believe he simply fabricated it.[14] Many years later, however, a tenjōname appeared in Mizuki's catalogs, illustrated in a remarkably similar fashion. But Mizuki's description is very different:

> There is a yōkai called "tenjōname." You would think that it would be a great help for neatly licking clean the ceiling, which normally does not get cleaned—but this is not the case. It is fine that this "ceiling licker" licks the ceiling, but when it licks, it inversely causes dirty stains to adhere. When there is nobody around in an old house, temple, or shrine, it comes out and licks with its long tongue. . . . It seems that if they found stains on the ceiling, people in the old days thought it was the handiwork of the tenjōname.

Mizuki goes on to explain how he first learned about the creature: "When I was a child," he writes, "there was an old woman in the neighborhood who was particularly knowledgeable about yōkai. On occasion, she used to stay at our place, and she looked at the stains on the ceiling of our house and said, 'Look! The tenjōname comes out at night and makes those stains.'"[15]

If Sekien did create the tenjōname, was his invention later incorporated into oral tradition and village folklore to become, centuries later, an explanation for stains on the ceiling? Or was this part simply made up by Mizuki, effectively transforming an individual artistic creation into a folk product of collective imagination? In fact there are several other records of the tenjōname. In a 1929 collection of yōkai-related material, for example, folklorist Fujisawa Morihiko noted that "in old houses and old halls, stains on the ceiling are the result of this yōkai." And writer and folklorist Yamada Norio (1922–2012) tells a legend of a tenjōname captured in the house of a retainer of the Tatebayashi clan, who brought it to Tatebayashi Castle and put it to work licking up spider webs. Unfortunately, however, neither Fujisawa nor Yamada provides any sources for this material, so the origins remain obscure.[16] Whatever the case, the work of Sekien and Mizuki, as well as of folklorists and other writers, demonstrates the dynamic and nonlinear relationship between the oral and literate (and visual), as well as the lively interplay of tradition and individual creativity in the making of monsters.

BAKU

Tapir or Dream-Eater

In Japan, the *baku* is a generally benevolent yōkai endowed with the power to eat nightmares.

Knowledge of the creature came from China as early as 834 in a poetry collection by the Tang-period poet Bai Juyi (772–846). There it is described as having the nose of an elephant, the eyes of a rhinoceros, the tail of an ox, and the legs of a tiger. The text goes on to explain, "If you lay out the skin when you sleep, you can avoid epidemics, and by drawing an image of the baku you can avoid misfortune. People with chronic headaches can protect their heads by using a screen with an image of a baku when they go to sleep."[17] This association with sleep and prevention of bad fortune took hold in Japan, and by the Edo period the baku had become a full-fledged devourer of nightmares, a guardian creature charged with protecting the vulnerable sleeper as he or she ventured into the otherworld of dreams. For this purpose, an image of a baku might be placed near the pillow at night. There were even pillows made in the shape of baku.[18]

The *Three Realms* includes an entry on the baku with a line drawing and an extended reference to the Chinese materia medica text *Bencao gangmu*. The creature is described as it is here, but with a few more details attesting to its particular strengths. For example, its teeth and bones are incredibly strong and its "urine can melt iron and turn it into water."[19]

One theory posits that the baku is based on the tapir, a real mammal found in South and Central America and Southeast Asia and also called baku in Japanese (with the same kanji). The yōkai version most resembles the Malayan tapir, the only species native to Asia. Although some scholars argue that the "zoological baku is not related to the baku of legend,"[20] the image of the baku with its long snout does indeed resemble the animal version.

Regardless of whether the zoological baku influenced the naming of the yōkai baku or vice versa, descriptions of the creature exemplify the way in which yōkai are often constructed as hybrids. The baku is generally described as a composite of animals—a tiger, elephant, rhinoceros, and ox. It is a chimera, a zoological collage. This explanation by analogy (tail like an ox, legs like a tiger) is a common way of describing yōkai and, by extension,

Figure 29. Baku and makura-gaeshi. Original illustrations by Shinonome Kijin.

part of the process of their construction. In a sense, then, a yōkai such as the baku fits somewhere between the real and imaginary; all its parts are derived from real animals, but their combination is imaginary.

But the baku in particular complicates this even further. To people living in Japan during the Edo period or earlier, the very parts from which the creature was constructed were as strange and foreign as their unnatural combination. Elephants, rhinoceroses, and tigers were not native to Japan; the average Japanese person during this time would have seen one only in illustrations and books (if at all), the same places that might also have images of a baku. That is, a baku was presumably no more mysterious, and also no less real, than a rhinoceros.

MAKURA-GAESHI

Pillow Shifter

You wake up in the morning to discover that your pillow has been mysteriously flipped over or moved from your head to your feet or to some other place in the room. Or perhaps you find your entire futon was moved to a different position after you went to sleep. This is the handiwork of a pillow-shifting yōkai called the makura-gaeshi.

An early image of the makura-gaeshi appears without commentary in Sekien's earliest catalog, so we can assume that it was fairly well known during the mid-Edo period. Sekien's picture shows a samurai waking up, with a confused look on his face, to find his pillow at his feet. Hovering faintly in the background above him is a demonic little creature (similar in appearance to traditional images of the thunder god Raijin or even to Sekien's own yanari from the same catalog), presumably the culprit who shifted his pillow. The figure is drawn hazily, as if it might be an image lingering from the samurai's dream.

Murakami Kenji points out that despite Sekien's illustration, few concrete examples of this yōkai dating from the Edo period can be found; however, examples are abundant in more recent local folklore, where the makura-gaeshi is often described as a childlike figure and, in some regions, called a *makura-kozō* (pillow urchin). Sometimes the shifting of pillows is also blamed on house spirits, such as zashiki-warashi.

Murakami also points out that the position of one's pillow has been a matter of concern since at least the late Heian period; it was considered important to shift the direction of a corpse so that the head, and the pillow, faced north.[21] This notion of the *kita-makura,* or "north-pillow," is commonly connected with the fact that the historical Buddha is said to have died lying down with his head to the north—so north came to be the direction associated with the sleep of death. Even today, common custom in Japan dictates that you avoid sleeping with your head to the north, because by the mechanism of sympathetic magic, this would mean your sleeping position replicates the position of death, which you would therefore be tempting.

Although the north-pillow concept is rarely mentioned in conjunction with the makura-gaeshi, occasionally the relationship between the two is explicit. A story collected in Kōchi, for example, tells of somebody waking up to find that while he slept, his position was turned around entirely so that his head and pillow were to the north.[22] In other instances, the makura-gaeshi just seems to be having fun, with no malicious intent or effect.

The connection between sleeping and death, and between consciousness and the loss of self that comes with sleep, is no coincidence. As Miyata Noboru suggests, a pillow is a kind of threshold device through which a person can cross into another world. As the mind starts to dream, the spirit and the physical body seem to separate. Before the modern period, many pillows in Japan were hard and boxlike; sometimes incense was placed inside or underneath them with the idea that the fragrance would lull the sleeper into dreams. In other words, the pillow was a sort of magical device through which a person could travel to another world. Pillows should, therefore, be treated with respect, and it was considered taboo to kick or throw one around. In this context, we can understand why it might have been frightening to wake up and find your pillow moved from one place to another or flipped over, as if somebody or something had shifted around the entire world.[23]

The experience of sleeping, and dreaming, is also connected with the idea that the spirit leaves the physical body in which it resides most of the time. By altering the position of your pillow while you are asleep, the makura-gaeshi makes it possible that your spirit may be unable to return home to the body. A similar idea can be found in the case of the rokurokubi.

ZASHIKI-WARASHI

House Spirit or House Familiar

Zashiki-warashi are most commonly associated with the Tohoku region in northeast Japan, particularly Iwate Prefecture. Translated literally, the name means "parlor child" or "little boy of the house"; and accordingly, zashiki-warashi reside inside the house. They usually resemble a boy between three and thirteen years of age, but there are also examples of female zashiki-warashi. There are numerous variant and regional names for this yōkai, such as *zashiki-bokko, heya-bokko, kura-warashi,* and *kome-tsuki-warashi.*[24]

Not all houses have a zashiki-warashi, but it is said that if one takes up residence the family will prosper. If it departs, however, household fortunes will decline. Zashiki-warashi generally refrain from showing themselves directly to the family, but rather, they perform mischief in all sorts of subtle ways: flipping pillows over while people are sleeping, yanking on the bedcovers, making noises throughout the house. If the resident zashiki-warashi suddenly does appear, this may be considered a sign of his impending departure and an omen that the house will fall on hard times.

A zashiki-warashi recorded in Aomori Prefecture was said to look like a little girl wearing a red chanchanko (sleeveless kimono vest) and to shift the pillows of visitors. She was considered a "protective spirit" (*mamori-gami*) of the household.[25] In his famous collection from Tōno (in Iwate Prefecture), Yanagita Kunio recorded several zashiki-warashi tales:

> The mother of Kizen Sasaki was sewing alone one day when she heard the sound of paper rustling in the next room. That room was only for the master of the house, but he was in Tokyo. Thinking it strange, she opened the door and looked in, but no one was there. Having sat down for a short while, she now heard the sound of someone sniffing in the next room. She concluded that it must be Zashikiwarashi. It has been rumored for sometime [*sic*] that Zashikiwarashi resided in this house. A house that this kami (spirit) lives in is said to become rich and prestigious.[26]

In some cases zashiki-warashi may be related to the practice of *mabiki*, or infanticide, which was carried out for population control in parts of rural Japan through at least the eighteenth century. A newborn baby was not necessarily considered a full-fledged human, so the dead infant might not be memorialized in the traditional fashion. Instead, for example, the body might be interred within the house itself, where it came to be thought of as a protective spirit.[27] Although this interpretation of the zashiki-warashi is speculative, it is clear that by having one less mouth to feed, the household in question would be a little more prosperous than otherwise— exactly the effect a resident zashiki-warashi is said to bring.

Although zashiki-warashi are most commonly associated with the Tohoku region, similar yōkai or protective house spirits are found elsewhere, such as the *ainukaisei* in Hokkaido and the *akagantā* in Okinawa.

TSUKUMOGAMI

Object Monsters or Utensil Yōkai

Tsukumogami is a general term referring to all sorts of household utensils, musical instruments, and other human-made objects that have become yōkai. The *Tsukumogami-ki,* a Muromachi-period otogizōshi tale, explains that "when an object reaches one hundred years, it transforms, obtaining a spirit [*seirei*] and deceiving people's hearts; this is called tsukumogami."[28]

A related set of sixteenth-century picture scrolls owned by a temple in Gifu Prefecture warns,

> There are tools and other objects that change into spirits after a span of one hundred years and often deceive people. These spirits are called *tsukumogami.* . . . At year's end families discard old furniture and utensils and pile them up at the side of the road. Then at New Year's—when it is time to renew the hearth fire and draw new water—the clothing, household utensils, and other objects transform in shape. They become angry at the extravagance of wealthy families. These *tsukumogami* should be treated with caution.[29]

The scrolls offer a story of Buddhist salvation, following a troop of discarded tools on their journey to seek revenge against human beings. Eventually the transformed objects are converted to the way of the Buddha and themselves finally attain Buddhahood.[30]

Since the Muromachi period, if not earlier, there seems to have been a belief that objects not treated with respect, or objects disposed of improperly, might become animated and seek revenge against the humans who mistreated them. As with many yōkai-related beliefs, the number one hundred seems to be instrumental in this transformation. The word *tsukumogami* itself may derive from complex wordplay associated with the number: *tsukumogami* is read the same as *tsukumo-gami* 九十九髪, in which case the kanji for *tsukumo* 九十九 indicates the number ninety-nine, and *gami* (*kami* 髪) denotes hair. The phrase then could be translated as "ninety-nine[-year-old] hair" and would refer to the white hair of an old woman and, by extension, to old age more generally. (The number ninety-nine is, of course, one short of one hundred; the character for *white* 白 is similarly one stroke short of the character for *one hundred* 百, hence connecting it to whiteness.) *Kami,* meaning "hair," is also a homonym for *kami* meaning deity.[31] The numbers here are not necessarily meant to be exact; both ninety-nine and one hundred may simply indicate that a very long time has passed, the assumption being that when any normal thing exists for long enough it can transform into something not so normal. An old tanuki might develop nasty magical powers, an old cat might turn into a bakeneko, an old human might become an oni, and even old objects can morph into yōkai.

This process of animation may reflect an animistic worldview, in which everything, including nonliving objects, potentially possess spirits. The transformation of *things* into yōkai articulates the essence of what it means to be a bakemono—a thing that changes. As Komatsu points out, one of the many interesting aspects of the tsukumogami scrolls noted earlier is that the ultimate objective of transformation is for each object to turn into a full-fledged oni. The scrolls illustrate the *process* of this transformation—they depict objects developing facial features and growing arms and legs.[32]

If becoming an oni is the goal of the transformation, however, then tsukumogami—at least in this example—are stuck in the middle, no longer objects, but not yet oni either. They are adolescent monsters, as it were, caught midtransformation. The fact that *tsukumo* is associated with the number ninety-nine also adds to the implication that these objects have almost—but not quite—completed their metamorphosis.

Just as the animate nature of all things suggests an animistic understanding of the world, so too the potential to transform reflects a Buddhist perspective in which there is always the possibility, in theory, of transformation into a Buddha.[33] In the case of tsukumogami, whether the object becomes a benevolent kami or a maleficent yōkai depends on how humans treat it: whether they respect it or, inversely, chuck it away as garbage. Even today in Japan, memorial services (*kuyō*) are performed for certain objects, particularly household goods such as brooms, brushes, needles, dolls, and eyeglasses that have dedicated their "lives" to helping humans. To an extent this attitude reflects a kind of ecological sensibility, perhaps born of necessity, in which nothing should be taken for granted. It also may reflect an economic, practical perspective, in which increased consumption of goods was facilitated by ritualistically handling "the disposal of used, exhausted objects."[34]

On a popular-culture level, certainly the idea of animate inanimate objects provides an entertaining and comical subject and the potential for social commentary. The most famous early images of tsukumogami

Figure 30. Tsukumogami: half-transformed objects. From *Tsukumogami ekotoba* (Edo period; artist unknown). Courtesy of International Research Center for Japanese Studies.

appear in the playful Muromachi-period *Hyakkiyagyō emaki,* but the idea has been reinvented over and over into the modern period. One early-twentieth-century version, for example, lightheartedly reflects a particular anxiety of the time: a procession of tsukumogami candles, lanterns, and torches runs in frenzied terror from a new, and frighteningly powerful, object-yōkai in the shape of an electric lightbulb.[35] It is all too easy to imagine an early-twenty-first-century version, full of discarded computers and cell phones, wide-eyed and animated, haunting our every step.

Epilogue

MONSTERFUL

Monsterful is an archaic word defined by the *Oxford English Dictionary* online as meaning "rare, marvelous, and extraordinary." Even though the word may be all but forgotten today, it seems an appropriate adjective to apply to the yōkai pantheon. In part this is because yōkai are akin to *monsters* in the modern sense—strange, anomalous manifestations of otherness. But most important, *monsterful* is associated with the marvelous and rare. It describes a sense of wonder—indeed, our contemporary equivalent might simply be *wonderful*. Wonders, of course, are things that transcend easy categorization and understanding, things beyond our powers of comprehension. *Wonder* is also a verb—expressing not only the intellectual act of contemplation but also an emotional, spiritual, affective sense of awe. And if *wonderful* and *monsterful* are synonymous, then in a sense, *monster* must also be a kind of feeling.

But what good is this monsterful world of yōkai in a real world racked by wars, ethnic tension, religious strife, economic crisis, and potentially catastrophic climate change? In Japan, the 2011 cataclysm of earthquake, tsunami, and ongoing nuclear emergency reminds us not just that the natural environment is beyond the control of humans but also, more devastatingly, that we humans have created monsters over which we have no control. The study of yōkai will not, of course, solve any of these problems. But because yōkai emerge from the process of thinking through the unknown, they can perhaps offer a small metaphor for considering these immense challenges. As I have argued implicitly throughout this book, yōkai are born from the dual acts of reading and writing the world around us; they develop from symbiotic processes of *interpretation* and *creation*.

If the monsterful is about wonder and the possibility of the inconceivable, it reminds us that there are otherworlds out there—sounds we have never heard, wavelengths of light human eyes cannot see, entire structures of thought yet to be imagined. As the human world contends with seemingly insurmountable twenty-first-century challenges, the otherworld of yōkai may provide an escapist dream of fantasy and lighthearted play. But more significantly, with its variety and abundance and endless change, it can also offer a metaphor for imagining the unknown, and for the possibility of transforming amorphous hopes into solid futures. Whether these futures turn out to be monstrous or monsterful, however, is the responsibility not of the yōkai but of the humans who do the transforming.

Notes

Throughout the notes and bibliography, unless otherwise specified all works in Japanese were published in Tokyo.

PREFACE

1. Terada Torahiko, "Bakemono no shinka," in *Terada Torahiko zuihitsushū,* ed. Komiya Toyotaka (Iwanami bunko, 1993), 2:204.

1. INTRODUCING YŌKAI

1. There are many recent English-language publications on monsters. See, for example, Marie-Hélène Huet, *Monstrous Imagination* (Cambridge, MA: Harvard University Press, 1993); Jeffrey Jerome Cohen, ed., *Monster Theory: Reading Culture* (Minneapolis: University of Minnesota Press, 1996); David Williams, *Deformed Discourse: The Function of the Monster in Mediaeval Thought and Literature* (Montreal: McGill-Queen's Press, 1999); David D. Gilmore, *Monsters: Evil Beings, Mythical Beasts, and All Manner of Imaginary Terror* (Philadelphia: University of Pennsylvania Press, 2003); Stephen T. Asma, *On Monsters: An Unnatural History of Our Worst Fears* (Oxford: Oxford University Press, 2011); Asa Simon Mittman and Peter Dendle, *Ashgate Research*

Companion to Monsters and the Monstrous (Surrey, UK: Ashgate, 2012); Jeffrey Andrew Weinstock, ed., *The Ashgate Encyclopedia of Literary and Cinematic Monsters* (Surrey, UK: Ashgate, 2014).

2. Thoms suggested the word as a substitute for "Popular Antiquities, or Popular Literature." See "Folk-Lore," *Anthanaeum* (August 22, 1846). Reprinted in *Journal of Folklore Research* 33, no. 3 (September–December 1996): 187–189.

3. See the discussion of the "twin laws" in Barre Toelken, *The Dynamics of Folklore* (Logan: Utah State University Press, 1996), 39–52.

4. Sometimes lack of "ownership" is the very thing that makes folklore the subject of disputes about intellectual property law and indigenous rights. See, for example, Michael F. Brown, *Who Owns Native Culture?* (Cambridge, MA: Harvard University Press, 2003).

5. Alan Dundes, "Who Are the Folk?" In *Interpreting Folklore*, ed. Alan Dundes (Bloomington: Indiana University Press, 1980), 6–7.

6. Doris G. Bargen, *A Woman's Weapon: Spirit Possession in* The Tale of Genji (Honolulu: University of Hawai'i Press, 1997), 20.

7. Takemitsu Makoto, *Nihonjin nara shitte okitai: 'Mono-no-ke' to Shintō* (Kawade shobō shinsha, 2011), 9; Yamauchi Hisashi, *Mono-no-ke*, vol. 1 of Mono to ningen no bunkashi 122 (Hōsei Daigaku shuppankyoku, 2004), 15–17. Bargen suggests the translation "mystery matter" (*Woman's Weapon*, 20).

8. English translation in D. E. Mills, *A Collection of Tales from Uji: A Study and Translation of Uji Shūi Monogatari* (Cambridge: Cambridge University Press, 1970), 154–155. For the Japanese, see Miki Sumito, Asami Kazuhiko, Nakamura Yoshio, and Kouchi Kazuaki, eds., *Uji shūi monogatari: Kohon setsuwa shū*, Shin Nihon koten bungaku taikei (Iwanami shoten 1990), 42:30–32.

9. Helen Craig McCullough, trans., *Ōkagami, the Great Mirror: Fujiwara Michinaga (966–1027) and His Times* (Princeton, NJ: Princeton University Press, 1980), 136.

10. See Ningen Bunka Kenkyū Kikō, Kokuritsu Rekishi Minzoku Hakubutsukan, Kokubungaku Kenkyū Shiryōkan, and Kokusai Nihon Bunka Kenkyū Sentā, eds., *Hyakkiyagyō no sekai: Ningen bunka kenkyū kikō renkei tenji* (Kadokawa gakugei shuppan, 2009), 10–13.

11. For images and discussion of different "Hyakkiyagyō emaki," see ibid.; Tanaka Takako, "'Hyakkiyagyō emaki' wa nao mo kataru," in *Zusetsu: Hyakkiyagyō emaki o yomu*, ed. Tanaka Takako, Hanada Kiyoteru, Shibusawa Tatsuhiko, and Komatsu Kazuhiko (Kawade shobō shinsha, 1999), 17–33. For historical context, see Tanaka Takako, *Hyakkiyagyō no mieru toshi* (Chikuma gakugei bunko, 2002).

12. For *bakemono*, see Komatsu, "Yōkai: Kaisetsu," in *Yōkai*, ed. Komatsu Kazuhiko (Kawade shobō shinsha, 2000), 436; also Adam Kabat (Adamu Kabatto), "Bakemono zukushi no kibyōshi no kōsatsu: Bakemono no gainen o megutte," in *Yōkai*, ed. Komatsu Kazuhiko (Kawade shobō shinsha, 2000), 141–164.

I should mention here a popular English-language website called The Obakemono Project, which seems to use the word *obakemono* as a creative mash-up of *obake* and *bakemono*. This is not a Japanese word per se, but it seems to have become a kind of regional (English-language) variant word for *yōkai*.

13. Aoki Kazuo, Inaoka Kōji, Sasayama Haruo, and Shirafuji Noriyuki, eds., *Shoku Nihongi*, Shin Nihon koten bungaku taikei 16 (Iwanami shoten, 1998), 5:33.

14. Komatsu, "Yōkai: Kaisetsu," 435–436. See also Kyōgoku Natsuhiko, "Yōkai to iu kotoba ni tsuite (sono 2)," *Kai* 12 (December 2001): 296–307.

15. Jason Ânanda Josephson, *The Invention of Religion in Japan* (Chicago: University of Chicago Press, 2012).

16. Mark Teeuwen and Bernhard Scheid, "Tracing Shinto in the History of Kami Worship: Editors' Introduction," *Japanese Journal of Religious Studies* 29, No. 3–4 (Fall 2002): 199.

17. John Breen and Mark Teeuwen, "Introduction: Shinto Past and Present," in *Shinto in History: Ways of the Kami*, ed. John Breen and Mark Teeuwen (Honolulu: University of Hawai'i Press, 2000), 7.

18. Komatsu Kazuhiko, "Yōkai to wa nanika," in *Yōkaigaku no kiso chishiki*, ed. Komatsu Kazuhiko (Kadokawa gakugei shuppan, 2011), 16–17.

19. Yanagita Kunio, *Teihon Yanagita Kunio shū* (Chikuma shobō, 1969), 5:125; Komatsu Kazuhiko, *Yōkaigaku shinkō: Yōkai kara miru Nihonjin no kokoro* (Shōgakukan, 1994), 33–40, 162–173.

20. Komatsu, "Yōkai to wa nanika," 16.

21. See Robert Borgen, *Sugawara no Michizane and the Early Heian Court* (Cambridge, MA: Council on East Asian Studies, Harvard University, 1986), 307–325.

22. Komatsu, "Yōkai to wa nanika," 10.

23. D. Felton, "Rejecting and Embracing the Monstrous in Ancient Greece and Rome," in Mittman and Dendle, *Ashgate Research Companion*, 104. For a thoughtful recent discussion of monsters, see Asa Simon Mittman, "Introduction: The Impact of Monsters and Monster Studies," in Mittman and Dendle, *Ashgate Research Companion*, 1–14.

24. For more on this, see Michael Dylan Foster, *Pandemonium and Parade: Japanese Monsters and the Culture of Yōkai* (Berkeley: University of California Press, 2009), 160–163. For distinctions between yōkai and kaijū, see Saitō Jun, "Yōkai to kaijū," in *Yōkai-henge*, ed. Tsunemitsu Tōru (Chikuma shobō, 1999), 66–101. For Godzilla and other monster movies, see William Tsutsui, *Godzilla on My Mind: Fifty Years of the King of Monsters* (New York: Palgrave Macmillan, 2004).

25. Yanagita Kunio, "Yōkai dangi" in *Teihon Yanagita Kunio shū* (Chikuma shobō, 1970), 4:292–293. For translation and analysis of this passage, see Foster, *Pandemonium*, 153–154.

26. Komatsu, "Yōkai to wa nanika," 27–29.

27. C. D. Stevinson and S. J. Biddle, "Cognitive Orientations in Marathon Running and 'Hitting the Wall,'" *British Journal of Sports Medicine* 32, no. 3 (September 1998): 229. For a discussion stressing the importance of somatic experience as the source for supernatural belief, see David J. Hufford's classic work, *The Terror That Comes in the Night: An Experience-Centered Study of Supernatural Assault Traditions* (Philadelphia: University of Pennsylvania Press), 1982.

28. This discussion is primarily from Komatsu, "Yōkai to wa nanika," 12–22, but similar analyses can be found throughout his work.

2. SHAPE-SHIFTING HISTORY

1. For a discussion of early writing in Japan, see David B. Lurie, *Realms of Literacy: Early Japan and the History of Writing* (Cambridge, MA: Harvard University Press, 2011), 13–212. On *mokkan,* see Joan R. Piggott, "*Mokkan:* Wooden Documents from the Nara Period," *Monumenta Nipponica* 45, no. 1 (1990): 449–470.

2. Donald L. Philippi, trans., *Kojiki* (Tokyo: University of Tokyo Press, 1968), 89–90. For versions from the *Nihonshoki,* see William G. Aston, trans., *Nihongi: Chronicles of Japan from the Earliest Times to A.D. 697* (1896; reprint, Tokyo: Tuttle, 1972), 53–58. For swords in Japanese history and literature, see Elizabeth Oyler, *Swords, Oaths, and Prophetic Visions: Authoring Warrior Rule in Medieval Japan* (Honolulu: University of Hawai'i Press, 2006), especially 115–137.

Interestingly, a careful reading of the Yamata no Orochi passage, with its multiple repetitions of the number eight, suggests that the creature actually drinks sixty-four barrels of wine! (I thank Bonita Hurd for bringing this to my attention.) It is probable, however, that the number eight is invoked here not as an exact amount but as a signifier of abundance and because of its great symbolic value as a sacred and propitious number in both Japanese and Chinese cultures. For a discussion of the importance of the number eight in Japanese tradition, see Gunji Masakatsu, *Wasūkō* (Hakusuisha, 2001), 125–142.

3. See Komatsu Kazuhiko, Miyata Noboru, Kamata Tōji, and Minami Shinbō, eds., *Nihon ikai emaki* (Chikuma bunko 1999), 75–76.

4. For history and definitions of setsuwa, see Michelle Osterfeld Li, *Ambiguous Bodies: Reading the Grotesque in Japanese Setsuwa Tales* (Stanford, CA: Stanford University Press, 2009), 15–30. For yōkai that appear in setsuwa, see Itō Shingo, "Setsuwa bungaku no naka no yōkai," in *Yōkaigaku no kiso chishiki,* ed. Komatsu Kazuhiko (Kadokawa gakugei shuppan, 2011), 77–107.

5. For a reproduction of the *Tsuchigumo-zōshi,* see Komatsu Shigemi, ed., *Tsuchigumo-zōshi, Tengu-zōshi, Ōeyama-ekotoba* (Zoku Nihon emaki taisei 19)

(Chūōkōronsha, 1984), 1–11. For yōkai in otogizōshi, see Tokuda Kazuo, "Otogizō-shi to yōkai," in Komatsu, ed. *Yōkaigaku no kiso*, 109–140.

6. Hayashi Makoto and Matthias Hayek suggest "the Way of divination" or "the Way of yin-yang" as the most accurate English translations of Onmyōdō. "Editors' Introduction: Onmyōdō in Japanese History," *Japanese Journal of Religious Studies* 40, no. 1 (2013): 2–3.

7. Shigeta Shin'ichi, *Abe no Seimei: Onmyōji-tachi no Heian jidai* (Yoshikawa kōbunkan, 2006), 23.

8. William H. McCullough and Helen Craig McCullough trans., *A Tale of Flowering Fortunes: Annals of Japanese Aristocratic Life in the Heian Period* (Stanford, CA: Stanford University Press, 1980), 807; Laura Miller, "Extreme Makeover for a Heian-Era Wizard," *Mechademia 3: Limits of the Human* (2008): 33.

9. Shigeta Shin'ichi, "A Portrait of Abe no Seimei," *Japanese Journal of Religious Studies* 40, no. 1 (2013): 87, 96.

10. Komatsu, in Komatsu et al., *Nihon ikai emaki*, 55–56. There are many versions of this legend; it seems to have been around since at least the medieval period but became popular during the Edo period (Shigeta, *Abe no Seimei*, 9–10). The fox is called Kuzunoha, and numerous legends and dramas have developed around her. Setting aside the question of whether Seimei's mother was a fox, even his paternity is disputed, with some evidence that his father was not Yasuna but Abe no Masuki. Okano Reiko, Yumemakura Baku, Komatsu Kazuhiko, and Togashi Rintarō, *Onmyōdō* (Tokuma shoten, 2000), 46–47. For more on Kuzunoha, Seimei, and Edo-period plays concerning them, see Janet E. Goff, "Conjuring Kuzunoha from the World of Abe no Seimei," in *A Kabuki Reader: History and Performance*, ed. Samuel L. Leiter (Armonk, NY: M. E. Sharpe, 2002), 269–283. For more on Seimei legends, see Takahara Toyoaki, "Abe Seimei densetsu: Kyō no Seimei densetsu o chūshin ni," *Shūkyō minzoku kenkyū* 5 (1995): 9–24; Takahara, *Seimei densetsu to Kibi no Onmyōji* (Iwata shoin, 2001).

11. Komine Kazuaki, ed., *Konjaku monogatari shū*, vol. 4 of Shin Nihon koten bungaku taisei 36 (Iwanami shoten, 1994), 411–414; Shimura Kunihiro, ed., *Nihon misuteriasu yōkai, kaiki, yōjin jiten* (Bensei shuppan, 2012), 207.

12. This story is found in a text from the 1580s; see Shimura Kunihiro, *Onmyōji Abe no Seimei* (Kadokawa gakugei shuppan, 1995), 56–57. A version of the episode is recounted on a panel at the Seimei Shrine in Kyoto.

13. Though sometimes attributed to the Noh master Zeami Motokiyo (1363–1443), authorship of this drama is uncertain. For an English translation, see Eileen Kato, *The Iron Crown (Kanawa)*, in *Twenty Plays of the Nō Theatre*, ed. Donald Keene (New York: Columbia University Press, 1970), 193–205.

14. Okano et al., *Onmyōdō*, 212–213.

15. Momose Meiji, *Gendai ni ikiru sennen no "yami": "Abe no Seimei" warudō* (Koara bukkusu, 1999), 230–233.

16. Shigeta, "Portrait," 93. For analysis of shikigami in history, literature, and popular culture, see Carolyn Pang, "Uncovering *Shikigami:* The Search for the Spirit Servant of Onmyōdō," *Japanese Journal of Religious Studies* 40, no. 1 (2013): 99–129.

17. Miller, "Extreme Makeover," 31. The Seimei obsession may have been inspired by, in addition to Yumemakura's contribution, Aramata Hiroshi's mid-1980s novel, *Teito monogatari*, which features a twentieth-century descendant of Seimei and introduced Onmyōdō concepts. See Tanaka Takako, *Abe no Seimei no issen nen: Seimei genshō o yomu* (Kōdansha, 2003), 14–22; Shigeta, *Abe no Seimei*, 2–3; Kyōgoku Natsuhiko, *Taidanshū: Yōkai daidangi* (Kadokawa shoten, 2005), 70–71. But while these fictional versions of Onmyōdō and Seimei certainly fueled popular interest, the authors and illustrators of these texts were surely influenced by academic research; in 1985, for example, Komatsu Kazuhiko and Naitō Masatoshi discussed Onmyōdō and Seimei in a popular nonfiction book. See *Oni ga tsukutta kuni Nihon: Rekishi o ugokashite kita "yami" no chikara to wa* (Kōbunsha, 1985), 99–133.

18. There seems to be a battle over who "owns" Seimei; a sign at the shrine strictly warns that the items for sale at the shop next door are not officially endorsed.

19. Komatsu, *Tsuchigumo-zōshi*, 1–11.

20. Susan B. Hanley, "Urban Sanitation in Preindustrial Japan," *Journal of Interdisciplinary History* 18, no. 1 (1987): 1.

21. Sumie Jones, with Kenji Watanabe, eds., *An Edo Anthology: Literature from Japan's Mega-City, 1750–1850* (Honolulu: University of Hawai'i Press, 2013), 22.

22. Asai Ryōi, *Otogibōko*, in Shin Nihon koten bungaku taikei (Iwanami shoten, 2001), 75:395. A 1718 text describes the procedure: "First light one hundred lamps (wicks) with blue paper around them, and hide all weapons. Now, for each frightening tale, extinguish one lamp (wick). . . . When all one hundred flames have been extinguished, a *bakemono* will most definitely appear." *Wakan kaidan hyōrin*, in Tachikawa Kiyoshi, ed., *Hyaku-monogatari kaidan shūsei* (Kokusho kankōkai, 1995), 354.

23. Nakazawa Shin'ichi suggests the number "clearly possesses a qualitative meaning," underscoring a sense of wonder at the abundance and variety of yōkai. "Yōkai-ga to hakubutsugaku," in Komatsu, *Yōkai*, 79.

24. Komatsu Kazuhiko, *Shuten dōji no kubi* (Serika shobō, 1997), 251.

25. Takada Mamoru, *Edo gensō bungakushi* (Chikuma gakugei bunko, 1999), 9–24. Published collections of tales can be found in Tachikawa, *Hyaku-monogatari* and Tachikawa Kiyoshi ed., *Zoku hyaku-monogatari kaidan shūsei* (Kokusho kankōkai, 1993). Tachikawa (*Hyaku-monogatari kaidan shūsei*, 354) and Komatsu (*Shuten dōji*, 251) both suggest the written collections grew out of the oral practice, but Takeda Tadashi notes the difficulty of determining the

relationship between the written and oral. "Hyaku-monogatari: Sono seiritsu to hirogari," in Komatsu, *Yōkai*, 112–118.

26. Noriko T. Reider, "The Appeal of *Kaidan:* Tales of the Strange," *Asian Folklore Studies* 59, no. 2 (2000): 268; Reider, "The Emergence of *Kaidan-shū:* The Collection of Tales of the Strange and Mysterious in the Edo Period," *Asian Folklore Studies* 60, no. 1 (2001): 79–99.

27. Aramata Hiroshi, "Obake kenkyū ga hajimatta koro," *Hyakkiyagyō no sekai: Ningen bunka kenkyū kikō renkei tenji*, ed. Bunka kenkyū sentā (Kadokawa gakugei shuppan, 2009), 44.

28. Kyōgoku Natsuhiko, "Yōkai zukan no yōkaiga," *Yōkai zukan*, ed. Kyōgoku Natsuhiko and Tada Katsumi (Kokusho kankōkai, 2000), 14.

29. See Aramata, "Obake," 44.

30. *Bencao gangmu* (Japanese: *Honzō kōmoku*) was compiled by Li Shizhen and published in the late 1500s; it is fifty-two volumes and contains 1,903 entries. It is believed to have entered Japan in the very early 1600s. Nishimura Saburō, *Bunmei no naka no hakubutsugaku: Seiyō to Nihon* (Kinokuniya shoten, 1999), 1:105–108. For a broad discussion of the relationship between encyclopedias and yōkai, see Michael Dylan Foster, *Pandemonium and Parade: Japanese Monsters and the Culture of Yōkai* (Berkeley: University of California Press, 2009), 30–76.

31. Terajima Ryōan, *Wakan-sansaizue* (Heibonsha, 1994), 7:183–184.

32. All four texts are reproduced in Inada Atsunobu and Tanaka Naohi, eds., *Toriyama Sekien gazu hyakkiyagyō* (Kokusho kankōkai, 1999).

33. The emaki is part of the Bigelow Collection at the Boston Museum of Fine Arts and is reproduced in Yumoto Kōichi, *Zoku yōkai zukan* (Kokusho kankōkai, 2006), 6–37.

34. Peter Kornicki, *The Book in Japan: A Cultural History from the Beginnings to the Nineteenth Century* (Honolulu: University of Hawai'i Press, 2001), 44.

35. Tada Katsumi, *Hyakki kaidoku* (Kōdansha, 1999), 20.

36. Ibid, 19–22.

37. Jones and Watanabe, *Edo Anthology*, 29–31. For a study of kibyōshi with examples in translation, see Adam L. Kern, *Manga from the Floating World: Comicbook Culture and the Kibyōshi of Edo Japan* (Cambridge, MA: Harvard University Asia Center, 2006).

38. Jones and Watanabe, *Edo Anthology*, 137–167.

39. On yōkai and kibyōshi, see the following works by Adam Kabat (Adamu Kabatto): *Edo bakemono zōshi* (Shōgakukan, 1999); *Ōedo bakemono saiken* (Shōgakukan, 2000); *Ōedo bakemono zufu* (Shōgakukan, 2000); "Bakemono zukushi no kibyōshi no kōsatsu: Bakemono no gainen o megutte," in Komatsu, *Yōkai*, 141–164; *Edo kokkei bakemono zukushi* (Kōdansha, 2003); *Edo no kawairashii bakemono-tachi* (Shōdensha, 2011).

40. See Kagawa Masanobu, *Edo no yōkai kakumei* (Kawade shobō shinsha, 2005), 181–239; Iwata Noriko, "Bakemono to asobu: 'Nankenkeredomo bakemono sugoroku,'" *Tōkyō-to Edo-Tōkyō hakubutsukan hōkoku* 5 (February 2000): 39–52; Tada Katsumi, *Edo yōkai karuta* (Kokusho kankōkai, 1998). For yōkai-related magic tricks, see Yokoyama Yasuko, *Yōkai tejina no jidai* (Seikyūsha, 2012).

41. Yokoyama Yasuko, *Yotsuya kaidan wa omoshiroi* (Heibonsha, 1997), 238. See also Satoko Shimazaki, "The End of the 'World': Tsuruya Nanboku IV's Female Ghosts and Late-Tokugawa Kabuki," *Monumenta Nipponica* 66, no. 2 (2011): 209–246. For more on the local legends on which the play was based, see Hirosaka Tomonobu, *Edo kaiki ibunroku* (Kirinkan, 1999), 137–144.

42. Aramata, "Obake," 44.

43. Gerald Figal invokes the word *monsterology* in his discussion of Enryō. *Civilization and Monsters: Spirits of Modernity in Meiji Japan* (Durham, NC: Duke University Press, 1999).

44. Itakura Kiyonobu, *Yōkai hakase: Enryō to yōkaigaku no tenka* (Kokusho kankōkai, 1983), 6–8. Unless otherwise noted, details of Enryō's life are from Itakura, *Yōkai hakase;* Kathleen M. Staggs, "'Defend the Nation and Love the Truth': Inoue Enryō and the Revival of Meiji Buddhism," *Monumenta Nipponica* 38, no. 3 (Autumn 1983), 251–281; Figal, *Civilization;* Jason Ânanda Josephson, "When Buddhism Became a 'Religion': Religion and Superstition in the Writings of Inoue Enryō," *Japanese Journal of Religious Studies* 33, no. 1 (2006), 143–168.

45. Staggs, "Defend," 259. For a list of Enryō's courses, see Miura Setsuo, "Kaisetsu: Inoue Enryō to yōkaigaku no tanjō," *Inoue Enryō, Yōkaigaku zenshū,* ed. Tōyō Daigaku Inoue Enryō kinen gakujutsu sentā (Kashiwa shobō, 2001), 6:472.

46. Ichiyanagi Hirotaka, "'Yōkai' to iu ba: Inoue Enryō, 'yōkaigaku' no ichi," in *Nihon shisō no kanōsei,* ed. Suzuki Tadashi and Yamaryō Kenji (Satsuki shobō, 1997), 85–87. For Fushigi kenkyūkai members, see Itakura, *Yōkai hakase,* 24; Figal, *Civilization,* 44–45; for minutes from the meetings, see Miura, "Kaisetsu," 476–477.

47. Inoue, quoted in Itakura, *Yōkai hakase,* 25.

48. Inoue Enryō, *Yōkaigaku kōgi,* in *Inoue Enryō, Yōkaigaku zenshū,* ed. Tōyō Daigaku Inoue Enryō kinen gakujutsu sentā (Kashiwa shobō, 1999), 1:19–20.

49. Koizumi Bon, *Minzokugakusha Koizumi Yakumo: Nihon jidai no katsudō kara* (Kōbunsha, 1995), 179–180.

50. Paul Murray, *A Fantastic Journey: The Life and Literature of Lafcadio Hearn* (Folkestone, Kent, UK: Japan Library, 1993), 14. The biographical information about Hearn comes primarily from Murray, *Fantastic Journey;* Koizumi, *Minzokugakusha;* Koizumi Toki and Koizumi Bon, eds., *Bungaku arubamu: Koizumi Yakumo.* (Kōbunsha, 2000).

51. Koizumi, *Minzokugakusha,* 124–125; Murray, *Fantastic Journey,* 144.

52. The earliest Japanese translation of *Kwaidan* I have found is Koizumi Yakumo, *Kaidan*, trans. Takahama Chōkō (Sumiya shoten, 1910). Several tales from *Kwaidan* were made into a successful film, *Kwaidan*, directed by Kobayashi Masaki (1965).

53. In Lafcadio Hearn, *Kwaidan: Stories and Studies of Strange Things* (Boston: Houghton Mifflin, 1904), n.p. For Hearn's relationship with identity, nationalism, and the politics of the time, see Roy Starrs, "Lafcadio Hearn as Japanese Nationalist," *Japan Review* 18 (2006): 181–213.

54. Starrs, "Lafcadio Hearn," 206.

55. Ema Tsutomu, *Ema Tsutomu chosaku shū* (Chūōkōronsha, 1977), 6:367–368.

56. Ibid, 367.

57. Ibid, 414–418, 450.

58. For a related but slightly different analysis of Yanagita's methodology, see Komatsu Kazuhiko, *Yōkaigaku shinkō: Yōkai kara miru Nihonjin no kokoro* (Shōgakukan, 1994), 15. For more on Yanagita's yōkai theories, see Michael Dylan Foster, "Yōkai and Yanagita Kunio Viewed from the 21st Century," in *Yanagita Kunio and Japanese Folklore Studies in the 21st Century*, ed. Ronald A. Morse (Tokyo: Japanime, 2012), 20–35. Yanagita's early essays on yōkai are in *Santō mintan shū* of 1914 (*Teihon Yanagita Kunio shū* [Chikuma shobō, 1970], 27:41–179); *Hitotsume kozō sono ta* (in *Teihon*, 5:113–340). See also "Tanuki to demonorojii," of 1918 (in *Teihon* 22:467–473), and "Yūrei shisō no hensen," of 1917 (in *Teihon* 15:562–568). *Yōkai dangi* (Discussions of monsters), a collection of some thirty essays originally published between 1910 and 1939, was released as a collection in 1956; for a newly annotated paperback version, see Yanagita Kunio, *Shintei yōkai dangi* (Kadokawa gakukei shuppan, 2013).

59. Originally published in the journal *Minkan denshō*, "Yōkai meii" is reprinted in *Teihon*, 4:424–438, and Yanagita, *Shintei yōkai dangi*, 243–301.

60. Yanagita, "Yōkai dangi," in *Teihon*, 4:292–293. See Komatsu, *Yōkaigaku shinkō*, 16–17, for examples of how scholars have refined Yanagita's ideas.

61. Yanagita, "Hitotsume-kozō," in *Teihon*, 5:125. "Hitotsume-kozō" was first published in August 1917 in the *Tokyo nichi nichi shinbun* (newspaper) and reprinted in 1934 with a number of other essays by Yanagita in a separate volume titled *Hitotsume-kozō sono ta*.

62. For explanation of this attitude in Yanagita's minzokugaku, see Alan Christy, *A Discipline on Foot: Inventing Japanese Native Ethnography, 1910–1945* (Lanham, MD: Rowman & Littlefield, 2012), especially 205–208.

63. The Fifteen-Year War is the series of conflicts that began with the Manchurian Incident of 1931 and ended with Japan's surrender to the Allied Powers in 1945.

64. Adachi Noriyuki, *Yōkai to aruku: Hyōden, Mizuki Shigeru* (Bungei shunjū, 1994), 58.

65. Hirabayashi Shigeo, *Mizuki Shigeru to Kitarō hensenshi* (YM Bukkusu: 2007). Kamishibai, literally "paper theater," was a popular form of entertainment from the 1920s through the 1960s, described concisely as "a set of pictures used by a performer to tell a story to an audience, usually of children aged four to twelve"; Sharalyn Orbaugh, "*Kamishibai* and the Art of the Interval," *Mechademia* 7 (2012), 78. For more on kamishibai and manga, see Fujishima Usaku, *Sengo manga no minzokugaku shi* (Kawaii shuppan, 1990), 2–18; 46–76.

66. "Terebi-kun" was published in *Bessatsu shōnen magajin*, August 15, 1965.

67. Hirabayashi, *Mizuki Shigeru to Kitarō*, 108; Mizuki Shigeru, *Nonnonbā to ore* (Chikuma bunko, 1997), 28. Apparently the title *Hakaba Kitarō* was derived from a much earlier kamishibai of the same name (but slightly different kanji) written by Itō Masami and released in 1932. Hirabayashi, *Mizuki Shigeru to Kitarō*, 13–14.

68. According to one manga episode, Medama-oyaji is the sole remnant of Kitarō's father, who has disintegrated through disease. The eyeball remains to watch over Kitarō as he grows up. See Mizuki Shigeru, *Chūkō aizōban Gegege no Kitarō* (Chūōkōronsha, 1994), 1:5–49. There are, however, several variations on Kitarō's genesis (Hirabayashi, *Mizuki Shigeru to Kitarō*, 89–107).

69. Aramata Hiroshi, *Shin Nihon yōkai junreidan: Kaiki no kuni Nippon* (Shūeisha, 1997), 180. For more on Sakaiminato, see Michael Dylan Foster, "Haunted Travelogue: Hometowns, Ghost Towns, and Memories of War," *Mechademia* 4 (2009): 164–181; Jitsugyō no Nihonsha ed., *Yōkai no machi, Sakaiminato: Kōshiki gaidobukku* (Jitsugyō no Nihonsha, 2007).

70. Iikura Yoshiyuki, "Yōkai kenkyū bukkugaido," in *Yōkaigaku no kiso chishiki*, ed. Komatsu Kazuhiko (Kadokawa gakugei shuppan, 2011), 261.

71. Miyata Noboru, *Yōkai no minzokugaku: Nihon no mienai kūkan* (Iwanami shoten, 1990), 248.

72. Komatsu Kazuhiko, *Ijinron: Minzoku shakai no shinsei* (Seidosha, 1985).

73. Komatsu, *Yōkaigaku shinkō*, 8

74. Komatsu has continued his research on Izanagi-ryū throughout his career; see his major work: *Izanagi-ryū no kenkyū: Rekishi no naka no Izanagi-ryū dayū* (Kadokawa gakugei shuppan, 2011).

75. These two paragraphs are based on my interview with Komatsu Kazuhiko, June 6, 2013.

76. Personal communication, June 6, 2013.

77. See Bernard Faure, "The Kyoto School and Reverse Orientalism," in *Japan in Traditional and Postmodern Perspectives*, ed. Charles Wei-Hsun Fu and Steven Heine (Albany: State University of New York Press, 1995), 265–266.

78. *Kai* sells four to five thousand copies of each issue. Gunji Satoshi, editor, personal communication, February 23, 2013.

79. "Hobonichi no suimin-ron: Kyōgoku Natsuhiko wa itsu neru no ka," *Hobo Nikkan Itoi shinbun*, December 17, 2007, www.1101.com/suimin/kyogoku/.

3. YŌKAI PRACTICE/YŌKAI THEORY

1. Gilles Deleuze and Félix Guattari, *A Thousand Plateaus: Capitalism and Schizophrenia*, trans. Brian Massumi (Minneapolis: University of Minnesota Press, 1987), 7. The ramifications of thinking of culture in terms of rhizomes are more complex than my use of the term here, but I invoke it to emphasize a web of relations built around yōkai in terms of interconnectedness and mutual influence. This also allows us to transcend questions of "origins" or "authenticity" that can obstruct interpretation of the multifacetedness of yōkai culture.

2. For examples of local uses of yōkai for tourism and similar purposes, see Saitō Tsugio, *Yōkai toshi keikaku ron: Obake kara no machi zukuri* (Sairyūsha, 1996). On tourism in Tōno, see Marilyn Ivy, *Discourses of the Vanishing: Modernity, Phantasm, Japan* (Chicago: University of Chicago Press, 1995), 98–140.

3. "Osusume no guzzu," Gegege tsūshin, www.mizukipro.com/goods/osusume/.

4. Schumann Shigeoka, *Yōkai kai-uta: Kaishi kyoku kashi shū* (self-published, 2012), n.p. Schumann Shigeoka is a pen name for Shigeoka Hidemitsu, a yōkai manga artist; see "Shigeoka Hidemitsu no obake no jikan," http://ameblo.jp/shigeoka-h/. Altering song lyrics like this, known as *kae-uta*, is a long-standing folk practice often done playfully or in parody.

5. Dan Ben-Amos, "Toward a Definition of Folklore in Context," *Journal of American Folklore* 84 (1971): 13.

6. See Kaisakusen, ed., *Yōkai shashinshū: Gōka gesuto no dai 4 kan* (self-published, 2012). The booklet is produced by a core group of three artist friends, collectively called Kaisakusen, with the assistance of a number of others. See also Kaisakusen, http://ranryoutei.blog.shinobi.jp/.

7. Benedict Anderson, *Imagined Communities: Reflections on the Origins and Spread of Nationalism*, rev. ed. (London: Verso, 1991).

8. The name of the event plays on the title of Maurice Sendak's famous *Where the Wild Things Are* (1963), translated into Japanese by Shingū Teruo as *Kaijū-tachi no iru tokoro* (1975).

9. Stephen T. Asma, *On Monsters: An Unnatural History of Our Worst Fears* (Oxford: Oxford University Press, 2011), 287.

10. Pascal Boyer, *Religion Explained: The Evolutionary Origins of Religious Thought* (New York: Basic Books, 2001), 145.

11. Abe Kōbō, "Hebi ni tsuite II," in *Abe Kōbō zenshū* (Shinchōsha, 1999), 19:132.

12. Freud explores this dynamic between the familiar and the unfamiliar in his famous treatise on the uncanny. "The Uncanny," in *Writings on Art and Literature* (Stanford, CA: Stanford University Press, 1997), 193–233.

13. Angela Tinwell, Mark Grimshaw, and Andrew Williams. "The Uncanny Wall," *International Journal of Arts and Technology* 4, no. 3 (2011): 327.

14. Mori Masahiro, "The Uncanny Valley," trans. K. F. MacDorman and Norri Kageki, *IEEE Robotics and Automation Magazine* 19, no. 2 (2012): 98–100. (Originally published in 1970).

15. "Yōkai dangi," in *Teihon Yanagita Kunio shū* (Chikuma shobō, 1970), 4:291–307; "Kawatare-toki," 4:308–310.

16. For more on the encyclopedic and ludic modes, see Michael Dylan Foster, *Pandemonium and Parade: Japanese Monsters and the Culture of Yōkai* (Berkeley: University of California Press, 2009), 30–55.

17. Mizuko Ito, "Mobilizing the Imagination in Everyday Play: The Case of Japanese Media Mixes," in *Mashup Cultures*, ed. Stefan Sonvilla-Weiss (Vienna: Springer-Verlag, 2010), 86.

18. Shunsuke Nozawa, "Characterization," *Semiotic Review 3: Open Issue 2013* (November 2013): 11, www.semioticreview.com/pdf/open2013/nozawa_characterization.pdf.

19. Shinonome Kijin, interview by author, Tokyo, August 2012.

20. For the Hachiōji character, see Hachiōji-shi, www.city.hachioji.tokyo.jp/kanko/8457/036245.html.

21. Although there had long been similar local mascots, the yuru-kyara name and idea were established through a weekly magazine feature started in 2003 by manga artist and essayist Miura Jun, who also happens to be a regular contributor to the journal *Kai*. See Oricon Style, November 27, 2009, www.oricon.co.jp/news/71089/. Debra J. Occhi uses the term *wobbly character* in her exploration of the phenomenon. "Wobbly Aesthetics, Performance, and Message: Comparing Japanese *Kyara* with their Anthropomorphic Forebears," *Asian Ethnology* 71, no. 1 (2012): 109–132.

22. Hiroki Azuma [Azuma Hiroki], *Otaku: Japan's Database Animals*, trans. Jonathan Abel and Shion Kono (Minneapolis: University of Minnesota Press, 2009).

23. See Yamada Shōji, "'Yurui' to 'katai' no aida: Nihon no 'yuru-kyara' masukotto o kangaeru," in *Understanding Contemporary Japan, International Symposium in Indonesia* (Kyoto: International Research Center for Japanese Studies, 2010), 157–166.

24. Yasui Manami of Tenri University, presentation at *Tradition and Creation of Yōkai Culture: Moving towards Expanding the Parameters of the Field* Research Symposium, International Research Center for Japanese Studies, Kyoto, Japan, March 23, 2013.

25. See Erika Griffin, "10 Bizarre Japanese Mythological Creatures," Cracked, n.d., www.cracked.com/funny-6080-10-bizarre-japanese-mythological-creatures/, accessed May 28, 2014; also Christy Golden, "5 Bizarre Legendary Creatures from Japan," Mysterious Universe, August 8, 2013, http://mysteriousuniverse.org/2013/08/5-bizarre-legendary-creatures-from-japan/.

26. On Nihonjinron, see Harumi Befu, *Hegemony of Homogeneity: An Anthropological Analysis of Nihonjinron* (Melbourne: Transpacific Press, 2001). 27. Kickstarter, www.kickstarter.com/projects/osarusan/the-night-parade-of-one-hundred-demons; www.kickstarter.com/projects/osarusan/the-hour-of-meeting-evil-spirits?ref = card. Matthew Meyer, *The Night Parade of One Hundred Demons: A Field Guide to Japanese Yokai* (self-published, 2012).

YŌKAI CODEX

1. Colin H. Roberts and T. C. Skeat, *The Birth of the Codex* (London: Oxford University Press, 1983), 1.

4. THE ORDER OF YŌKAI

1. There are many books like this, but the one I used is Toyoda Naoyuki, *Chōgyo zukan*, Jitsuyō Mini Books (Nihon bungeisha, 2011).

2. See International Commission on Zoological Nomenclature, *International Code of Zoological Nomenclature*, updated January 1, 2012, www.nhm.ac.uk/hosted-sites/iczn/code/.

3. See Takada Mamoru, "'Hyakkiyagyō' sōsetsu: Jo ni kaete," in *Toriyama Sekien gazu hyakkiyagyō*, ed. Inada Atsunobu and Tanaka Naohi (Kokusho kankōkai, 1999), 11–12. For the *Shanhaijing*, see Richard E. Strassberg, ed. and trans., *A Chinese Bestiary: Strange Creatures from the Guideways through Mountains and Seas* (Berkeley: University of California Press, 2002).

4. See Katsuhisa Moriya, "Urban Networks and Information Networks," in *Tokugawa Japan: The Social and Economic Antecedents of Modern Japan*, ed. Chie Nakane and Shinzaburō Oishi (Tokyo: University of Tokyo Press, 1990), 97–123; Peter Kornicki, *The Book in Japan: A Cultural History from the Beginnings to the Nineteenth Century* (Honolulu: University of Hawai'i Press, 2001), 169–276; Mary Elizabeth Berry, *Japan in Print: Information and Nation in the Early Modern Period* (Berkeley: University of California Press, 2006); Richard Rubinger, *Popular Literacy in Early Modern Japan* (Honolulu: University of Hawai'i Press, 2007).

5. Berry, *Japan in Print*, 15.

6. See, for example, Richard Freeman, *The Great Yokai Encyclopedia: The A-Z of Japanese Monsters* (North Devon, UK: CFZ Press, 2010); Matthew Meyer, *The Night Parade of One Hundred Demons: A Field Guide to Japanese Yokai* (self-published, 2012); Hiroko Yoda and Matt Alt, *Yōkai Attack! The Japanese Monster Survival Guide*, rev. ed. (Tokyo: Tuttle, 2012).

7. See *Gensō dōbutsu no jiten*, www.toroia.info.

8. See, respectively, Mizuki Shigeru, *Yōkai gadan* (Iwanami shoten, 1994); Mizuki, *Zusetsu Nihon yōkai taizen* (Kōdansha, 1994); Murakami Kenji, *Yōkai jiten* (Mainichi shinbunsha, 2000); Chiba Mikio, *Zenkoku yōkai jiten* (Shōgakukan, 1995); Itō Ryōhei, "Yōkai no hakubutsushi," in *Yōkaigaku no kiso chishiki*, ed. Komatsu Kazuhiko (Kadokawa gakugei shuppan, 2011), 212–238; Komatsu Kazuhiko, Tsunemitsu Tōru, Yamada Shōji, and Iikura Yoshiyuki, eds., *Nihon kaii yōkai daijiten* (Tōkyōdō shuppan, 2013).

9. For a more complex use of "contact zone" in relation to colonial discourses, see Mary Louise Pratt, *Imperial Eyes: Travel Writing and Transculturation* (London: Routledge, 1992).

5. WILDS

1. Inada Atsunobu and Tanaka Naohi, eds., *Toriyama Sekien gazu hyakkiyagyō* (Kokusho kankōkai, 1992), 28–29.

2. Zília Papp, *Anime and Its Roots in Early Japanese Monster Art* (Folkestone, UK: Global Oriental, 2010), 14.

3. *Meikyō kokugo jiten* (Taishūkan shoten, 2002), s.v. "kodama."

4. Komatsu Kazuhiko, "Oni: Kaisetsu," in *Oni*, ed. Komatsu Kazuhiko (Kawade shobō shinsha, 2000), 458.

5. Shimura Kunihiro, ed., *Nihon misuteriasu yōkai, kaiki, yōjin jiten* (Bensei shuppan, 2012), 134.

6. Komatsu, "Oni: Kaisetsu," 459.

7. See Komatsu Shigemi, "Jigoku zōshi," in *Gaki zōshi, Jigoku zōshi, Yamai zōshi, Kusōshi emaki*. Nihon no emaki 7 (Chūōkōronsha, 1987), 40–66. For discussion of this picture scroll, see Michelle Osterfeld Li, "Human of the Heart: Pitiful Oni in Medieval Japan," in *Ashgate Research Companion to Monsters and the Monstrous*, ed. Asa Simon Mittman and Peter Dendle (Surrey, UK: Ashgate, 2012), 177–178.

8. Komatsu, "Oni: Kaisetsu," 459.

9. Noriko T. Reider, *Japanese Demon Lore: Oni from Ancient Times to the Present* (Logan: Utah State University Press, 2010), 2–14. For a concise discussion of the varied ways in which oni appear in medieval setsuwa, see Li, "Human of the Heart."

10. Even today, relatively few houses built in Japan have an entrance facing in this direction; see Mizusawa Tatsuki, *Nihon no matsurowanu tami: Hyōhakusuru sansetsumin no zankon* (Shin jinbutsu ōraisha, 2011), 224–235.

11. For association of oni with marginalized peoples, see, for example, Wakao Itsuo, *Oni-densetsu no kenkyū* (Yamato shobō, 1981); Komatsu Kazuhiko and Naitō Masatoshi, *Oni ga tsukutta kuni Nihon: Rekishi o ugokashite kita "yami" no chikara to wa* (Kōbunsha, 1985).

12. Quotations here are from the Shibukawa edition of the narrative as translated by Reider in *Japanese Demon Lore*, 191, 200. For different versions, see 32–35.

13. For oni as "marginalized other," see Li, "Human of the Heart"; Reider, *Japanese Demon Lore*, 42–45.

14. Keigo Seki, ed., *Folktales of Japan*, trans. Robert J. Adams (London: Routledge and Kegan Paul, 1963), 54.

15. There are hundreds of versions of this tale; for an English translation of one collected in Aomori Prefecture, see ibid., 40–43.

16. See Klaus Antoni, "Momotarō (the Peach Boy) and the Spirit of Japan: Concerning the Function of a Fairy Tale in Japanese Nationalism of the Early Shōwa Age," *Asian Folklore Studies* 50 (1991): 155–188; John W. Dower, *War without Mercy: Race and Power in the Pacific War* (New York: Pantheon, 1986), 234–261; Robert Thomas Tierney, *Tropics of Savagery: The Culture of Japanese Empire in Comparative Frame* (Berkeley: University of California Press, 2010), 110–146.

17. Donald L. Philippi, trans., *Kojiki* (Tokyo: University of Tokyo Press, 1968), 62. Philippi uses the expression "hags of Yomi," explaining that *shikome* literally means "ugly woman" (64); see also William G. Aston, trans., *Nihongi: Chronicles of Japan from the Earliest Times to A.D. 697* (Tokyo: Tuttle, 1972), 1:24–26.

18. Also known as Shōgetsubō. See Rajyashree Pandey, "Women, Sexuality, and Enlightenment: *Kankyo no tomo*," *Monumenta Nipponica* 50, no. 3 (1995): 325–334. Summary and quotations from the tale are taken from Pandey's translation, 339–340.

19. Li, "Human of the Heart," 175. For more on female oni, see Reider, *Japanese Demon Lore*, 53–89.

20. For more on Namahage, see Michael Dylan Foster, "Inviting the Uninvited Guest: Ritual, Festival, Tourism, and the Namahage of Japan," *Journal of American Folklore* 126, no. 501 (2013), 302–334.

21. Beans have long been valued both for nutrition and for ritual power. Throwing beans to ward off oni during Setsubun has probably been practiced since at least the Muromachi period; some scholars posit that rather than (or in addition to) their role in banishing evil, beans were presented as offerings to the gods. Sasaki Kōkan, Miyata Noboru, and Yamaori Tetsuo, eds., *Nihon minzoku shūkyō jiten* (Tōkyōdō, 1998), 318. This double function—both weapon and offering—is evident at setsubun as beans are thrown to ward off oni even as they invite in good fortune. When the ritual is performed at a temple or shrine, the beans are often thrown not at the oni but to the visitors, who reach out excitedly to grab them.

22. Komatsu Kazuhiko, "Setsubun no oni," in *Bukkyō gyōji saijiki: Nigatsu setsubun*, ed. Setouchi Jakuchō, Fujii Masao, and Miyata Noboru (Daiichi hōki, 1988), 23–24. For more on tsuina, see Fujii Masao, "Setsubun to tsuina no girei,"

in Setouchi, Fujii, and Miyata, *Bukkyō gyōji saijiki*, 29–34. Comments here are based on my own observations of tsuina ceremonies at Yoshida Shrine and Rozan Temple in Kyoto, on February 2 and 3, respectively, in 2013.

23. Komatsu, "Setsubun no oni," 21.

24. See Inada and Tanaka, *Toriyama*, 31. For yamabiko in emaki, see Kyōgoku Natsuhiko and Tada Katsumi, eds., *Yōkai zukan* (Kokusho kankōkai, 2000), 154.

25. Murakami Kenji, *Yōkai jiten* (Mainichi shinbunsha, 2000), 222. For the portrayal of tsuchigumo in the fudoki, see Akiko Yoshie, "Gender in Early Classical Japan: Marriage, Leadership, and Political Status in Village and Palace," trans. Janet Goodwin, *Monumenta Nipponica* 60, no. 4 (Winter 2005), 463–464.

26. Komatsu Shigemi, ed., *Tsuchigumo-zōshi, Tengu-zōshi, Ōeyama-ekotoba*, Zoku Nihon emaki taisei 19 (Chūōkōronsha, 1984), 1–11.

27. Melinda Takeuchi, "Kuniyoshi's *Minamoto Raikō and the Earth Spider*: Demons and Protest in Late Tokugawa Japan," *Ars Orientalis* 17 (1987): 5–23.

28. M. W. de Visser, "The Tengu," *Transactions of the Asiatic Society of Japan* 36, no. 2 (1908): 27.

29. Aston, *Nihongi*, 2:167.

30. Haruko Wakabayashi, *The Seven Tengu Scrolls: Evil and the Rhetoric of Legitimacy in Medieval Japanese Buddhism* (Honolulu: University of Hawai'i Press, 2012), 4.

31. See ibid., 4; also de Visser, "Tengu," 48–50, for Sutoku's tengu attributes in other texts.

32. Wakabayashi, *The Seven*, 13–19.

33. Royall Tyler, ed. and trans., *Japanese Tales* (New York: Pantheon, 1987), 181–182.

34. Wakabayashi, *The Seven*, 32.

35. Ibid., 46. Wakabayashi describes this text and analyzes the Tengu-dō in the context of Buddhism at the time (32–51). For the original text, see Koizumi Hiroshi, Yamada Shōzen, Kojima Takayuki, and Kinoshita Motoichi, eds., *Hōbutsushū, Kankyo no tomo, Hirasan kojin reitaku*, Shin Nihon koten bungaku taikei 40 (Iwanami shoten, 1993), 455–482.

36. For analysis of this dynamic, see Wakabayashi, *The Seven*.

37. Quoted in de Visser, "Tengu," 47.

38. Quotes from Asahara Yoshiko and Kitahara Yasuo, eds., *Mae no hon* (Iwanami shoten, 1994), 306, 311.

39. Komatsu Kazuhiko, *Yōkai bunka nyūmon* (Serika shobō, 2006), 165.

40. Ibid., 166–167. See also Komatsu Kazuhiko, ed., *Nihon no yōkai* (Natsume-sha, 2009), 60–63.

41. Watanabe Shōgo, *Nihon densetsu taikei* (Mizuumi shobō, 1982), 7:150.

42. Ibid., 7:148.

43. Yanagita Kunio, *Teihon Yanagita Kunio shū* (Chikuma shobō, 1968), 4:78.

44. Ibid., 4:77.

45. The title translation here is from Carmen Blacker, "Supernatural Abductions in Japanese Folklore," *Asian Folklore Studies* 26, no. 2 (1967): 111–148. For *Senkyō ibun* in historic and religious context, see Wilburn Hansen, *When Tengu Talk: Hirata Atsutane's Ethnography of the Other World* (Honolulu: University of Hawai'i Press, 2008).

46. See Birgit Staemmler, "Virtual *Kamikakushi*: An Element of Folk Belief in Changing Times and Media," *Japanese Journal of Religious Studies* 32, no. 2 (2005): 341–352. For a thorough discussion of the kamikakushi phenomenon in history and folklore, see Komatsu Kazuhiko, *Kamikakushi: Ikai kara no izanai* (Kōbundō, 1991).

47. Takao-san Yakuō-in, www.takaosan.or.jp/index.html.

48. See Murakami, *Yōkai jiten*, 325. A much more elaborate version of the story is found in the *Tawara no Tōta emaki*, from the Edo period; see *Tawara no Tōta emaki*, www2.osaka-ohtani.ac.jp/tawaranotouta/index.html. The story has many different versions and a complicated textual history; see Kiribayashi Hiromichi, "Fujiwara no Hidesato mukade taiji densetsu seiritsu no ichikōsatsu: Taiheiki shoshū setsuwa o chūshin ni," *Udai kokugo ronken* 11 (1999): 41–52.

49. Murakami, *Yōkai jiten*, 325–326.

50. Yanagita, "Yōkai meii," in *Teihon*, 4:431.

51. Kodama Yōmi, *Ōita-ken shi, minzokugaku hen* (Ōita-ken, 1986), 360–361.

52. Mizuki Shigeru, *Zusetsu Nihon yōkai taizen* (Kōdansha, 1994), 337.

53. "Gegege no 'nurikabe,' konna sugata? Edo-ki no emaki ni tōjō," *Asahi shinbun*, August 7, 2007.

54. Murakami, *Yōkai jiten*, 317–318.

55. Yanagita, *Teihon*, 4:433.

56. Terajima Ryōan, *Wakan-sansaizue* (Heibonsha, 1994), 6:151.

57. Inada and Tanaka, *Toriyama*, 77.

58. See Adam Kabat, *Ōedo bakemono saiken* (Shōgakukan, 2000), 139–150.

59. Murakami, *Yōkai jiten*, 318.

60. Seki, *Folktales of Japan*, 55.

61. Komatsu, *Yōkai bunka nyūmon*, 170; Murakami, *Yōkai jiten*, 345.

62. These include most famously a 1976 short story by Ōba Minako, "The Smile of a Mountain Witch" [Yamamba no bisho], trans. Noriko Mizuta Lippit, assisted by Mariko Ochi, in *Japanese Women Writers: Twentieth Century Short Fiction*, ed. Noriko Mizuta Lippit and Kyoko Iriye Selden (Armonk, NY: M. E. Sharpe, 1991), 194–206. See also Mizuta Noriko and Kitada Sachie, eds., *Yamamba-tachi no monogatari: Josei no genkei to katarinaoshi* (Gakugei shorin, 2002).

63. See Seki, *Folktales of Japan*, 54–57.

64. Komatsu, *Yōkai bunka nyūmon*, 171. For more on the "yamamba's curse," or "yamamba possession," see Komatsu, *Hyōrei shinkō ron* (Kōdansha gakujutsu bunko, 1994), 278–313.

65. Mizuta Noriko, "Yamamba no yume: Josetsu toshite," in Mizuta and Kitada, *Yamamba-tachi no monogatari*, 9.

66. He suggests that she was first an attendant (*miko*) of the deity and then became his wife; see Orikuchi Shinobu, "Okina no hassei," in *Orikuchi Shinobu zenshū* (Chūōkōronsha, 1995), 2:363.

67. Komatsu, *Yōkai bunka nyūmon*, 174. The first known text to contain the yamamba birth motif is *Kinpira tanjō-ki* (1661). For yamamba and Kintoki legends during the Edo period, see Reider, *Japanese Demon Lore*, 69–84.

68. Watanabe Shōgo, *Nihon densetsu taikei* (Mizuumi shobō, 1982), 7:165–166.

69. Reider, *Japanese Demon Lore*, 63.

70. For more on the relationship between the "hags of Yomi" episode and yamamba folklore, see Yoshida Atsuhiko, *Yōkai to bijo no shinwa-gaku* (Meicho kankōkai, 1989), 5–177.

71. Tada Katsumi, *Nihon to sekai no "yūrei, yōkai" ga yoku wakaru hon* (PHP kenkyūjo, 2007), 108.

72. Murakami, *Yōkai jiten*, 131–132.

73. Recounted in Ōi Kōtarō, "Okinawa no shokubutsu bunkaron: Shokubutsu to shinkō," *Okidai keizai ronsō* 4, no. 1 (1980): 8–9.

74. See "Kijimunaa Fesuta ni tsuite," www.kijimuna.org/.

75. Mizuki, *Zusetsu Nihon yōkai taizen*, 249.

76. Inada and Tanaka, *Toriyama*, 191.

77. Terajima, *Wakan-sansaizue*, 3: 319.

78. See, for example, "Iskandar at the Talking Tree," by an unknown artist from the fourteenth century, which shows a man on a white horse seemingly in conversation with a tree with human heads (and the heads of a few other animals as well): Freer/Sackler: The Smithsonian's Museums of Asian Art, www.asia.si.edu/explore/shahnama/F1935.23.asp; accessed February 2, 2014. For the Wakwak Tree, see David Williams, *Deformed Discourse: The Function of the Monster in Mediaeval Thought and Literature* (Montreal: McGill-Queen's University Press, 1999), 210.

79. See the classic study by Rudolf Wittkower, "Marvels of the East: A Study in the History of Monsters," *Journal of the Warburg and Courtauld Institutes* 5 (1942): 159–197.

6. WATER

1. Kojima Noriyuki, Naoki Kōjirō, Nishimiya Kuzutami, Kuranaka Susumu, and Mōri Masamori, eds., *Nihonshoki* (Shōgakukan, 1996), 2:575. Translation is

mine, but I have also consulted William G. Aston, trans., *Nihongi: Chronicles of Japan from the Earliest Times to* A.D. *697* (Tokyo: Tuttle, 1972), 2:147.

2. Yumoto Kōichi, *Nihon genjū zusetsu* (Kawade shobōshinsha, 2005), 40–46; Murakami Kenji, *Yōkai jiten* (Mainichi shinbunsha, 2000), 255; for the ningyo's power of prophecy, see Satō Sami, "Kami no oshie: Minkan setsuwa 'ningyo to tsunami' no shiza yori," *Onomichi Daigaku Nihon bungaku ronsō* 2 (2006): 51–71.

3. Yumoto, *Nihon genjū*, 44. The original print is in the possession of the Tsubouchi Memorial Theatre Museum at Waseda University.

4. This version of the tale is told on the Obama City website; see Happyaku bikuni monogatari, n.d., www.city.obama.fukui.jp/KIKAKU/800bikuni/index. html; accessed July 1, 2013. See also Yanagita's comments in Yanagita Kunio, *Yukiguni no haru: Yanagita Kunio ga aruita Tōhoku* (Kadogawa gakugei shuppan, 2011), 228–234. There are many versions of the legend, such as one in Okayama Prefecture in which the heroine is called the "thousand-year nun." See Imamura Katsuhiko, "Mitsugun mukashi banashi," *Mukashi banashi kenkyū* 1, no. 8 (1935): 25–28. For the religious context of these legends, see Hank Glassman, "At the Crossroads of Birth and Death: The Blood-Pool Hell and Postmortem Fetal Extraction," in *Death and the Afterlife in Japanese Buddhism*, ed. Jacqueline I. Stone and Mariko Namba Walter (Honolulu: University of Hawai'i Press, 2009), 182–183.

5. For Edo-period animal hoaxes, see Andrew L. Markus, "The Carnival of Edo: Misemono Spectacles from Contemporary Accounts," *Harvard Journal of Asiatic Studies* 45, no. 2 (1985): 528–529.

6. Jan Bondeson, *The Feejee Mermaid and Other Essays in Natural and Unnatural History* (Ithaca, NY: Cornell University Press, 1999), 41.

7. For a history of the Feejee Mermaid, see ibid., 36–63; also James W. Cook, *The Arts of Deception: Playing with Fraud in the Age of Barnum* (Cambridge, MA: Harvard University Press, 2001), 73–118.

8. See "Yamaguchi kenchō no hori ni 'jinmengyo,'" *Asahi Shimbun Digital*, April 9, 2008, www.asahi.com/komimi/SEB200804090009.html.

9. Ishikawa Jun'ichirō, *Shinpan kappa no sekai* (Jiji tsūshinsha, 1985), 41–64; for other attempts, see also Ōno Katsura, *Kappa no kenkyū* (San'ichi shobō, 1994), 22–28; Iikura Yoshiyuki, ed., *Nippon no kappa no shōtai* (Shinjinbutsu ōraisha, 2010), 39–45.

10. Komatsu Kazuhiko, *Yōkai bunka nyūmon* (Serika shobō, 2006), 109–110.

11. Itō Ryōhei, "Yōkai no hakubutsushi," in *Yōkaigaku no kiso chishiki*, ed. Komatsu Kazuhiko (Kadokawa gakugei shuppan, 2011), 220–221.

12. Aston, *Nihongi*, 1:298–99; Maruyama Rinpei, ed., *Teihon Nihonshoki* (Kōdansha, 1966), 2:245–246. *Mizuchi, midochi, medochi,* and *medotsu* are local names for the kappa in Aomori, Iwate, and Miyagi Prefectures. Iikura, *Nippon no kappa*, 46.

13. Iikura, *Nippon no kappa*, 70.

14. Terajima Ryōan, *Wakan-sansaizue* (Heibonsha, 1994), 6:159.

15. Kagawa Masanobu, "Kappa imēji no hensen," in *Kappa to wa nanika: Dai 84-kai rekihaku fōramu*, ed. Kokuritsu rekishi minzoku hakubutsukan (Sakura-shi, Chiba: Kokuritsu rekishi minzoku hakubutsukan, 2012), 6. The kawatarō image is in volume 3 of the five-volume *Nihon sankai meibutsu zue*. For a digitally scanned version held by Kyushu University Library, see *Nihon sankai meibutsu zue*, Hirose bunkobon 3, Kyushu University Library website, n.d., http://catalog.lib.kyushu-u.ac.jp/en/recordID/411729?hit=3&caller=xc-search, accessed June 20, 2014.

16. Kagawa, "Kappa imēji," 6–7.

17. See Ishida Eiichirō, *The Kappa Legend: A Comparative Ethnological Study on the Japanese Water Spirit Kappa and Its Habit of Trying to Lure Horses into the Water*, trans. Yoshida Ken'ichi, *Folklore Studies* 9 (1950): 33–34.

18. The "kappa bridegroom" tale has been classified as tale type Ikeda-AaTh 312B. See Hiroko Ikeda, *A Type and Motif Index of Japanese Folk-Literature* (Helsinki: Suomalainen tiedeakatemia, 1971), 74–75.

19. Cited in Iikura, *Nippon no kappa*, 19–20. For more about kappa losing their arms and providing bone-setting secrets, see Nakamura Teiri, *Kappa no Nihonshi* (Nihon Editāsukūru shuppanbu, 1996), 81–101. See also Ishikawa, *Kappa no sekai*, 217–230.

20. Ishikawa, *Kappa no sekai*, 120.

21. Akutagawa Ryūnosuke, *Kappa* (Iwanami shoten, 1996).

22. For changes in the kappa image, see Michael Dylan Foster, "The Metamorphosis of the Kappa: Transformation from Folklore to Folklorism in Japan," *Asian Folklore Studies* 57 (Fall 1998): 1–24.

23. J. K. Rowling, *Harry Potter and the Prisoner of Azkaban* (New York: Scholastic Press, 1999); J. K. Rowling [Newt Scamander], *Fantastic Beasts & Where to Find Them* (New York: Scholastic Press, Arthur A. Levine Books, 2001).

24. Murakami, *Yōkai jiten*, 122.

25. See John R. Platt, "Japanese River Otter Declared Extinct," *Scientific American*, September 5, 2012, http://blogs.scientificamerican.com/extinction-countdown/2012/09/05/japanese-river-otter-declared-extinct/.

26. Murakami, *Yōkai jiten*, 289–290; Chiba Mikio, *Zenkoku yōkai jiten* (Shōgakukan, 1995), 219–220.

27. Inada Atsunobu and Tanaka Naohi, eds., *Toriyama Sekien gazu hyakki-yagyō* (Kokusho kankōkai, 1992), 79; Kyōgoku Natsuhiko and Tada Katsumi, eds., *Yōkai zukan* (Kokusho kankōkai, 2000), 144–145.

28. Data from residents in these paragraphs based on personal communications with the author in February and March 2012.

29. Takakuwa Fumiko, "Shimo-Koshiki no minzoku: Shinkō densetsu o chūshin ni," Shimo-Koshiki-son kyōdo-shi hensan iinkai ed., *Shimo-Koshiki-son kyōdo-shi* (Shimo-Koshiki-son: Shimo-Koshiki-son kyōdo-shi hensan iinkai, 2004), 1007; the same name was also reported by a current resident of Teuchi in

his early fifties, personal communication with the author, February 15, 2012. In his massive kappa dictionary, Wada Hiroshi includes "gameshirō" as one of many variant names for kappa-like creatures in the Kagoshima area; see *Kappa denshō daijiten* (Iwata shoin, 2005), 696.

30. For *game*, see Murakami, *Yōkai jiten*, 117.

31. Ibid., 329–330.

32. Nakamura Tekisai, *Kinmōzui* (Waseda Daigaku shuppanbu, 1975), 75.

33. Terajima, *Wakan-sansaizue*, 6:156–157.

34. Inada and Tanaka, *Toriyama*, 157.

35. For description and comparison of images, see Zília Papp, *Anime and Its Roots in Early Japanese Monster Art* (Folkestone, UK: Global Oriental, 2010), 86, 89.

36. Kyōgoku Natsuhiko, *Mōryō no hako* (Kōdansha, 1999).

37. Murakami, *Yōkai jiten*, 12–13.

38. Tada Katsumi, ed., *Takehara Shunsen: Ehon hyaku-monogatari—Tōsanjin yawa* (Kokusho kankōkai, 1997), 99–101; Mizuki, *Zusetsu Nihon yōkai taizen*, 26–27. For a comparison of images, see Papp, *Anime*, 108; Zília Papp, *Traditional Monster Imagery in Manga, Anime and Japanese Cinema* (Folkestone, UK: Global Oriental, 2010), 136–137.

39. *Nihon kokugo daijiten*, 2nd ed. (Shōgakukan, 2000) 1:341; 8:1411.

7. COUNTRYSIDE

1. Yanagita Kunio, *Teihon Yanagita Kunio shū* (Chikuma shobō, 1968), 4:428.

2. Kondō Masaki, "Yōkai no meikan," in *Zusetsu: Nihon no yōkai, shinsōban*, ed. Iwai Hiromi and Kondō Masaki (Kawade shobō shinsha, 2000), 103.

3. See, for example, Mizuki Shigeru, *Zoku yōkai jiten* (Tōkyōdō shuppan, 1984), 30–31.

4. This information comes from Murakami Kenji, *Yōkai jiten* (Mainichi shinbunsha, 2000), 356.

5. Inada Atsunobu and Tanaka Naohi, eds., *Toriyama Sekien gazu hyakkiyagyō* (Kokusho kankōkai, 1992), 67.

6. Lafcadio Hearn, *Kwaidan: Stories and Studies of Strange Things* (Boston: Houghton, Mifflin, 1904), iii.

7. Ibid., 18.

8. Lafcadio Hearn, *The Japanese Letters of Lafcadio Hearn*, edited with an introduction by Elizabeth Bisland (Boston: Houghton Mifflin, 1910), 56–57.

9. Yoko Makino, "Lafcadio Hearn's 'Yuki-Onna' and Baudelaire's 'Les Bienfaits de la Lune,'" *Comparative Literature Studies* 28, no. 3, East-West Issue (1991): 234–244. See also Komatsu Kazuhiko, ed., *Nihon no yōkai* (Natsumesha, 2009), 114–115.

10. Murakami, *Yōkai jiten*, 114–115.

11. Chiba Mikio, *Zenkoku yōkai jiten* (Shōgakukan, 1995), 81.

12. Steven R. Sheffield and Carolyn M. King, "Mustela nivalis," *Mammalian Species* 454 (June 2, 1994): 6.

13. Chiba, *Zenkoku yōkai jiten*, 115.

14. Murakami, *Yōkai jiten*, 115.

15. "An Epitome of Current Medical Literature," *British Medical Journal* 2, no. 2646 (September 16, 1911): 37.

16. For the fox in China, particularly in literature from the sixteenth to nineteenth centuries, see Rania Huntington, *Alien Kind: Foxes and Late Imperial Chinese Narrative*, Harvard East Asian Monographs 222 (Cambridge, MA: Harvard University Asia Center), 2003.

17. M. W. de Visser suggests that in Chinese texts the term *kori* referred exclusively to foxes. "The Fox and Badger in Japanese Folklore," *Transactions of the Asiatic Society of Japan* 36, no. 3 (1908): 1. The first appearance of the term in a Japanese text is in the thirteenth-century *Gukanshō* (41).

18. Serge Larivière and Maria Pasitschniak-Arts, "Vulpes vulpes," *Mammalian Species*, no. 537 (December 27, 1996): 2.

19. See de Visser, "Fox and Badger," 11–19.

20. Kyoko Motomochi Nakamura, trans., *Miraculous Stories from the Japanese Buddhist Tradition: The Nihon Ryōiki of the Monk Kyōkai* (Cambridge, MA: Harvard University Press, 1973), 105.

21. Royall Tyler, ed. and trans., *Japanese Tales* (New York: Pantheon, 1987), 116–118. There is also a Muromachi-period emaki, called *Kitsune-zōshi*, based on this tale; see Komatsu Kazuhiko, *Ikai to Nihonjin: Emonogatari no sōzōryoku* (Kadokawa shoten, 2003), 133–147.

22. See Janet E. Goff, "Conjuring Kuzunoha from the World of Abe no Seimei," in *A Kabuki Reader: History and Performance*, ed. Samuel L. Leiter (Armonk, NY: M. E. Sharpe, 2002), 269–283.

23. Yanagita Kunio, *Nihon no mukashibanashi* (Kadokawa gakugei shuppan 2013), 118–119. *Shippo o dasu* ("showing one's tail") is a common Japanese expression meaning to show one's true self, usually with a negative connotation, that presumably derives from narratives of kitsune, tanuki, and similar mammalian shape-shifters who suddenly, inadvertently, reveal themselves.

24. See Karen Smyers, *The Fox and the Jewel: Shared and Private Meanings in Contemporary Japanese Inari Worship* (Honolulu: University of Hawai'i Press, 1999), and particularly 73–86 for theories on why the fox and Inari are connected.

25. Komatsu, *Ikai to Nihonjin*, 136. For fox possession through history, see Hiruta Genshirō, "Kitsune-tsuki no shinseishi," in *Tsukimono*, ed. Komatsu Kazuhiko (Kawade shobō shinsha, 2000), 67–90.

26. D. E. Mills, *A Collection of Tales from Uji: A Study and Translation of Uji Shūi Monogatari* (Cambridge: Cambridge University Press, 1970), 218–219.

27. Nakamura, *Miraculous Stories*, 225.

28. Cited in Sasama Yoshihiko, *Kaii kitsune hyaku-monogatari* (Yūzankaku, 1998), 213.

29. Shigeyuki Eguchi, "Between Folk Concepts of Illness and Psychiatric Diagnosis: *Kitsune-tsuki* (Fox Possession) in a Mountain Village of Western Japan," *Culture, Medicine and Psychiatry* 14, no. 4 (December 1991): 422. See Eguchi also for more recent examples of kitsune-tsuki and different ways to interpret such phenomena.

30. Lafcadio Hearn, *Glimpses of Unfamiliar Japan* (Boston: Houghton Mifflin, 1894), 1:324.

31. See Kawamura Kunimitsu, *Genshi suru kindai kūkan: Meishin, byōki, zashikirō, aruiwa rekishi no kioku* (Seikyūsha, 1997), 61–121; S. Bānzu (Susan Burns), "Toritsukareta shintai kara kanshi sareta shintai e: Seishin igaku no hassei," *Edo no shisō* 6 (May 1997): 48–62; Gerald Figal, *Civilization and Monsters: Spirits of Modernity in Meiji Japan* (Durham, NC: Duke University Press, 1999), 96–99; Jason Ānanda Josephson, *The Invention of Religion in Japan* (Chicago: University of Chicago Press, 2012), 183–185.

32. See Carmen Blacker, *The Catalpa Bow: A Study of Shamanistic Practices in Japan* (London: George Allen and Unwin, 1975), 51–68; also Michael Bathgate, *The Fox's Craft in Japanese Religion and Folklore: Shapeshifters, Transformations and Duplicities* (New York: Routledge, 2004), 120–133.

33. Terajima Ryōan, *Wakan-sansaizue* (Heibonsha, 1994), 6:96.

34. Ibid., 6:94–95.

35. Murakami, *Yōkai jiten*, 134.

36. Tyler, *Japanese Tales*, 298–299.

37. Murakami, *Yōkai jiten*, 134. A fox wedding procession is vividly portrayed in Kurosawa Akira's film *Yume* (*Dreams*: 1990).

38. *Raccoon dog* is probably the most appropriate term because tanuki are canids, in the same family as dogs, Linnaean classification *Nyctereutes procyonoides*. Three subspecies have been identified: *Nyctereutes procyonoides procyonoides* and *N. p. ussuriensis* in continental Asia, and *N. p. viverrinus* in Japan. See Kaarina Kauhala, "The Raccoon Dog: A Successful Canid," *Canid News* 2 (1994): 37–40, http://archive.today/SMcM; also Oscar G. Ward and Doris H. Wurster-Hill, "Nyctereutes procyonoides," *Mammalian Species*, no. 358 (October 23, 1990): 1–5; Nakamura Teiri, *Tanuki to sono sekai* (Asahi shinbunsha, 1990), 236–244; Inoue Tomoji, *Tanuki to Nihonjin* (Nagoya: Reimei shobō, 1980), 34–51.

39. The figure is generally associated with the Shigaraki pottery style. For more on this style and the tanuki's large testicles, see Nakamura, *Tanuki*, 107–129.

40. The relationship between mujina and tanuki is often confusing. In contemporary biological terms, *mujina* generally refers to an *anaguma*, or Japanese

badger, native to parts of Japan. In some regions, however, tanuki were also called mujina, and the two are often conflated in folklore. See Murakami, *Yōkai jiten*, 326; Nakamura, *Tanuki*, 236–244; Inoue, *Tanuki to Nihonjin*, 57–61.

41. For English translations see Tyler, *Japanese Tales*, 174–175; Mills, *Tales from Uji*, 297–299. Michelle Osterfeld Li discusses this tale in relation to similar animal-related setsuwa (*Ambiguous Bodies: Reading the Grotesque in Japanese Setsuwa Tales* [Stanford, CA: Stanford University Press, 2009], 192–233).

42. See n. 17.

43. This version is from Nagano Prefecture. Fanny Hagin Mayer, trans., *Ancient Tales in Modern Japan: An Anthology of Japanese Folk Tales* (Bloomington: Indiana University Press, 1984), 139–140.

44. Inoue, *Tanuki to Nihonjin*, 106–112.

45. See Mayer, *Ancient Tales*, 301–302. Also Keigo Seki, "Types of Japanese Folktales," *Asian Folklore Studies* 25 (1966): 39–40. For more on tanuki in English, see U.A. Casal, "The Goblin Fox and Badger and Other Witch Animals of Japan," *Folklore Studies* 18 (1959): 1–93.

46. Konno Ensuke, *Nihon kaidan shū, yōkai hen* (Shakai shisōsha, 1999), 144.

47. Yanagita Kunio, "Tanuki to demonorojii," *Yanagita Kunio zenshū* (Chikuma shobō, 2000), 25:314; also Matsutani Miyoko, *Gendai minwakō* (Rippū shobō, 1985), 3:14–15; Konno Ensuke, *Nihon kaidan shū, yūrei hen* (Shakai shisōsha, 1999), 236–237.

48. Terajima, *Wakan-sansaizue*, 6:92–93.

49. From *Shokoku hyaku-monogatari* compiled by an unknown editor in 1677; see Tachikawa Kiyoshi, ed., *Hyaku-monogatari kaidan shūsei* (Kokusho kankōkai, 1995), 81.

50. "Kori no kisha"; reprinted in Yumoto Kōichi, *Meijiki kaii yōkai kiji shiryō shūsei* (Kokusho kankōkai, 2009), 209. In another version of the legend, from Yamagata Prefecture, railroad workers similarly dine on soup made from the carcass of the mischievous tanuki (Matsutani, *Gendai minwakō*, 3:21–22).

51. I am grateful to Torii Keijirō, an excellent storyteller, for sharing this anecdote with me. Interview by author in Teuchi, Shimo-Koshikijima, Kagoshima Prefecture, January 17, 2001, minidisk recording. For analysis of this story and the phantom train narratives, see Michael Dylan Foster, "Haunting Modernity: *Tanuki*, Trains, and Transformation in Japan," *Asian Ethnology* 71, no. 1 (2012): 3–29.

52. For more on *Pom Poko*, and also the tanuki musical films of the 1950s, see Melek Ortabasi, "(Re)animating Folklore: Raccoon Dogs, Foxes, and Other Supernatural Japanese Citizens in Takahata Isao's *Heisei tanuki gassen pompoko*," *Marvels & Tales* 27, no. 2 (2013): 254–275.

53. See Nakamura Teiri, *Tanuki to sono sekai*, 237–252; Inoue, *Tanuki to Nihonjin*, 57–61.

54. Kojima Noriyuki, Naoki Kōjirō, Nishimiya Kuzutami, Kuranaka Susumu, and Mōri Masamori, eds., *Nihonshoki* (Shōgakukan, 1996), 2:551; William G. Aston, trans., *Nihongi: Chronicles of Japan from the Earliest Times to A.D. 697* (Tokyo: Tuttle, 1972), 2:155.

55. Shimura Kunihiro, ed., *Nihon misuteriasu yōkai, kaiki, yōjin jiten* (Bensei shuppan, 2012), 96.

56. Inada and Tanaka, *Toriyama*, 158.

57. Terajima, *Wakan-sansaizue*, 6:100.

58. Shiota Fukashi, ed., *Sato-son kyōdo shi (jōkan)* (Sato-son: Sato-son kyōdo-shi hensan iinkai, 1985), 679.

59. For a detailed list of kubi-kire-uma legends, distribution, and interpretation, see Nagayoshi Keiko, "'Toshidon' to kubi-nashi-uma denshō," *Mukashibanashi densetsu kenkyū* 25 (2005): 50–69. For analysis of this yōkai and the places it appears, see Sasaki Takahiro, *Kaii no fūkeigaku: Yōkai bunka no minzoku chiri* (Kokon shoten. 2009), 35–50.

60. Murakami, *Yōkai jiten*, 255–256; Hino Iwao, *Dōbutsu yōkai tan: Shumi kenkyū* (Yōkendō, 1926), 234.

61. Elizabeth Oyler, "The Nue and Other Monsters in *Heike monogatari*," *Harvard Journal of Asiatic Studies* 68, no. 2 (2008): 3.

62. Royall Tyler, trans., *The Tale of the Heike* (New York: Viking, 2012), 243.

63. Thomas Blenman Hare, *Zeami's Style: The Noh Plays of Zeami Motokiyo* (Stanford, CA: Stanford University Press, 1986), 239.

64. See Inada and Tanaka, *Toriyama*, 154.

65. Murakami, *Yōkai jiten*, 362–363.

66. Yoshioka Ikuo, "Raijū kō," *Hikaku minzoku kenkyū* 21 (March 2007), 35–36.

67. Yumoto Kōichi, *Nihon genjū zusetsu* (Kawade shobōshinsha, 2005), 50–51.

68. Yoshioka, "Raijū kō."

69. For more on UMA, see Kawasaki-shi shimin myūjiamu, ed., *Nihon no genjū: Mikakunin seibutsu shutsugen roku* (Kawasaki: Kawasaki-shi shimin myūjiamu, 2004).

70. Itō Ryōhei, *Tsuchinoko no minzokugaku: Yōkai kara mikakunin dōbutsu e* (Seikyūsha, 2008), 51–52.

71. Murakami, *Yōkai jiten*, 223.

72. From *Hokkoku kidan junjōki* by Chōsuidai Hokkei; quoted in Itō, *Tsuchinoko*, 53–54.

73. See Itō, *Tsuchinoko*.

74. See, for example, Ishizaka Masao, "Watashi mimashita, tsuchinoko to neko no kenka," *Shūkan pureibōi*, October 24, 2000, 54.

75. See Akaiwa-shi: Tsuchinoko jōhō, www.city.akaiwa.lg.jp/tutinoko/index.html.

8. VILLAGE AND CITY

1. See Jo Gyu-heon, "Akujin saishi no shinsō: Kantō chiiki no 'kotoyōka' girei ni miru Nihonjin no fukkakan," *Ningen kagaku kenkyū* 18, no. 2 (2005): 215–228.

2. Murakami Kenji, *Yōkai jiten* (Mainichi shinbunsha, 2000), 284.

3. Quotations from Yanagita Kunio, *Teihon Yanagita Kunio shū* (Chikuma shobō, 1968), 5:119, 134, 151–152. "Hitotsume-kozō" was first published in August 1917 in *Tokyo nichi nichi shinbun* and reprinted in 1934, with other essays, in a volume titled *Hitotsume-kozō sono ta*. See ibid., 113–340. This essay should not be confused with another, shorter essay also titled "Hitotsume-kozō," originally published several months earlier and reprinted later (see *Teihon* 4:411–412). For more on hitotsume-kozō, see Iijima Yoshiharu, *Hitotsume-kōzo to hyōtan: Sei to gisei no fōkuroa* (Shinyōsha, 2001), 18–43.

4. See Kyōgoku Natsuhiko and Tada Katsumi, eds., *Yōkai zukan* (Kokusho kankōkai, 2000), 110, 173.

5. The emaki can be accessed at International Research Center for Japanese Studies, Emakimono dētabēsu, http://kikyo.nichibun.ac.jp/emakimono/index.html.

6. Murakami, *Yōkai jiten*, 56–57; Miyata Noboru, *Yōkai no minzokugaku: Nihon no mienai kūkan* (Iwanami shoten, 1990), 22–24.

7. Chiba Mikio, *Zenkoku yōkai jiten* (Shōgakukan, 1995), 49, 80.

8. *Konjaku monogatari shū*, vol. 25 of Nihon koten bungaku taikei (Iwanami shoten, 1965), 539–541.

9. For insightful analysis of ubume historically and in Kabuki and literature, see Satoko Shimazaki, "The End of the 'World': Tsuruya Nanboku IV's Female Ghosts and Late-Tokugawa Kabuki," *Monumenta Nipponica* 66, no. 2 (2011): 209–246.

10. *Nihon kokugo daijiten*, 2nd ed. (Shogakukan, 2000), 2:402.

11. Terajima Ryōan, *Wakan-sansaizue* (Heibonsha, 1994), 6:342. In the *Three Realms* the ubume is in a section titled "birds of the mountains."

12. Inada Atsunobu and Tanaka Naohi, eds., *Toriyama Sekien gazu hyakki-yagyō* (Kokusho kankōkai, 1992), 57. For more on the ubume image, see Shimazaki, "The End"; Tada Katsumi, *Hyakki kaidoku* (Kōdansha, 1999), 27–34; Shibuya Yōichi, "Bakemono zōshi no kenkyū: Yōkai kenkyū e no shikiron" (undergraduate thesis, Chiba University, 2000), 24–30.

13. Murakami, *Yōkai jiten*, 159–160.

14. For a discussion of the ubume and similar legends within a religious context, see Hank Glassman, "At the Crossroads of Birth and Death: The Blood-Pool Hell and Postmortem Fetal Extraction," in *Death and the Afterlife in Japanese Buddhism*, ed. Jacqueline I. Stone and Mariko Namba Walter, 175–206 (Honolulu: University of Hawai'i Press, 2009).

15. Kyōgoku Natsuhiko, *Ubume no natsu* (Kōdansha bunko, 1998). For an English translation, see Kyōgoku Natsuhiko, *The Summer of the Ubume*, trans. Alexander O. Smith with Elye J. Alexander (New York: Vertical 2009).

16. Mizuki Shigeru, *Zusetsu Nihon yōkai taizen* (Kōdansha, 1994), 341.

17. Kyōgoku and Tada, *Yōkai zukan*, 152; Shimura Kunihiro, ed., *Nihon misuteriasu yōkai, kaiki, yōjin jiten* (Bensei shuppan, 2012), 72–73.

18. Lafcadio Hearn, *Kwaidan: Stories and Studies of Strange Things* (Boston: Houghton Mifflin, 1904), 77–80.

19. Shimura, *Nihon misuteriasu*, 73.

20. Kimura Yūshō, *Higo mukashi-banashi shū*, Zenkoku mukashi-banashi shiryō shūsei 6 (Iwasaki bijutsusha, 1974), 90.

21. Tada Katsumi, "Kaisetsu," in Kyōgoku and Tada, *Yōkai zukan*, 152; Shimura, *Nihon misuteriasu*, 72–73.

22. Kikuoka Senryō, *Shokoku rijindan*, in *Nihon zuihitsu taisei dainiki*, ed. Nihon zuihitsu taisei henshūbu (Yoshikawa kōbunkan, 1975), 24:452–453.

23. Miyata, *Yōkai no minzokugaku*, 202–204.

24. Kyōgoku and Tada, *Yōkai zukan*, 172. For this collection of urban legends and other anecdotes from Edo, see Negishi Yasumori, *Mimi bukuro*, 3 vols. (Iwanami shoten, 1991).

25. Murakami, *Yōkai jiten*, 116–117.

26. Inada and Tanaka, *Toriyama*, 40–41.

27. Adam Kabat, *Ōedo bakemono zufu* (Shōgakukan , 2000), 32.

28. Ibid., 30.

29. Komatsu Kazuhiko, *Nihon no yōkai* (Natsume-sha, 2009), 124; Kabat, *Ōedo bakemono zufu*, 30–51.

30. See Takehara Tadamichi, "Tōfu kozō to tennendō ni tsuite," *Nihon ishigaku zasshi* 55, no. 2 (2009): 161.

31. The incident is in *Meigetsuki* (Record of a clear moon), a diary kept by aristocrat and poet Fujiwara Sadaie (also known as Teika) for over fifty years.

32. Murakami, *Yōkai jiten*, 261–262.

33. Inada and Tanaka, *Toriyama*, 35.

34. Murakami, *Yōkai jiten*, 271.

35. A compelling English-language retelling, titled "The Vampire Cat of Nabéshima," can be found in A. B. Mitford, *Tales of Old Japan* (London: Macmillan, 1893), 200–207.

36. Yumoto Kōichi, *Nihon genjū zusetsu* (Kawade shobōshinsha), 66.

37. See Murakami, *Yōkai jiten*, 143. For this image and commentary, see Yumoto, *Nihon genjū*, 66–69. Kawaraban were a sort of Edo-period predecessor to the modern-day newspaper. They were single sheets of papers printed from a carved clay tile or woodblock. Often simply illustrated, kawaraban generally reported on news and emergency information.

38. Komatsu, *Nihon no yōkai*, 130; Yumoto, *Nihon genjū*, 66–70; also Kihara Hirokatsu, "Hakken: Yōkai-kudan," *Kai* 17 (October 2004): 2–7, 230–235. For a modern twist on the kudan, see the short story "Kudan no haha": Komatsu Sakyō, "The Kudan's Mother," trans. Mark Gibeau, in *Kaiki: Uncanny Tales from Japan*, vol. 2, *Country Delights*, ed. Higashi Masao (Fukuoka: Kurodahan Press, 2011), 197–229.

39. Satō Kenji, *Ryūgen higo: Uwasabanashi o yomitoku sahō* (Yūshindō, 1995), 147–209; Komatsu, *Nihon no yōkai*, 130.

40. Murakami, *Yōkai jiten*, 255. Also Kyōgoku and Tada, *Yōkai zukan*, 149–150; Inada and Tanaka, *Toriyama*, 84.

41. Mizuki, *Zusetsu*, 344–345.

42. Tada, "Kaisetsu," 149.

43. Chiba, *Zenkoku yōkai jiten*, 177; Murakami, *Yōkai jiten*, 258.

44. *Kōjien*, 6th ed. (Iwanami shoten, 2008), 2163. (The phrase in question is *hyōtan-namazu*.)

45. Tada Katsumi, "Yōkai shitsumon bako," *Discover yōkai: Nihon yōkai daihyakka* (Kōdansha 2008), 10:34.

46. Matsutani Miyoko, *Gendai minwakō* (Rippū shobō, 1987), 7:97.

47. See Tsunemitsu Tōru, *Gakkō no kaidan: Kōshō bungei no tenkai to shosō* (Kyoto: Mineruva, 1993). Films based on the legend are *Toire no Hanako-san* (dir. Matsuoka Jōji, 1995); *Shinsei Toire no Hanako-san* (dir. Tsutsumi Yukihiko, 1998); *Toire no Hanako-san shin gekijō ban* (dir. Yamada Masafumi 2013). See also Ichiyanagi Hirotaka, ed., *"Gakkō no kaidan" wa sasayaku* (Seikyūsha, 2005).

48. The Bloody Mary ritual practiced by American girls has similarly been analyzed in terms of anxiety toward puberty and menstruation. See Alan Dundes, "Bloody Mary in the Mirror: A Ritual Reflection of Pre-Pubescent Anxiety," *Western Folklore* 57, no. 2–3 (Spring–Summer 1998): 119–135.

49. Terajima, *Wakan-sansaizue*, 3:305–307.

50. See Adam Kabat, *Ōedo bakemono saiken* (Shōgakukan, 2000), 139–150; Komatsu, *Nihon no yōkai*, 122–123.

51. Hearn, *Kwaidan*, 90.

52. Quoted in Saitō Shūhei, "Uwasa no fōkuroa: Kuchi-sake-onna no denshō oboegaki," *Kenkyū kiyō* 7 (March 30, 1992): 90.

53. Asakura Kyōji, "Ano 'Kuchi-sake-onna' no sumika o Gifu sanchū ni mita!" in *Uwasa no hon*, vol. 92 of Bessatsu takarajima, ed. Ishii Shinji (JICC Shuppan kyoku, 1989), 140.

54. Ibid., 138–140. Asakura's data is from *Shūkan asahi* (Weekly Asahi), which claims the rumor started in the town of Yaotsuchō in Gifu Prefecture. See Hiraizumi Etsurō, "Zenkoku no shō-chū-gakusei o osoresaseru 'Kuchi-sake-onna' fūsetsu no kiki kaikai," *Shūkan asahi*, June 29, 1979, 16–20; also *Gifu nichi nichi shinbun*, January 26, 1979.

55. Kinoshita Tomio, "Gendai no uwasa kara kōtōdenshō no hassei mekanizumu o saguru: 'Kuchi-sake-onna' no uwasa o daizai toshite," in *Ryūgen, uwasa, soshite jōhō: Uwasa no kenkyūshū taisei*, ed. Satō Tatsuya (Shibundō, 1999), 14. For more on the spread of the legend, see Miyamoto Naokazu, "'Kodomo no ryūgen' kenkyū: Otona no miru kodomo no genjitsu to kodomo no genjitsu" (PhD diss., Kanagawa University Graduate School of History and Folk Culture Studies, 1998).

56. Nomura Jun'ichi, *Nihon no sekenbanashi* (Tōkyō shoseki, 1995), 69; *Edo Tōkyō no uwasa-banashi: "Konna ban" kara "Kuchi-sake-onna" made* (Taishūkan shoten, 2005), 125–128.

57. This story was collected in Tochigi Prefecture, in Saitō, "Uwasa no fōkuroa," 91.

58. Nomura, *Nihon no sekenbanashi*, 51.

59. See, for example, Miyata, *Yōkai no minzokugaku*, 20. For a general description of the education mama, see Anne Allison, *Permitted and Prohibited Desires: Mothers, Comics, and Censorship in Japan* (Boulder, CO: Westview Press, 1996), 106.

60. Masks were first used publicly in Japan in 1918 to protect against the Spanish influenza. Shimokawa Kōshi and Katei sōgō kenkyūkai, ed., *Meiji Taishō kateishi nenpyō 1868–1925* (Kawade shobō shinsha, 2000), 429.

61. For more on these perspectives, see Michael Dylan Foster, "The Question of the Slit-Mouthed Woman: Contemporary Legend, the Beauty Industry, and Women's Weekly Magazines in Japan." *Signs: Journal of Women in Culture and Society* 32, no. 3 (Spring 2007): 699–726.

62. Komatsu, *Nihon no yōkai*, 134.

63. Murakami, *Yōkai jiten*, 195.

64. Komatsu, *Nihon no yōkai*, 134.

65. Ibid.

66. Murakami, *Yōkai jiten*, 195.

67. Yumoto, *Nihon genjū*, 66.

9. HOME

1. Inada Atsunobu and Tanaka Naohi, eds., *Toriyama Sekien gazu hyakkiyagyō* (Kokusho kankōkai, 1992), 56.

2. See Ningen bunka kenkyū kikō, Kokuritsu rekishi minzoku hakubutsukan, Kokubungaku kenkyū shiryōkan, and Kokusai Nihon bunka kenkyū sentā, eds., *Hyakkiyagyō no sekai: Ningen bunka kenkyū kikō renkei tenji* (Kadokawa gakugei shuppan, 2009), 18–23.

3. The board game was called "Mukashi banashi bakemono sugoroku." For more on this game and yōkai sugoroku in general, see Kagawa Masanobu, *Edo*

no yōkai kakumei (Kawade shobō shinsha, 2005), 183–189; see also Iwata Noriko, "Bakemono to asobu: 'Nankenkeredomo bakemono sugoroku,'" *Tōkyō-to Edo-Tōkyō hakubutsukan hōkoku* 5 (February 2000): 39–52.

4. See Zília Papp, *Anime and Its Roots in Early Japanese Monster Art* (Folkestone, UK: Global Oriental, 2010), 110.

5. See Inada and Tanaka, *Toriyama*, 240.

6. For a detailed interpretation of this yōkai, see Tada Katsumi, *Hyakki kaidoku* (Kōdansha, 1999), 174–177.

7. Murakami Kenji, *Yōkai jiten* (Mainichi shinbunsha, 2000), 332.

8. Mizuki Shigeru, *Zusetsu Nihon yōkai taizen* (Kōdansha, 1994), 447; also Mizuki, *Yōkai gadan* (Iwanami shoten, 1994), 46–47.

9. Yamada Norio, *Tōhoku kaidan no tabi* (Jiyū kokuminsha, 1974), 145.

10. Murakami, *Yōkai jiten*, 7–8; Tachikawa Kiyoshi, ed., *Zoku hyaku-monogatari kaidan shūsei* (Kokusho kankōkai, 1995), 34–35.

11. Mizuki, *Yōkai gadan*, 40–41.

12. Donald Keene, trans., *Essays in Idleness: The Tsurezuregusa of Kenkō* (New York: Columbia University Press, 1967), 50–51.

13. Inada and Tanaka, *Toriyama*, 273. Tada suggests the tenjōname's appearance is a visual pun on the Edo-period fire companies: the clothing, mane, and fingers resemble a *matoi*, the frilly flaglike banner carried by firemen. Tada Katsumi, "Etoki gazu hyakkiyagyō no yōkai," *Kai* 12 (December 2001): 320–321.

14. Komatsu Kazuhiko, *Yōkaigaku shinkō: Yōkai kara miru Nihonjin no kokoro* (Shōgakukan, 1994), 63; Murakami, *Yōkai jiten*, 235.

15. Mizuki Shigeru, *Zoku yōkai jiten* (Tōkyōdō shuppan, 1984), 152–153.

16. Fujisawa Morihiko, *Yōkai gadan zenshū, Nihon hen jō* (Chūō bijutsu sha, 1929), 10; Yamada Norio, "Nihon no yōkai, henge, majintachi," in *Yōkai, majin, shinsei no sekai*, ed. Yamamuro Shizuka (Jiyū kokuminsha, 1974), 22.

17. Quoted in Shimura Kunihiro, ed., *Nihon misuteriasu yōkai, kaiki, yōjin jiten* (Bensei shuppan, 2012), 77. The Japanese title of the collection is *Hakushimonjū* (also *Hakushibunshū*).

18. Hino Iwao, *Dōbutsu yōkai tan: Shumi kenkyū* (Yōkendō, 1926), 394.

19. Terajima Ryōan, *Wakan-sansaizue* (Heibonsha, 1994), 6:55.

20. Hino, *Dōbutsu*, 394.

21. Murakami, *Yōkai jiten*, 310–311.

22. Chiba Mikio, *Zenkoku yōkai jiten* (Shōgakukan, 1995), 210–211.

23. Miyata Noboru, *Yōkai no minzokugaku: Nihon no mienai kūkan* (Iwanami shoten, 1990), 60–64.

24. Murakami, *Yōkai jiten*, 179.

25. Chūō Daigaku minzoku kenkyūkai, ed., "Aomori-ken Sannohe-gun Nangyō-mura Shimamori-chiku chōsa hōkokusho," *Jōmin* 17 (1980): 141.

26. Yanagita Kunio, *The Legends of Tono: 100th Anniversary Edition*, trans. Ronald A. Morse (Lanham, MD: Lexington Books, 2008), 20–21. Sasaki Kizen

(1886–1933) was the Tōno resident and scholar from whom Yanagita collected these tales.

27. Murakami, *Yōkai jiten*, 179. For *mabiki*, see Fabian Drexler, *Mabiki: Infanticide and Population Growth in Eastern Japan, 1660–1950* (Berkeley: University of California Press, 2013).

28. Quoted in Komatsu Kazuhiko, *Hyōrei shinkō ron* (Kōdansha gakujutsu bunko, 1994), 329. For more on tsukumogami, see Komatsu, *Nihon yōkai ibunroku* (Shōgakukan, 1995), 175–212; Komatsu, *Ikai to Nihonjin: Emonogatari no sōzōryoku* (Kadokawa shoten, 2003), 149–162; also Shibusawa Tatsuhiko, "Tsukumogami," in *Yōkai*, ed. Komatsu Kazuhiko (Kawade shobō shinsha, 2000), 65–78.

29. Quoted and translated in Elizabeth Lillehoj, "Man-Made Objects as Demons in Japanese Scrolls," *Asian Folklore Studies* 54, no. 1 (1995): 21–22. The picture scrolls are at Sūfuki-ji Temple.

30. Ibid., 21–24. There are several related texts concerning tsukumogami, variously titled *Tsukumogami-ki*, *Tsukumogami emaki*, or *Tsukumogami ekotoba*; most are Buddhist narratives in which nonsentient beings attain salvation. See Tanaka Takako, *Hyakkiyagyō no mieru toshi* (Chikuma gakugei bunko, 2002), 162–190; also Noriko T. Reider, "Animating Objects: *Tsukumogami ki* and the Medieval Illustration of Shingon Truth," *Japanese Journal of Religious Studies* 36, no. 2 (2009): 231–257. *Tsukumogami ekotoba* can be accessed at International Research Center for Japanese Studies, Emakimono dētabēsu, http://kikyo.nichibun.ac.jp/emakimono/index.html/.

31. The connection with an old woman may also relate to a poem from the thirteenth-century *Ise monogatari* (Tales of Ise). Reider, "Animating Objects," 247–249.

32. Komatsu Kazuhiko, *Yōkai bunka nyūmon* (Serika shobō, 2006), 18.

33. I do not want to oversimplify the relationships between objects, Buddhism, and animism; for a nuanced discussion of these issues, see Fabio Rambelli, *Buddhist Materiality: A Cultural History of Objects in Japanese Buddhism* (Stanford, CA: Stanford University Press, 2007).

34. Ibid., 246. For this kind of kuyō, see also Angelika Kretschmer, "Mortuary Rites for Inanimate Objects: The Case for *Hari Kuyō*. *Japanese Journal of Religious Studies* 27, no. 3–4 (Fall 2000): 379–404.

35. Artist unknown; see Fukuoka-shi hakubutsukan, ed., *Yūrei, yōkaiga daizenshū: Bi to kyōfu to yūmoa* (Fukuoka: Yūrei, yōkaiga daizenshū jikkōiinkai, 2012), 101.

Bibliography

Unless otherwise specified, all works in Japanese were published in Tokyo.

Abe Kōbō. "Hebi ni tsuite II." In *Abe Kōbō zenshū*. Vol. 19, 131–133. Shinchōsha, 1999.

Adachi Noriyuki. *Yōkai to aruku: Hyōden, Mizuki Shigeru.* Bungei shunjū, 1994.

Akutagawa Ryūnosuke. *Kappa.* Iwanami shoten, 1996.

Allison, Anne. *Permitted and Prohibited Desires: Mothers, Comics, and Censorship in Japan.* Boulder, CO: Westview Press, 1996.

Anderson, Benedict. *Imagined Communities: Reflections on the Origins and Spread of Nationalism.* Rev. ed. London: Verso, 1991.

Andō Misao and Seinō Fumio. *Kappa no keifu.* Satsuki shobō, 1993.

"An Epitome of Current Medical Literature." *British Medical Journal* 2, no. 2646 (September 16, 1911): 37–40.

Antoni, Klaus. "Momotarō (the Peach Boy) and the Spirit of Japan: Concerning the Function of a Fairy Tale in Japanese Nationalism of the Early Shōwa Age." *Asian Folklore Studies* 50 (1991): 155–188.

Aoki Kazuo, Inaoka Kōji, Sasayama Haruo, and Shirafuji Noriyuki, eds. *Shoku Nihongi.* Vol. 5 of Shin Nihon koten bungaku taikei 16. Iwanami shoten, 1998.

Aramata Hiroshi. "Obake kenkyū ga hajimatta koro." In *Hyakkiyagyō no sekai: Ningen bunka kenkyū kikō renkei tenji,* edited by Ningen bunka kenkyū kikō, Kokuritsu rekishi minzoku hakubutsukan, Kokubungaku kenkyū shiryōkan, and Kokusai Nihon bunka kenkyū sentā, 44. Kadokawa gakugei shuppan, 2009.

———. *Shin Nihon yōkai junreidan: Kaiki no kuni Nippon.* Shūeisha, 1997.

Asahara Yoshiko and Kitahara Yasuo, eds. *Mae no hon.* Iwanami shoten, 1994.

Asahi shinbun. "Gegege no 'nurikabe,' konna sugata? Edo-ki no emaki ni tōjō." August 7, 2007.

Asai Ryōi. *Otogibōko.* Shin Nihon koten bungaku taikei 75. Iwanami shoten, 2001.

Asakura Kyōji. "Ano 'Kuchi-sake-onna' no sumika o Gifu sanchū ni mita!" In *Uwasa no hon.* Vol. 92 of Bessatsu takarajima, edited by Ishii Shinji, 132–149. JICC Shuppan kyoku, 1989.

Asma, Stephen T. *On Monsters: An Unnatural History of Our Worst Fears.* Oxford: Oxford University Press, 2011.

Aston, William G., trans. *Nihongi: Chronicles of Japan from the Earliest Times to A.D. 697.* 2 vols. Tokyo: Tuttle, 1972.

Azuma, Hiroki. *Otaku: Japan's Database Animals.* Translated by Jonathan Abel and Shion Kono. Minneapolis: University of Minnesota Press, 2009.

Bargen, Doris G. *A Woman's Weapon: Spirit Possession in* The Tale of Genji. Honolulu: University of Hawai'i Press, 1997.

Bathgate, Michael. *The Fox's Craft in Japanese Religion and Folklore: Shapeshifters, Transformations and Duplicities.* New York: Routledge, 2004.

Befu, Harumi. *Hegemony of Homogeneity: An Anthropological Analysis of Nihonjinron.* Melbourne: Transpacific Press, 2001.

Ben-Amos, Dan. "Toward a Definition of Folklore in Context." *Journal of American Folklore* 84 (1971): 3–15.

Berry, Mary Elizabeth. *Japan in Print: Information and Nation in the Early Modern Period.* Berkeley: University of California Press, 2006.

Blacker, Carmen. *The Catalpa Bow: A Study of Shamanistic Practices in Japan.* London: George Allen and Unwin, 1975.

———. "Supernatural Abductions in Japanese Folklore." *Asian Folklore Studies* 26, no. 2 (1967): 111–148.

Bondeson, Jan. *The Feejee Mermaid and Other Essays in Natural and Unnatural History.* Ithaca, NY: Cornell University Press, 1999.

Borgen, Robert. *Sugawara no Michizane and the Early Heian Court.* Cambridge, MA: Council on East Asian Studies, Harvard University, 1986.

Boyer, Pascal. *Religion Explained: The Evolutionary Origins of Religious Thought.* New York: Basic Books, 2001.

Breen, John, and Mark Teeuwen. "Introduction: Shinto Past and Present." In *Shinto in History: Ways of the Kami,* ed. John Breen and Mark Teeuwen, 1–12. Honolulu: University of Hawai'i Press, 2000.

Brown, Michael F. *Who Owns Native Culture?* Cambridge, MA: Harvard University Press, 2003.

Burns, Susan [S. Bānzu]. "Toritsukareta shintai kara kanshi sareta shintai e: Seishin igaku no hassei." *Edo no shisō* 6 (May 1997): 48–62.

Casal, U. A. "The Goblin Fox and Badger and Other Witch Animals of Japan." *Folklore Studies* 18 (1959): 1–93.

Chiba Mikio. *Zenkoku yōkai jiten.* Shōgakukan, 1995.

Christy, Alan. *A Discipline on Foot: Inventing Japanese Native Ethnography, 1910–1945.* Lanham, MD: Rowman & Littlefield, 2012.

Chūō Daigaku minzoku kenkyūkai, ed. "Aomori-ken Sannohe-gun Nangyō-mura Shimamori-chiku chōsa hōkokusho." *Jōmin* 17 (1980): 1–153.

Cohen, Jeffrey Jerome, ed. *Monster Theory: Reading Culture.* Minneapolis: University of Minnesota Press, 1996.

Cook, James W. *The Arts of Deception: Playing with Fraud in the Age of Barnum.* Cambridge, MA: Harvard University Press, 2001.

Deleuze, Gilles, and Félix Guattari. *A Thousand Plateaus: Capitalism and Schizophrenia.* Translated by Brian Massumi. Minneapolis: University of Minnesota Press, 1987.

de Visser, M. W. "The Fox and Badger in Japanese Folklore." *Transactions of the Asiatic Society of Japan* 36, no. 3 (1908): 1–159.

———. "The Tengu." *Transactions of the Asiatic Society of Japan* 36, no. 2 (1908): 25–99.

Dower, John W. *War without Mercy: Race and Power in the Pacific War.* New York: Pantheon, 1986.

Drexler, Fabian. *Mabiki: Infanticide and Population Growth in Eastern Japan, 1660–1950.* Berkeley: University of California Press, 2013.

Dundes, Alan. "Bloody Mary in the Mirror: A Ritual Reflection of Pre-Pubescent Anxiety." *Western Folklore* 57, no. 2–3 (Spring–Summer 1998): 119–135.

———. "Who Are the Folk?" In *Interpreting Folklore*, edited by Alan Dundes, 1–19. Bloomington: Indiana University Press, 1980.

Eguchi, Shigeyuki. "Between Folk Concepts of Illness and Psychiatric Diagnosis: *Kitsune-tsuki* (Fox Possession) in a Mountain Village of Western Japan." *Culture, Medicine and Psychiatry* 14, no. 4 (December 1991): 421–451.

Ema Tsutomu. *Ema Tsutomu chosaku shū.* Vol. 6. Chūōkōronsha, 1977.

Faure, Bernard. "The Kyoto School and Reverse Orientalism." In *Japan in Traditional and Postmodern Perspectives,* edited by Charles Wei-Hsun Fu and Steven Heine, 245–281. Albany: State University of New York Press, 1995.

Felton, D. "Rejecting and Embracing the Monstrous in Ancient Greece and Rome." In *Ashgate Research Companion to Monsters and the Monstrous,* edited by Asa Simon Mittman and Peter Dendle, 104–131. Surrey, UK: Ashgate, 2012.

Figal, Gerald. *Civilization and Monsters: Spirits of Modernity in Meiji Japan.* Durham, NC: Duke University Press, 1999.

Foster, Michael Dylan. "Haunted Travelogue: Hometowns, Ghost Towns, and Memories of War." *Mechademia* 4 (2009): 164–181.

———. "Haunting Modernity: *Tanuki,* Trains, and Transformation in Japan." *Asian Ethnology* 71, no. 1 (2012): 3–29.

———. "Inviting the Uninvited Guest: Ritual, Festival, Tourism, and the Namahage of Japan." *Journal of American Folklore* 126, no. 501 (2013): 302–334.

———. "The Metamorphosis of the Kappa: Transformation from Folklore to Folklorism in Japan." *Asian Folklore Studies* 57 (Fall 1998): 1–24.

———. *Pandemonium and Parade: Japanese Monsters and the Culture of Yōkai.* Berkeley: University of California Press, 2009.

———. "The Question of the Slit-Mouthed Woman: Contemporary Legend, the Beauty Industry, and Women's Weekly Magazines in Japan." *Signs: Journal of Women in Culture and Society* 32, no. 3 (Spring 2007): 699–726.

———. "Yōkai and Yanagita Kunio Viewed from the 21st Century." In *Yanagita Kunio and Japanese Folklore Studies in the 21st Century,* edited by Ronald A. Morse, 20–35. Tokyo: Japanime, 2012.

Freeman, Richard. *The Great Yokai Encyclopedia: The A-Z of Japanese Monsters.* North Devon, UK: CFZ Press, 2010.

Freud, Sigmund. "The Uncanny." In *Writings on Art and Literature,* 193–233. Stanford, CA: Stanford University Press, 1997.

Fujii Masao. "Setsubun to tsuina no girei." In *Bukkyō gyōji saijiki: Nigatsu setsubun,* edited by Setouchi Jakuchō, Fujii Masao, and Miyata Noboru, 29–34. Daiichi hōki, 1988.

Fujisawa Morihiko. *Yōkai gadan zenshū, Nihon hen jō.* Chūō bijutsu sha, 1929.

Fujishima Usaku. *Sengo manga no minzokugakushi.* Kawaii shuppan, 1990.

Fukuoka-shi hakubutsukan, ed. *Yūrei, yōkaiga daizenshū: Bi to kyōfu to yūmoa.* Fukuoka: Yūrei, yōkaiga daizenshū jikkōiinkai, 2012.

Gifu nichi nichi shinbun. January 26, 1979.

Gilmore, David D. *Monsters: Evil Beings, Mythical Beasts, and All Manner of Imaginary Terror.* Philadelphia: University of Pennsylvania Press, 2003.

Glassman, Hank. "At the Crossroads of Birth and Death: The Blood-Pool Hell and Postmortem Fetal Extraction." In *Death and the Afterlife in Japanese Buddhism,* edited by Jacqueline I. Stone and Mariko Namba Walter, 175–206. Honolulu: University of Hawai'i Press, 2009.

Goff, Janet E. "Conjuring Kuzunoha from the World of Abe no Seimei." In *A Kabuki Reader: History and Performance,* edited by Samuel L. Leiter, 269–283. Armonk, NY: M. E. Sharpe, 2002.

Gunji Masakatsu. *Wasūkō.* Hakusuisha, 2001.

Hanley, Susan B. "Urban Sanitation in Preindustrial Japan." *Journal of Interdisciplinary History* 18, no. 1 (1987): 1–26.

Hansen, Wilburn. *When Tengu Talk: Hirata Atsutane's Ethnography of the Other World*. Honolulu: University of Hawai'i Press, 2008.

Hare, Thomas Blenman. *Zeami's Style: The Noh Plays of Zeami Motokiyo*. Stanford, CA: Stanford University Press, 1986.

Hayashi, Makoto, and Matthias Hayek. "Editors' Introduction: Onmyōdō in Japanese History." *Japanese Journal of Religious Studies* 40, no. 1 (2013): 1–18.

Hearn, Lafcadio. *Glimpses of Unfamiliar Japan*. Boston: Houghton Mifflin, 1894.

———. *The Japanese Letters of Lafcadio Hearn*. Edited with an introduction by Elizabeth Bisland. Boston: Houghton Mifflin, 1910.

———. *Kwaidan: Stories and Studies of Strange Things*. Boston: Houghton Mifflin, 1904.

Hino Iwao. *Dōbutsu yōkai tan: Shumi kenkyū*. Yōkendō, 1926.

Hirabayashi Shigeo. *Mizuki Shigeru to Kitarō hensenshi*. YM Bukkusu, 2007.

Hiraizumi Etsurō. "Zenkoku no shō-chū-gakusei o osoresaseru 'Kuchi-sake-onna' fūsetsu no kiki kaikai." *Shūkan asahi*, June 29, 1979, 16–20.

Hirosaka Tomonobu. *Edo kaiki ibunroku*. Kirinkan, 1999.

Hiruta Genshirō. "Kitsune-tsuki no shinseishi." In *Tsukimono*, edited by Komatsu Kazuhiko, 67–90. Kawade shobō shinsha, 2000.

Huet, Marie-Hélène. *Monstrous Imagination*. Cambridge, MA: Harvard University Press, 1993.

Hufford, David J. *The Terror That Comes in the Night: An Experience-Centered Study of Supernatural Assault Traditions*. Philadelphia: University of Pennsylvania Press, 1982.

Huntington, Rania. *Alien Kind: Foxes and Late Imperial Chinese Narrative*. Harvard East Asian Monographs 222. Cambridge, MA: Harvard University Asia Center, 2003.

Ichiyanagi Hirotaka, ed. *"Gakkō no kaidan" wa sasayaku*. Seikyūsha, 2005.

———. "'Yōkai' to iu ba: Inoue Enryō, 'yōkaigaku' no ichi." In *Nihon shisō no kanōsei*, edited by Suzuki Tadashi and Yamaryō Kenji, 71–90. Satsuki shobō, 1997.

Iijima Yoshiharu. *Hitotsume-kōzo to hyōtan: Sei to gisei no fōkuroa*. Shinyōsha, 2001.

Iikura Yoshiyuki, ed. *Nippon no kappa no shōtai*. Shinjinbutsu ōraisha, 2010.

———. "Yōkai kenkyū bukkugaido." In *Yōkaigaku no kiso chishiki*, edited by Komatsu Kazuhiko, 255–272. Kadokawa gakugei shuppan, 2011.

Ikeda, Hiroko. *A Type and Motif Index of Japanese Folk-Literature*. Helsinki: Suomalainen tiedeakatemia, 1971.

Imamura Katsuhiko. "Mitsugun mukashi banashi." *Mukashi banashi kenkyū* 1, no. 8 (1935): 25–28.

Inada Atsunobu and Tanaka Naohi, eds. *Toriyama Sekien gazu hyakkiyagyō*. Kokusho kankōkai, 1992.

Inoue Enryō. *Inoue Enryō, Yōkaigaku zenshū*. Edited by Tōyō Daigaku Inoue Enryō kinen gakujutsu sentā. 6 vols. Kashiwa shobō, 1999–2001.

Inoue Tomoji. *Tanuki to Nihonjin*. Nagoya: Reimei shobō, 1980.

Ishida Eiichirō. *The Kappa Legend: A Comparative Ethnological Study on the Japanese Water Spirit Kappa and Its Habit of Trying to Lure Horses into the Water*, translated by Yoshida Ken'ichi. *Folklore Studies* 9 (1950): 1–152.

Ishikawa Jun'ichirō. *Shinpan kappa no sekai*. Jiji tsūshinsha, 1985.

Ishizaka Masao. "Watashi mimashita, tsuchinoko to neko no kenka." *Shūkan pureibōi*, October 24, 2000, 54–57.

Itakura Kiyonobu. *Yōkai hakase: Enryō to yōkaigaku no tenka*. Kokusho kankōkai, 1983.

Ito, Mizuko. "Mobilizing the Imagination in Everyday Play: The Case of Japanese Media Mixes." In *Mashup Cultures*, edited by Stefan Sonvilla-Weiss, 79–97. Vienna: Springer-Verlag, 2010.

Itō Ryōhei. *Tsuchinoko no minzokugaku: Yōkai kara mikakunin dōbutsu e*. Seikyūsha, 2008.

———. "Yōkai no hakubutsushi." In *Yōkaigaku no kiso chishiki*, edited by Komatsu Kazuhiko, 212–238. Kadokawa gakugei shuppan, 2011.

Itō Shingo. "Setsuwa bungaku no naka no yōkai." In *Yōkaigaku no kiso chishiki*, edited by Komatsu Kazuhiko, 77–107. Kadokawa gakugei shuppan, 2011.

Ivy, Marilyn. *Discourses of the Vanishing: Modernity, Phantasm, Japan*. Chicago: University of Chicago Press, 1995.

Iwata Noriko. "Bakemono to asobu: 'Nankenkeredomo bakemono sugoroku.'" *Tōkyō-to Edo-Tōkyō hakubutsukan hōkoku* 5 (February 2000): 39–52.

Jitsugyō no Nihonsha, ed. *Yōkai no machi, Sakaiminato: Kōshiki gaidobukku*. Jitsugyō no Nihonsha, 2007.

Jo Gyu-heon. "Akujin saishi no shinsō: Kantō chiiki no 'kotoyōka' girei ni miru Nihonjin no fukkakan." *Ningen kagaku kenkyū* 18, no. 2 (2005): 215–228.

Jones, Sumie, with Kenji Watanabe, eds. *An Edo Anthology: Literature from Japan's Mega-City, 1750–1850*. Honolulu: University of Hawai'i Press, 2013.

Josephson, Jason Ânanda. *The Invention of Religion in Japan*. Chicago: University of Chicago Press, 2012.

———. "When Buddhism Became a 'Religion': Religion and Superstition in the Writings of Inoue Enryō." *Japanese Journal of Religious Studies* 33, no. 1 (2006): 143–168.

Kabat, Adam [Adamu Kabatto]. "Bakemono zukushi no kibyōshi no kōsatsu: Bakemono no gainen o megutte." In *Yōkai*, edited by Komatsu Kazuhiko, 141–164. Kawade shobō shinsha, 2000.

———. *Edo bakemono zōshi*. Shōgakukan, 1999.

———. *Edo kokkei bakemono zukushi*. Kōdansha, 2003.

———. *Edo no kawairashii bakemono-tachi.* Shōdensha, 2011.

———. *Ōedo bakemono saiken.* Shōgakukan, 2000.

———. *Ōedo bakemono zufu.* Shōgakukan, 2000.

Kagawa Masanobu. *Edo no yōkai kakumei.* Kawade shobō shinsha, 2005.

———. "Kappa imēji no hensen." In *Kappa to wa nanika: Dai 84-kai rekihaku fōramu,* edited by Kokuritsu rekishi minzoku hakubutsukan, 6–9. Sakura-shi, Chiba: Kokuritsu rekishi minzoku hakubutsukan, 2012.

Kaisakusen, ed. *Yōkai shashinshū: Gōka gesuto no dai 4 kan.* Self-published, 2012.

Kato, Eileen. *The Iron Crown (Kanawa).* In *Twenty Plays of the Nō Theatre,* edited by Donald Keene, 193–205. New York: Columbia University Press, 1970.

Kauhala, Kaarina. "The Raccoon Dog: A Successful Canid." *Canid News* 2 (1994): 37–40, http://archive.today/SMcM.

Kawamura Kunimitsu. *Genshi suru kindai kūkan: Meishin, byōki, zashikirō, aruiwa rekishi no kioku.* Seikyūsha, 1997.

Kawasaki-shi shimin myūjiamu, ed. *Nihon no genjū: Mikakunin seibutsu shutsugen roku.* Kawasaki: Kawasaki-shi shimin myūjiamu, 2004.

Keene, Donald, trans. *Essays in Idleness: The Tsurezuregusa of Kenkō.* New York: Columbia University Press, 1967.

Kern, Adam L. *Manga from the Floating World: Comicbook Culture and the Kibyōshi of Edo Japan.* Cambridge, MA: Harvard University Asia Center, 2006.

Kihara Hirokatsu. "Hakken: Yōkai-kudan." *Kai* 17 (October 2004): 2–7, 230–235.

Kikuoka Senryō. *Shokoku rijindan.* In *Nihon zuihitsu taisei dainiki,* edited by Nihon zuihitsu taisei henshūbu 24:413–511. Yoshikawa kōbunkan, 1975.

Kimura Yūshō. *Higo mukashi-banashi shū.* Zenkoku mukashi-banashi shiryō shūsei 6. Iwasaki bijutsusha, 1974.

Kinoshita Tomio. "Gendai no uwasa kara kōtōdenshō no hassei mekanizumu o saguru: 'Kuchi-sake-onna' no uwasa o daizai toshite." In *Ryūgen, uwasa, soshite jōhō: Uwasa no kenkyūshū taisei,* ed Satō Tatsuya, 13–30. Shibundō, 1999.

Kiribayashi Hiromichi. "Fujiwara no Hidesato mukade taiji densetsu seiritsu no ichikōsatsu: Taiheiki shoshū setsuwa o chūshin ni." *Udai kokugo ronken* 11 (1999): 41–52.

Kodama Yōmi. *Ōita-ken shi, minzokugaku hen.* Ōita-ken, 1986.

Koizumi Bon. *Minzokugakusha Koizumi Yakumo: Nihon jidai no katsudō kara.* Kōbunsha, 1995.

Koizumi Hiroshi, Yamada Shōzen, Kojima Takayuki, and Kinoshita Motoichi, eds. *Hōbutsushū, Kankyo no tomo, Hirasan kojin reitaku.* Shin Nihon koten bungaku taikei 40. Iwanami shoten, 1993.

Koizumi Toki and Koizumi Bon, eds. *Bungaku arubamu: Koizumi Yakumo.* Kōbunsha, 2000.

Koizumi Yakumo. *Kaidan*. Translated by Takahama Chōkō. Sumiya shoten, 1910.

Kōjien. 6th ed. Iwanami shoten, 2008.

Kojima Noriyuki, Naoki Kōjirō, Nishimiya Kuzutami, Kuranaka Susumu, and Mōri Masamori, eds. *Nihonshoki*. Vol. 2. Shōgakukan, 1996.

Kokuritsu rekishi minzoku hakubutsukan, Kokubungaku kenkyū shiryōkan, and Kokusai Nihon bunka kenkyū sentā, eds. *Hyakkiyagyō no sekai: Ningen bunka kenkyū kikō renkei tenji*. Kadokawa gakugei shuppan, 2009.

Komatsu Kazuhiko. *Hyōrei shinkō ron*. Kōdansha gakujutsu bunko, 1994.

———. *Ijinron: Minzoku shakai no shinsei*. Seidosha, 1985.

———. *Ikai to Nihonjin: Emonogatari no sōzōryoku*. Kadokawa shoten, 2003.

———. *Izanagi-ryū no kenkyū: Rekishi no naka no Izanagi-ryū dayū*. Kadokawa gakugei shuppan, 2011.

———. *Kamikakushi: Ikai kara no izanai*. Kōbundō, 1991.

———, ed. *Nihon no yōkai*. Natsume-sha, 2009.

———. *Nihon yōkai ibunroku*. Shōgakukan, 1995.

———. "Oni: Kaisetsu." In *Oni*, edited by Komatsu Kazuhiko, 457–474. Kawade shobō shinsha, 2000.

———. "Setsubun no oni." In *Bukkyō gyōji saijiki: Nigatsu setsubun*, edited by Setouchi Jakuchō, Fujii Masao, and Miyata Noboru, 21–28. Daiichi hōki, 1988.

———. *Shuten dōji no kubi*. Serika shobō, 1997.

———. *Tsukimono*. Kawade shobō shinsha, 2000.

———. *Yōkai bunka nyūmon*. Serika shobō, 2006.

———. *Yōkai bunka nyūmon*. Kadokawa gakugei shuppan, 2012.

———, ed. *Yōkaigaku no kiso chishiki*. Kadokawa gakugei shuppan, 2011.

———. *Yōkaigaku shinkō: Yōkai kara miru Nihonjin no kokoro*. Shōgakukan, 1994.

———. "Yōkai: Kaisetsu." In *Yōkai*, edited by Komatsu Kazuhiko, 433–449. Kawade shobō shinsha, 2000.

———. "Yōkai to wa nanika." In *Yōkaigaku no kiso chishiki*, edited by Komatsu Kazuhiko, 9–31. Kadokawa gakugei shuppan, 2011.

Komatsu Kazuhiko, Miyata Noboru, Kamata Tōji, and Minami Shinbō, eds. *Nihon ikai emaki*. Chikuma bunko, 1999.

Komatsu Kazuhiko and Naitō Masatoshi. *Oni ga tsukutta kuni Nihon: Rekishi o ugokashite kita "yami" no chikara to wa*. Kōbunsha, 1985.

Komatsu Kazuhiko, Tsunemitsu Tōru, Yamada Shōji, and Iikura Yoshiyuki, eds. *Nihon kaii yōkai daijiten*. Tōkyōdō shuppan, 2013.

Komatsu Sakyō. "The Kudan's Mother," translated by Mark Gibeau. In *Kaiki: Uncanny Tales from Japan*, edited by Higashi Masao. Vol. 2, *Country Delights*, 197–229. Fukuoka: Kurodahan Press, 2011.

Komatsu Shigemi, ed. *Gaki zōshi, Jigoku zōshi, Yamai zōshi, Kusōshi emaki*. Nihon no emaki 7. Chūōkōronsha, 1987.

———, ed. *Tsuchigumo-zōshi, Tengu-zōshi, Ōeyama-ekotoba*. Zoku Nihon emaki taisei 19. Chūōkōronsha, 1984.

Komine Kazuaki, ed. *Konjaku monogatari shū*. Vol. 4 of Shin Nihon kotenbungaku taisei 36. Iwanami shoten, 1994.

Kondō Masaki. "Yōkai no meikan." In *Zusetsu: Nihon no yōkai, shinsōban*, edited by Iwai Hiromi and Kondō Masaki, 101–108. Kawade shobō shinsha, 2000.

Konjaku monogatari shū. Vol. 25 of Nihon koten bungaku taikei. Iwanami shoten, 1965.

Konno Ensuke. *Nihon kaidan shū, yōkai hen*. Shakai shisōsha, 1999.

———. *Nihon kaidan shū, yūrei hen*. Shakai shisōsha, 1999.

Kornicki, Peter. *The Book in Japan: A Cultural History from the Beginnings to the Nineteenth Century*. Honolulu: University of Hawai'i Press, 2001.

Kretschmer, Angelika. "Mortuary Rites for Inanimate Objects: The Case for *Hari Kuyō*." *Japanese Journal of Religious Studies* 27, no. 3–4 (Fall 2000): 379–404.

"Kuchi-sake-onna o shōbai ni suru nante yūki ga iru no da to iu ohanashi." *Shūkan pureibōi*, July 31, 1979, 74.

Kyōgoku Natsuhiko. *Mōryō no hako*. Kōdansha, 1999.

———. *The Summer of the Ubume*. Translated by Alexander O. Smith and Elye J. Alexander. New York: Vertical, 2009.

———. *Taidanshū: Yōkai daidangi*. Kadokawa shoten, 2005.

———. "Tsūzoku 'yōkai' gainen no seiritsu ni kansuru ichi kōsatsu." In *Nihon yōkaigaku taizen*, edited by Komatsu Kazuhiko, 547–582. Shōgakukan, 2003.

———. *Ubume no natsu*. Kōdansha bunko, 1998.

———. "Yōkai to iu kotoba ni tsuite (sono 2)." *Kai* 12 (December 2001): 296–307.

———. "Yōkai zukan no yōkaiga." In *Yōkai zukan*, edited by Kyōgoku Natsuhiko and Tada Katsumi, 5–15. Kokusho kankōkai, 2000.

Kyōgoku Natsuhiko and Tada Katsumi, eds. *Yōkai zukan*. Kokusho kankōkai, 2000.

Kyōgoku Natsuhiko, Tada Katsumi, and Murakami Kenji. *Yōkai baka*. Shinchō OH! bunko, 2001.

Larivière, Serge, and Maria Pasitschniak-Arts. "Vulpes vulpes." *Mammalian Species*, no. 537 (December 27, 1996): 1–11.

Li, Michelle Osterfeld. *Ambiguous Bodies: Reading the Grotesque in Japanese Setsuwa Tales*. Stanford, CA: Stanford University Press, 2009.

———. "Human of the Heart: Pitiful Oni in Medieval Japan." In *Ashgate Research Companion to Monsters and the Monstrous*, edited by Asa Simon Mittman and Peter Dendle, 173–196. Surrey, UK: Ashgate, 2012.

Lillehoj, Elizabeth. "Man-Made Objects as Demons in Japanese Scrolls." *Asian Folklore Studies* 54, no. 1 (1995): 7–34.

Lurie, David B. *Realms of Literacy: Early Japan and the History of Writing.* Cambridge, MA: Harvard University Press, 2011.

Makino, Yoko. "Lafcadio Hearn's 'Yuki-Onna' and Baudelaire's 'Les Bienfaits de la Lune.'" East-West issue, *Comparative Literature Studies* 28, no. 3 (1991): 234–244.

Markus, Andrew L. "The Carnival of Edo: Misemono Spectacles from Contemporary Accounts." *Harvard Journal of Asiatic Studies* 45, no. 2 (December 1985): 499–541.

Maruyama Rinpei, ed. *Teihon Nihonshoki.* Vol. 2. Kōdansha, 1966.

Matsutani Miyoko. *Gendai minwakō.* Vol. 3. Rippū shobō, 1985.

———. *Gendai minwakō.* Vol. 7. Rippū shobō, 1987.

Mayer, Fanny Hagin, trans. *Ancient Tales in Modern Japan: An Anthology of Japanese Folk Tales.* Bloomington: Indiana University Press, 1984.

McCullough, Helen Craig, trans. *Ōkagami, the Great Mirror: Fujiwara Michinaga (966–1027) and His Times.* Princeton, NJ: Princeton University Press, 1980.

McCullough, William H., and Helen Craig McCullough, trans. *A Tale of Flowering Fortunes: Annals of Japanese Aristocratic Life in the Heian Period.* Stanford, CA: Stanford University Press, 1980.

Meikyō kokugo jiten. Taishūkan shoten, 2002.

Meyer, Matthew. *The Night Parade of One Hundred Demons: A Field Guide to Japanese Yokai.* Self-published, 2012.

Miki Sumito, Asami Kazuhiko, Nakamura Yoshio, and Kouchi Kazuaki, eds. *Uji shūi monogatari: Kohon setsuwa shū.* Vol. 42 of Shin Nihon koten bungaku taikei. Iwanami shoten, 1990.

Miller, Laura. "Extreme Makeover for a Heian-Era Wizard." *Mechademia 3: Limits of the Human* (2008): 20–45.

Mills, D. E. *A Collection of Tales from Uji: A Study and Translation of Uji Shūi Monogatari.* Cambridge: Cambridge University Press, 1970.

Mitford, A. B. *Tales of Old Japan.* London: Macmillan, 1893.

Mittman, Asa Simon. "Introduction: The Impact of Monsters and Monster Studies." In *Ashgate Research Companion to Monsters and the Monstrous,* edited by Asa Simon Mittman and Peter Dendle, 1–14. Surrey, UK: Ashgate, 2012.

Mittman, Asa Simon, and Peter Dendle, eds. *Ashgate Research Companion to Monsters and the Monstrous.* Surrey, UK: Ashgate, 2012.

Miura Setsuo. "Kaisetsu: Inoue Enryō to yōkaigaku no tanjō." In *Inoue Enryō, Yōkaigaku zenshū.* Vol. 6, edited by Tōyō Daigaku Inoue Enryō kinen gakujutsu sentā, 464–493. Kashiwa shobō, 2001.

Miyamoto Naokazu. "'Kodomo no ryūgen' kenkyū: Otona no miru kodomo no genjitsu to kodomo no genjitsu." PhD diss., Kanagawa University Graduate School of History and Folk Culture Studies, 1998.

Miyata Noboru. *Yōkai no minzokugaku: Nihon no mienai kūkan.* Iwanami shoten, 1990.

Mizuki Shigeru. *Chūkō aizōban Gegege no Kitarō.* Vol. 1. Chūōkōronsha, 1994.

———. *Nonnonbā to ore.* Chikuma bunko, 1997.

———. *Yōkai gadan.* Iwanami shoten, 1994.

———. *Zoku yōkai jiten.* Tōkyōdō shuppan, 1984.

———. *Zusetsu Nihon yōkai taizen.* Kōdansha, 1994.

Mizusawa Tatsuki. *Nihon no matsurowanu tami: Hyōhakusuru sansetsumin no zankon.* Shin jinbutsu ōraisha, 2011.

Mizuta Noriko. "Yamamba no yume: Josetsu toshite." In *Yamamba-tachi no monogatari: Josei no genkei to katarinaoshi,* edited by Mizuta Noriko and Kitada Sachie, 9–37. Gakugei shorin, 2002.

Mizuta Noriko and Kitada Sachie, eds. *Yamamba-tachi no monogatari: Josei no genkei to katarinaoshi.* Gakugei shorin, 2002.

Momose Meiji. *Gendai ni ikiru sennen no "yami": "Abe no Seimei" warudō.* Koara bukkusu, 1999.

Mori Masahiro. "The Uncanny Valley," translated by K. F. MacDorman and Norri Kageki. *IEEE Robotics and Automation Magazine* 19, no. 2 (2012): 98–100.

Moriya, Katsuhisa. "Urban Networks and Information Networks." In *Tokugawa Japan: The Social and Economic Antecedents of Modern Japan,* edited by Chie Nakane and Shinzaburō Oishi, 97–123. Tokyo: University of Tokyo Press, 1990.

Morris-Suzuki, Tessa. *Re-inventing Japan: Time, Space, Nation.* Armonk, NY: M. E. Sharpe, 1998.

Morse, Ronald A. *Yanagita Kunio and the Folklore Movement: The Search for Japan's National Character and Distinctiveness.* New York: Garland, 1990.

Murakami Kenji. *Yōkai jiten.* Mainichi shinbunsha, 2000.

Murray, Paul. *A Fantastic Journey: The Life and Literature of Lafcadio Hearn.* Folkestone, Kent, UK: Japan Library, 1993.

Nagayoshi Keiko. "'Toshidon' to kubi-nashi-uma denshō." *Mukashi-banashi densetsu kenkyū* 25 (2005): 50–69.

Nakamura, Kyoko Motomochi, trans. *Miraculous Stories from the Japanese Buddhist Tradition: The Nihon Ryōiki of the Monk Kyōkai.* Cambridge, MA: Harvard University Press, 1973.

Nakamura Teiri. *Kappa no Nihonshi.* Nihon Editāsukūru shuppanbu, 1996.

———. *Tanuki to sono sekai.* Asahi shinbunsha, 1990.

Nakamura Tekisai. *Kinmōzui.* Waseda Daigaku shuppanbu, 1975.

Nakazawa Shin'ichi. "Yōkai-ga to hakubutsugaku." In *Yōkai,* edited by Komatsu Kazuhiko, 79–86. Kawade shobō shinsha, 2000.

Negishi Yasumori. *Mimi bukuro.* 3 vols. Iwanami shoten, 1991.

Nihon kokugo daijiten. 2nd ed. Shōgakukan, 2000.

Ningen bunka kenkyū kikō, Kokuritsu rekishi minzoku hakubutsukan, Kokubungaku kenkyū shiryōkan, and Kokusai Nihon bunka kenkyū sentā, eds. *Hyakkiyagyō no sekai: Ningen bunka kenkyū kikō renkei tenji.* Kadokawa gakugei shuppan, 2009.

Nishimura Saburō. *Bunmei no naka no hakubutsugaku: Seiyō to Nihon.* Vol. 1. Kinokuniya shoten, 1999.

Nomura Jun'ichi. *Edo Tōkyō no uwasa-banashi: "Konna ban" kara "Kuchi-sake-onna" made.* Taishūkan shoten, 2005.

———. *Nihon no sekenbanashi.* Tōkyō shoseki, 1995.

Nozawa, Shunsuke. "Characterization." *Semiotic Review 3: Open Issue 2013* (November 2013): 1–31, www.semioticreview.com/pdf/open2013/nozawa_characterization.pdf.

Ōba Minako. "The Smile of a Mountain Witch," translated by Noriko Mizuta Lippit, assisted by Mariko Ochi. In *Japanese Women Writers: Twentieth Century Short Fiction*, edited by Noriko Mizuta Lippit and Kyoko Iriye Selden, 194–206. Armonk, NY: M. E. Sharpe, 1991.

Occhi, Debra J. "Wobbly Aesthetics, Performance, and Message: Comparing Japanese *Kyara* with their Anthropomorphic Forebears." *Asian Ethnology* 71, no. 1 (2012): 109–132.

Ōi Kōtarō. "Okinawa no shokubutsu bunkaron: Shokubutsu to shinkō." *Okidai keizai ronsō* 4, no. 1 (1980): 1–52.

Okano Reiko, Yumemakura Baku, Komatsu Kazuhiko, and Togashi Rintarō. *Onmyōdō.* Tokuma shoten, 2000.

Ōno Katsura. *Kappa no kenkyū.* San'ichi shobō, 1994.

Oppenheim, Janet. *The Other World: Spiritualism and Psychical Research in England, 1850–1914.* Cambridge: Cambridge University Press, 1985.

Orbaugh, Sharalyn. "*Kamishibai* and the Art of the Interval." *Mechademia* 7 (2012): 78–100.

Orikuchi Shinobu. "Okina no hassei." In *Orikuchi Shinobu zenshū* 2:348–388. Chūōkōronsha, 1995.

Ortabasi, Melek. "(Re)animating Folklore: Raccoon Dogs, Foxes, and Other Supernatural Japanese Citizens in Takahata Isao's *Heisei tanuki gassen pompoko*." *Marvels & Tales* 27, no. 2 (2013): 254–275.

Oyler, Elizabeth. "The Nue and Other Monsters in *Heike monogatari*." *Harvard Journal of Asiatic Studies* 68, no. 2 (2008): 1–32.

———. *Swords, Oaths, and Prophetic Visions: Authoring Warrior Rule in Medieval Japan.* Honolulu: University of Hawai'i Press, 2006.

Pandey, Rajyashree. "Women, Sexuality, and Enlightenment: *Kankyo no tomo*." *Monumenta Nipponica* 50, no. 3 (1995): 323–355.

Pang, Carolyn. "Uncovering *Shikigami*: The Search for the Spirit Servant of Onmyōdō." *Japanese Journal of Religious Studies* 40, no. 1 (2013): 99–129.

Papp, Zília. *Anime and Its Roots in Early Japanese Monster Art.* Folkestone, UK: Global Oriental, 2010.

———. *Traditional Monster Imagery in Manga, Anime and Japanese Cinema.* Folkestone, UK: Global Oriental, 2010.

Philippi, Donald L., trans. *Kojiki.* Tokyo: University of Tokyo Press, 1968.

Piggott, Joan R. "*Mokkan:* Wooden Documents from the Nara Period." *Monumenta Nipponica* 45, no. 1 (1990): 449–470.

Pratt, Mary Louise. *Imperial Eyes: Travel Writing and Transculturation.* London: Routledge, 1992.

Rambelli, Fabio. *Buddhist Materiality: A Cultural History of Objects in Japanese Buddhism.* Stanford, CA: Stanford University Press, 2007.

Reider, Noriko T. "Animating Objects: *Tsukumogami ki* and the Medieval Illustration of Shingon Truth." *Japanese Journal of Religious Studies* 36, no. 2 (2009): 231–257.

———. "The Appeal of *Kaidan*: Tales of the Strange." *Asian Folklore Studies* 59, no. 2 (2000): 265–283.

———. "The Emergence of *Kaidan-shū:* The Collection of Tales of the Strange and Mysterious in the Edo Period." *Asian Folklore Studies* 60, no. 1 (2001): 79–99.

———. *Japanese Demon Lore: Oni from Ancient Times to the Present.* Logan: Utah State University Press, 2010.

Robbins, Tom. *Villa Incognito.* New York: Bantam Books, 2003.

Roberts, Colin H., and T. C. Skeat. *The Birth of the Codex.* London: Oxford University Press, 1983.

Rowling, J. K. [Newt Scamander, pseud.]. *Fantastic Beasts & Where to Find Them.* New York: Scholastic Press, Arthur A. Levine Books, 2001.

———. *Harry Potter and the Prisoner of Azkaban.* New York: Scholastic Press, 1999.

Rubinger, Richard. *Popular Literacy in Early Modern Japan.* Honolulu: University of Hawai'i Press, 2007.

Saitō Jun. "Yōkai to kaijū." In *Yōkai henge*, edited by Tsunemitsu Tōru, 66–101. Chikuma shobō, 1999.

Saitō Shūhei. "Uwasa no fōkuroa: Kuchi-sake-onna no denshō oboegaki." *Kenkyū kiyō* 7 (March 30, 1992): 81–99.

Saitō Tsugio. *Yōkai toshi keikaku ron: Obake kara no machi zukuri.* Sairyūsha, 1996.

Sasaki Kōkan, Miyata Noboru, and Yamaori Tetsuo, eds. *Nihon minzoku shūkyō jiten.* Tōkyōdō, 1998.

Sasaki Takahiro. *Kaii no fūkeigaku: Yōkai bunka no minzoku chiri.* Kokon shoten, 2009.

Sasama Yoshihiko. *Kaii kitsune hyaku-monogatari.* Yūzankaku, 1998.

Satō Kenji. *Ryūgen higo: Uwasabanashi o yomitoku sahō.* Yūshindō, 1995.

Satō Sami. "Kami no oshie: Minkan setsuwa 'ningyo to tsunami' no shiza yori." *Onomichi Daigaku Nihon bungaku ronsō* 2 (2006): 51–71.

Seki, Keigo, ed. *Folktales of Japan*. Translated by Robert J. Adams. London: Routledge and Kegan Paul, 1963.

———. "Types of Japanese Folktales." *Asian Folklore Studies* 25 (1966): 1–220.

Sheffield, Steven R., and Carolyn M. King. "Mustela nivalis." *Mammalian Species* 454 (June 2, 1994): 1–10.

Shibusawa Tatsuhiko. "Tsukumogami." In *Yōkai*, edited by Komatsu Kazuhiko, 65–78. Kawade shobō shinsha, 2000.

Shibuya Yōichi. "Bakemono zōshi no kenkyū: Yōkai kenkyū e no shikiron." Undergraduate thesis, Chiba University, 2000.

Shigeoka, Schumann. *Yōkai kai-uta: Kaishi kyoku kashi shū*. Self-published, 2012.

Shigeta Shin'ichi. *Abe no Seimei: Onmyōji-tachi no Heian jidai*. Yoshikawa kōbunkan, 2006.

———. "A Portrait of Abe no Seimei." *Japanese Journal of Religious Studies* 40, no. 1 (2013): 77–97.

Shimazaki, Satoko. "The End of the 'World': Tsuruya Nanboku IV's Female Ghosts and Late-Tokugawa Kabuki." *Monumenta Nipponica* 66, no. 2 (2011): 209–246.

Shimokawa Kōshi and Katei sōgō kenkyūkai, eds. *Meiji Taishō kateishi nenpyō 1868–1925*. Kawade shobō shinsha, 2000.

Shimura Kunihiro, ed. *Nihon misuteriasu yōkai, kaiki, yōjin jiten*. Bensei shuppan, 2012.

———. *Onmyōji Abe no Seimei*. Kadokawa gakugei shuppan, 1995.

Shiota Fukashi, ed. *Sato-son kyōdo shi (jōkan)*. Sato-son: Sato-son kyōdo-shi hensan iinkai, 1985.

Smyers, Karen. *The Fox and the Jewel: Shared and Private Meanings in Contemporary Japanese Inari Worship*. Honolulu: University of Hawai'i Press, 1999.

Staemmler, Birgit. "Virtual *Kamikakushi*: An Element of Folk Belief in Changing Times and Media." *Japanese Journal of Religious Studies* 32, no. 2 (2005): 341–352.

Staggs, Kathleen M. "'Defend the Nation and Love the Truth': Inoue Enryō and the Revival of Meiji Buddhism." *Monumenta Nipponica* 38, no. 3 (Autumn 1983): 251–281.

Starrs, Roy. "Lafcadio Hearn as Japanese Nationalist." *Japan Review* 18 (2006): 181–213.

Stevinson, C. D., and S. J. Biddle. "Cognitive Orientations in Marathon Running and 'Hitting the Wall.'" *British Journal of Sports Medicine* 32, no. 3 (September 1998): 229–235.

Strassberg, Richard E., ed. and trans. *A Chinese Bestiary: Strange Creatures from the Guideways through Mountains and Seas*. Berkeley: University of California Press, 2002.

Suzuki Tadashi and Yamaryō Kenji, eds. *Nihon shisō no kanōsei*. Satsuki shobō, 1997.

Tachikawa Kiyoshi, ed. *Hyaku-monogatari kaidan shūsei*. Kokusho kankōkai, 1995.

———, ed. *Zoku hyaku-monogatari kaidan shūsei*. Kokusho kankōkai, 1993.

Tada Katsumi. *Edo yōkai karuta*. Kokusho kankōkai, 1998.

———. "Etoki gazu hyakkiyagyō no yōkai." *Kai* 12 (December 2001): 320–331.

———. *Hyakki kaidoku*. Kōdansha, 1999.

———. "Kaisetsu." In *Yōkai zukan*, edited by Kyōgoku Natsuhiko and Tada Katsumi, 130–182. Kokusho kankōkai, 2000.

———. *Nihon to sekai no "yūrei, yōkai" ga yoku wakaru hon*. PHP kenkyūjo, 2007.

———, ed. *Takehara Shunsen: Ehon hyaku-monogatari—Tōsanjin yawa*. Kokusho kankōkai, 1997.

———. "Yōkai shitsumon bako." In *Discover yōkai: Nihon yōkai daihyakka*. Vol. 10. Kōdansha, 2008.

Takada Mamoru. *Edo gensō bungakushi*. Chikuma gakugei bunko, 1999.

———. "'Hyakkiyagyō' sōsetsu: Jo ni kaete." In *Toriyama Sekien gazu hyakki-yagyō*, edited by Inada Atsunobu and Tanaka Naohi, 7–16. Kokusho kankō kai, 1999.

Takahara Toyoaki. "Abe Seimei densetsu: Kyō no Seimei densetsu o chūshin ni." *Shūkyō minzoku kenkyū* 5 (1995): 9–24.

———. *Seimei densetsu to Kibi no Onmyōji*. Iwata shoin, 2001.

Takakuwa Fumiko. "Shimo-Koshiki no minzoku: Shinkō densetsu o chūshin ni." In *Shimo-Koshiki-son kyōdo-shi*, edited by Shimo-Koshiki-son kyōdo-shi hensan iinkai, 985–1007. Shimo-Koshiki-son: Shimo-Koshiki-son kyōdo-shi hensan iinkai, 2004.

Takeda Tadashi. "Hyaku-monogatari: Sono seiritsu to hirogari." In *Yōkai*, edited by Komatsu Kazuhiko, 109–125. Kawade shobō shinsha, 2000.

Takehara Tadamichi. "Tōfu kozō to tennendō ni tsuite." *Nihon ishigaku zasshi* 55, no. 2 (2009): 161.

Takemitsu Makoto. *Nihonjin nara shitte okitai: 'Mono-no-ke' to Shintō*. Kawade shobō shinsha, 2011.

Takeuchi, Melinda. "Kuniyoshi's *Minamoto Raikō and the Earth Spider: Demons and Protest in Late Tokugawa Japan*." *Ars Orientalis* 17 (1987): 5–23.

Tanaka Takako. *Abe no Seimei no issen nen: Seimei genshō o yomu*. Kōdansha, 2003.

———. *Hyakkiyagyō no mieru toshi*. Chikuma gakugei bunko, 2002.

Tanaka Takako, Hanada Kiyoteru, Shibusawa Tatsuhiko, and Komatsu Kazuhiko, eds. *Zusetsu: Hyakkiyagyō emaki o yomu*. Kawade shobō shin-sha, 1999.

Teeuwen, Mark, and Bernhard Scheid. "Tracing Shinto in the History of Kami Worship: Editors' Introduction." *Japanese Journal of Religious Studies* 29, no. 3–4 (Fall 2002): 195–207.

Terada Torahiko. "Bakemono no shinka." In *Terada Torahiko zuihitsushū*, edited by Komiya Toyotaka, 2:193–206. Iwanami bunko, 1993.

Terajima Ryōan. *Wakan-sansaizue*. 18 vols. Heibonsha, 1994.

Thoms, William J. "Folk-Lore." *Anthanaeum* (August 22, 1846). Reprinted in *Journal of Folklore Research* 33, no. 3 (September–December 1996): 187–189.

Tierney, Robert Thomas. *Tropics of Savagery: The Culture of Japanese Empire in Comparative Frame*. Berkeley: University of California Press, 2010.

Tinwell, Angela, Mark Grimshaw, and Andrew Williams. "The Uncanny Wall." *International Journal of Arts and Technology* 4, no. 3 (2011): 326–341.

Toelken, Barre. *The Dynamics of Folklore*. Logan: Utah State University Press, 1996.

Tokuda Kazuo. "Otogizōshi to yōkai." In *Yōkaigaku no kiso chishiki*, edited by Komatsu Kazuhiko, 109–140. Kadokawa gakugei shuppan, 2011.

Toyoda Naoyuki. *Chōgyo zukan*. Jitsuyō mini books [Nihon bungeisha], 2011.

Tsunemitsu Tōru. *Gakkō no kaidan: Kōshō bungei no tenkai to shosō*. Kyoto: Mineruva, 1993.

Tsutsui, William. *Godzilla on My Mind: Fifty Years of the King of Monsters*. New York: Palgrave Macmillan, 2004.

Tyler, Royall, ed. and trans. *Japanese Tales*. New York: Pantheon, 1987.

———, trans. *The Tale of the Heike*. New York: Viking, 2012.

Wada Hiroshi. *Kappa denshō daijiten*. Iwata shoin, 2005.

Wakabayashi, Haruko. *The Seven Tengu Scrolls: Evil and the Rhetoric of Legitimacy in Medieval Japanese Buddhism*. Honolulu: University of Hawai'i Press, 2012.

Wakao Itsuo. *Oni-densetsu no kenkyū*. Yamato shobō, 1981.

Ward, Oscar G., and Doris H. Wurster-Hill. "Nyctereutes procyonoides." *Mammalian Species*, no. 358 (October 23, 1990): 1–5.

Watanabe Shōgo. *Nihon densetsu taikei*. Vol. 7. Mizuumi shobō, 1982.

Weinstock, Jeffrey Andrew, ed. *The Ashgate Encyclopedia of Literary and Cinematic Monsters*. Surrey, UK: Ashgate, 2014.

Williams, David. *Deformed Discourse: The Function of the Monster in Mediaeval Thought and Literature*. Montreal: McGill-Queen's University Press, 1999.

Wittkower, Rudolf. "Marvels of the East: A Study in the History of Monsters." *Journal of the Warburg and Courtauld Institutes* 5 (1942): 159–197.

Yamada Norio. "Nihon no yōkai, henge, majintachi." In *Yōkai, majin, shinsei no sekai*, edited by Yamamuro Shizuka. Jiyū kokuminsha, 1974.

———. *Tōhoku kaidan no tabi*. Jiyū kokuminsha, 1974.

Yamada Shōji. "'Yurui' to 'katai' no aida: Nihon no 'yurukyara' masukotto o kangaeru." In *Understanding Contemporary Japan, International Symposium in Indonesia,* 157–166. Kyoto: International Research Center for Japanese Studies, 2010.

Yamauchi Hisashi. *Mono-no-ke.* Vol. 1 of Mono to ningen no bunkashi 122. Hōsei Daigaku shuppankyoku, 2004.

Yanagita Kunio. *The Legends of Tono: 100th Anniversary Edition.* Translated by Ronald A. Morse. Lanham, MD: Lexington Books, 2008.

———. *Nihon no mukashibanashi.* Kadokawa gakugei shuppan, 2013.

———. *Shintei yōkai dangi.* Kadokawa gakukei shuppan, 2013.

———. "Tanuki to demonorojii." In *Yanagita Kunio zenshū.* Vol. 25. Chikuma shobō, 2000.

———. *Teihon Yanagita Kunio shū.* 31 vols. Chikuma shobō, 1968–1971.

———. *Yukiguni no haru: Yanagita Kunio ga aruita Tōhoku.* Kadogawa gakugei shuppan, 2011.

Yoda, Hiroko, and Matt Alt. *Yōkai Attack! The Japanese Monster Survival Guide.* Rev. ed. Tokyo: Tuttle, 2012.

Yokoyama Yasuko. *Yōkai tejina no jidai.* Seikyūsha, 2012.

———. *Yotsuya kaidan wa omoshiroi.* Heibonsha, 1997.

Yoshida Atsuhiko. *Yōkai to bijo no shinwa-gaku.* Meicho kankōkai, 1989.

Yoshie, Akiko. "Gender in Early Classical Japan: Marriage, Leadership, and Political Status in Village and Palace," translated by Janet Goodwin. *Monumenta Nipponica* 60, no. 4 (Winter 2005): 437–479.

Yoshioka Ikuo. "Raijū-kō." *Hikaku minzoku kenkyū* 21 (March 2007): 35–50.

Yumoto Kōichi. *Meijiki kaii yōkai kiji shiryō shūsei.* Kokusho kankōkai, 2009.

———. *Nihon genjū zusetsu.* Kawade shobō shinsha, 2005.

———. *Zoku yōkai zukan.* Kokusho kankōkai, 2006.

Alphabetized List of Yōkai in the Codex

Words in bold print have entries specifically dedicated to them; others are variant names or are mentioned only briefly within an entry. Kanji are included for yōkai in bold print when they are fairly standardized or particularly meaningful for understanding the phenomenon in question.

Index

Text: 10/14 Miller Text
Display: Miller Text
Compositor: IDS Infotech, Ltd.
Indexer: Alexander Trotter
Printer and binder: Maple Press